BEFORE I FORGET

One Man's Radar War

George Phelps in 1939

BEFORE I FORGET

One Man's Radar War

by

George E. Phelps

Being the story of my life in the Royal Air Force,
July 1941—September 1946

© 2014 Stephen Phelps

All rights reserved under International and Pan-American Copyright Conventions. No part of this book may be reproduced without permission in writing from the author, except by a reviewer who may quote brief passages in a review.

stephenphelps@blueyonder.co.uk

ISBN-13: 978-1500708122

Contents

FOREWORD..i
INTRODUCTION..1
Cardington 9
Skegness..17
Sir John Cass, Aldgate 23
Cranwell 31
Happisburgh..41
TRE Malvern...53
Trimingham...59
Tillywhim..85
Going Overseas..101
Flavion...105
Mons..111
Mutzig...115
Witry-les-Reims 145
POSTSCRIPT..165

One Man's Radar War

FOREWORD

I used to be slightly ashamed of my father. In the 50s and 60s when I was growing up in the London suburb of Chiswick, most of my friends had fathers who had fought in the war. They would come to school with tales of heroism and bravery. Of hand-to-hand fighting or flying in the belly of a bomber 15,000 feet above Nazi Germany. There were dark stories of Japanese prison camps and unspoken horrors endured. There was even a boy who claimed his father was one of only three survivors of the sinking of the mighty *HMS Hood* during the great sea battle with the *Bismarck*.

My father, on the other hand, when questioned about his role in the war, would proudly tell my brother and me that he'd never even *seen* a German. How well would that go down in the playground? I used, of course, to keep quiet about it – nothing much to boast about there. If ever we pressed him further he would tell us he used to work in Radar. And that he spent his war almost exclusively in England, at places which sounded as though they can have had little to do with the global struggle against the forces of fascism. Malvern, Trimingham and Tillywhim. Bawdsey Manor, Worth Matravers and Cardington. They sounded like places worth fighting for, for sure, but hardly names from the front line of battle.

"So what did you actually *do* there, Dad?" I would ask. First there would be a flippant reply about card games, and what seemed like nightly dances, with plenty of pretty young WAAFs in attendance – but then, as I grew older, he began to talk about the work he did "as a lowly mechanic"on a secret system called OBOE. This was the first ever blind-bombing system, he told me. A brilliant breakthrough in the use

i

BEFORE I FORGET

of radio transmission to pinpoint a bomber's position in the air and trigger the bomb release at the precise moment necessary to deliver it on to a target up to 35,000 feet below with an incredible degree of accuracy. It was thought at first that OBOE could only be used once before the Germans found a way to jam it, and this first substantial outing enabled the RAF's Pathfinder Force to score direct hits on the huge Krupps armaments factory at Essen. After that, OBOE continued to be used on a regular basis for some 18 months in the middle of the war, helping the RAF to carry out precision bombing raids on Germany's vital industrial heartland of the Ruhr. This top-secret system did much to help turn the tide of the Second World War, but like many of Britain's wartime scientific developments no-one talked about it much when the war was over, so deep did the culture of secrecy run.

Of course, I never heard all this. As a restless fourteen-year-old, worried about where to find the latest Rolling Stones single, or what sort of shoes I needed to buy with the money saved from my paper-round, I had glazed over even before the bombers had reached full altitude. And year after year his real story remained untold. There were tantalizing glimpses. He did see some Germans after all, but right at the end of the war, when the then brand-new technology of microwave transmission (antecedent of almost all the modern communications revolution) enabled the miniaturization of OBOE into mobile units which travelled (along with my Dad) across to Europe behind the advancing D-Day armies. Even then, though, my father's war seemed to consist mostly of softball matches organized by the Canadian airmen now attached to his unit, and dances. Always dances, and plenty of pretty girls – only this time they were in Alsace, newly liberated from Germany. And when his unit came anywhere near the enemy (as they did), he told me they had to pick everything up and run away as fast as they could. Clearly there was no way such state-of-the-art systems could be allowed to fall into enemy hands, but you try explaining that to the other kids in the playground, kids whose Dads had flown fighters or braved the icy seas of the Atlantic convoys. Or killed people.

One Man's Radar War

Years on, I found myself running a small television production company, making programs mainly for the UK's Channel 4. At the time they were running a series called Secrets of the Dead. Well my Dad wasn't dead, though he was by then approaching 80. Maybe his story, the story of OBOE, might be a suitable subject for a series dedicated to unearthing long-forgotten technological advances. So I began to look into the history of OBOE and the role it played in changing the nature of the aerial assault on Germany. A report commissioned by the UK government in 1941 showed that, before OBOE arrived, the bombers were missing their targets by as much as five miles – pretty useless if you're trying to hit factories, ammunition dumps, or troop transports. And of course I began to talk to my Dad. And to listen. The stories he told me did much to inform the program my company eventually made – *Birth of the Smart Bomber*.

But, more importantly I discovered that my father had recently written a memoir of his entire wartime service in the RAF. He called it *Before I Forget*, and when I sat down to read it, I found a rich and eminently readable account of the life of a young serviceman (his call-up came a month after his twentieth birthday) through five and a quarter years of war and into an uncertain future. This is the account I bring to you now, in this book. Just as I did, you will come to meet a young man determined to live life to the full while always trying to do the decent thing. War corrupts. But it also has the capacity to bring out the best in people, and in reading his memoir I watched my father mature into the fundamentally kind man I knew as I grew up. As you read his story you will meet my mother for the first time and watch their relationship develop under the cloud of war and enforced separation. You will be with them as David, my elder brother, is born during the Little Blitz while V1 flying-bombs rain down on London. And when the first of the V2 rockets strikes a few streets away from their home you will be with my Dad as he goes AWOL to spirit mother and baby away from London to safety in the countryside.

With the end of war, and my father's demobilization, his sense of optimism about the future is profound. Victory has delivered the free world from the Nazis, but through my father's development over those

BEFORE I FORGET

five years it is possible to discern the new spirit that began to permeate Europe, leading eventually to the creation of the European Community and an overwhelming desire that "we shall not go through this again". This is, above all a human story – wartime seen through a wide variety of individuals all making sense of it in their own different ways. There are football matches, black marketeers and US servicemen - "overpaid, oversexed and over here"- as the saying went at the time. But there are also glimpses of the awful realities of war – a sad insight into American losses on D-Day, a visit to a concentration camp, and a journey through the ruins of Essen, where the OBOE story began – now flattened and devastated by a series of thousand-bomber raids.

And yes, actually it turned out that my Dad was by no means isolated from, or absolved of, the killing. The top-secret systems he helped to maintain and operate made these huge bombing raids possible, and there were many nights when OBOE raids killed German civilians in their thousands. I might have boasted about this in the playground had I listened, but he certainly would not have done so. Reading *Before I Forget* has been fascinating. I got to know my father as a young man, and how people managed to have fun with the threat of fascism hanging over them, but I also learned much about the futility of war. All this through the prism of one man's war. I hope you enjoy the journey.

Stephen Phelps
Le Marche
ITALY

August 2014

One Man's Radar War

BEFORE I FORGET

INTRODUCTION
Before I Forget

Before setting out on a description of life as it was at the outbreak of war, it is perhaps a good idea to say briefly what kind of person I was. I was 18 at the time, working at Tribe Clarke Painter Darton and Co., a firm of accountants located at Broad Street Place in the City of London. I was an employed Clerk (i.e. not articled) and earning, I believe, 37s.6d. per week.

My chances of becoming a Chartered Accountant at that time were zero, as all potential CAs had to have a period of 5 years articled to a practising CA. This cost money and produced no (or very little) income – both criteria ruling me OUT as an articled Clerk.

My only opening, therefore, was to become an Incorporated Accountant – affiliated to a separate accounting body that allowed non-articled clerks to take their examinations after 9 years working with accredited accountancy firms. I had become disillusioned with this length of time, and had tried to switch my career to the Civil Service by taking a correspondence course leading to the Executive Officer Class examinations.

This course had made some desultory progress and wasn't looking very promising when, somehow or other, my boss had found out. He had me on the carpet and said I had got to make up my mind whether I wanted to move to the Civil Service or remain in Accountancy, more or less indicating that, if I chose the Civil Service, I could depart his employment. In those days, this was a very serious threat, and I had thus been blackmailed into giving up. However, I had done nothing further about studying accountancy, other than the R.S.A. certificates

BEFORE I FORGET

in Bookkeeping (Parts I and II), which I had obtained at school or just thereafter at Night School.

My one sporting activity at this time was cycling. I belonged to the Bayswater Wheelers (or "Wobblers" to insiders): rode on their Club Runs every Sunday (which started from the Victoria Gate, Hyde Park), and attended their Club Night at the Dorchester Arms, Bayswater; and my pride and joy was my Raleigh Charlie Holland special bike, for which I had paid £9.15s. in the preceding year. I also frequently rode out myself on Saturdays.

In July 1939 I had had my first holiday ever on my own. A week in Portsmouth – though I spent several days of it on the Isle of Wight, going over on an early ferry and returning late at night. I rode down to Portsmouth on my bike and also rode round the Isle of Wight. My digs in Portsmouth were bed and breakfast only, and cost me 25s. for the week. There were also a couple of other lads staying at the guest house, but the landlady preferred me – as she said "They put their tan on out of a bottle and it stains my pillows – but yours is a genuine tan."

I must admit that by this time I had begun to take an interest in girls, and part of my holiday objective was to "get off", as it used to be called, with some girls. I picked up a rather nice-looking girl from Erdington, Birmingham called Sheila in Shanklin, and in Portsmouth a rather plainer but perhaps nicer girl called Edna. She turned out to be one of the Plymouth Brethren, and I amused myself by inventing a totally false identity of a White Russian called Boris, whose mother had married again, bringing me from Paris, where we had previously lived, to London. For this I adopted a phoney French accent (based on Maurice Chevalier). Since my French was very sketchy, this was a hazardous procedure; but I got away with it. I actually corresponded with this girl for a few months thereafter; but the effort of trying to keep up this persona was too great, and I gave up.

The time I spent touring the Isle of Wight on my bike was very worthwhile, and I have always remained very fond of the island, even contemplating buying a bungalow and retiring there many years later. The whole holiday cost a total of £3.10s.: not bad for a week!

I was also a very keen supporter of what were then rather outlandish sports, particularly ice hockey in the winter. I supported the Earls Court Rangers, then playing on a rink since knocked down and replaced by the Admiralty Building. I followed them to most away games, riding my bike to Wembley, Harringay and Streatham. At Earls Court, I was part of a group containing a lad called Eric Turner (rather important to me, as we shall see later) to which I had introduced my cousin Lily and some of her friends. They became keen fans of the Rangers. I rather fancied a nice-looking girl called Joyce Lay; but my general shyness had prevented me from making any progress at all.

In the summertime I also supported the Wembley Speedway team, and followed them to Wimbledon and Harringay. There was also a baseball league, in which I supported the White City team; and whenever the Six-day Cycle Race was on at Wembley, I was there for every night of the week. I was a very active supporter. You might well ask how I managed this on 37s. 6d. a week; and I can only reply that seats were a lot cheaper then, and that I also managed to supplement my wages a little by fiddling the expenses. Before you read too much into that statement, the sort of thing I mean would be to get up early for a trip to Woolwich and catch a tram from Victoria with an all-day ticket for 1s. and then charge the train fare of say 2s. 6d. from Charing Cross.

So that's the sort of chap I was in those days. But what sort of world was I living in? I, of course, lived with my mother and father at 98 Thornton Avenue, Chiswick. At the outbreak of war, we had no other relatives staying with us, though my childhood had always been spent with some one or other of my aunts, uncles and cousins living with us. My parents were always very supportive of their family. My mother's brother Wal had lived with us until his marriage to Maud in 1928. My father's half-sister Jane had also lived with us until she got married sometime in the 1930s, and my cousin Dorothy, daughter of my mother's sister, Flo, had come to live with us when she was 15, which

BEFORE I FORGET

would have been in 1931. She also had left to share a flat with her friend Mavis, so that by 1939, there were only the 3 of us at 98.

The international situation at the outbreak of war was pretty chaotic. The previous autumn Chamberlain had returned from Munich brandishing Hitler's agreement following the surrender of the Sudetenland and saying it was "Peace In Our Time". I think most observant people did not believe it then; but in March 1939, when Hitler took over the remainder of Czechoslovakia, the hollowness of the claim became obvious to everyone. Of course Hitler repeatedly said "This is my last territorial claim in Europe"; but no one believed him. During the summer we were all issued with gas masks in cardboard boxes suspended on string, and the children were evacuated to the country. So when the Russo-German Pact was signed the invasion of Poland was already a certainty and the declaration of war by Britain and France inevitable - though Hitler apparently didn't think so.

At the outbreak of war, massive air raids were expected and the hospitals were all cleared for thousands of casualties – precautions that the dear old British Press reported in detail, thus thoroughly putting the wind up people. I remember that in the first few days there were occasional air raid warnings - always false alarms, but causing panic at 98 Thornton. We had decided to make the ground-floor bedroom the safe room (from gas attack), and so we rushed down there and endeavoured to hang soaking wet blankets over both door and window. God knows whether this would have been any good; but fortunately it was not put to the test. The gas masks were of a weird design, with the intake through a filter on the front and the exhalation being blown out at the sides of the mask and producing a well-rounded "raspberry". In fact a group of people wearing masks and exhaling in turn must have sounded hilarious; though I don't think we laughed much at the time. But after a few days it became apparent that Hitler was not going to start raiding, and so life gradually returned to near-normal.

Of course the ice hockey teams had disappeared; but we could still skate, and gradually some Canadian Army teams appeared and put on some games. At this time also I decided to take up dancing (ballroom variety) and enrolled in a little private school in Gunnersbury. There I learnt 3 or 4 steps in each dance, and found this a good investment, as I could always take to the floor with the minimum of damage to my partner.

All the external action was confined to naval clashes and some isolated and generally unsuccessful raids, including leaflet raids. The Allied armies confined themselves to patrol activities. The British took a long time to adjust themselves to conscription – so there was a very slow build-up of British forces in France. The USSR had seized the Baltic republics of Latvia, Lithuania and Estonia as a result of the deal with Hitler, and they now issued a series of demands on the Finns. Following their rejection by the Finns they invaded, and rapidly got bogged down in the Arctic winter. The Allies (Britain and France) complained bitterly to the Russians, and there was even talk of sending forces to help the Finns. Considering the terrible hidings that Hitler had in store for us, you can see that this would have been the height of stupidity.

The winter of 1939/40 was anyway very severe, and there were heavy snowfalls in London. On 7 January 1940 the aforesaid Eric Turner had his nineteenth birthday, and invited me to join his birthday party. He had at this time begun to go out with a girl called Cynthia Warneford, who lived in Sterndale Road, Hammersmith; and naturally she was invited too. She in turn brought with her a young lady who was originally from Northamptonshire but who was lodging with the Warnefords to be near her work at the Post Office Savings Bank. Her name was Mary Houghton. The party was organized largely by Eric's parents, and there were loads of things to eat. There must have been drinks, too, though I don't remember them flowing too freely. You must remember though that only the previous summer had I begun to drink shandy, and also only on the preceding Christmas Eve did I drink my first glass of beer. Wines and spirituous liquors were absolutely beyond my ken. In the light of present-day attitudes to booze this may seem incredible; but it was nevertheless true. The party was very much oriented towards party games – some dancing but not much; and the games were very decorous, such as passing the parcel and packing my trunk – none of your postman's knock or similar hanky-panky. But for me there was only one interest at that party and that was Mary Houghton. I could not take my eyes off her.

She was then 21, about 2 ¼ years older than me; and since girls matured much more rapidly than boys in their teens, she was much more sophisticated and self-confident. She had light brown hair with auburn tints in it and a fresh open sunny face with very light make-up. She wore a pink light-weight dress with a high neck and a tight waist with a loose swirling skirt. This showed off her slender figure and her shapely legs to perfection. But what impressed me the most was her sparkling personality. Some people become the centre of attention by showing off – she never did that, but simply by personality alone she became centre of all activities. I, by contrast, hung about the edges and looked inconspicuous. Most of the people present at the party came from Eric's involvement with the Scouts, and they included one Reg Hunter, a young man of about 21 or 22 who had the reputation of being a ladies' man. Again you must remember that such an expression in those days did not mean the degree of intimacy that it does today – merely that he chatted up girls and went out with them. His beady eye, as I discovered later, was also attracted by Mary Houghton; and before the end of the proceedings he had got a date with her.

Finally the party ended; and as I trudged back to 98 Thornton through the snow, alone, I could think of nothing else but Mary Houghton. I suppose in retrospect it was love at first sight; but she seemed so far beyond my reach that I dared not even think of it as that. I thought only that she was just the kind of girl that I would like to marry.

The following Saturday, I went to the Richmond Ice Rink for a skating session; and, to my delight, she and Cynthia turned up again – this time she was sporting a brown sweater and short skating skirt. I was a pretty useless skater, and she wasn't a lot better; but somehow we found ourselves skating in a long line with me on the outside and her just inside me, holding my hand! As the line whipped around the end of the rink, the outside man got swung around the fastest, and, as we turned the corner, she suddenly let go. I was projected off at a tangent at high speed; and, as my stopping ability was not great, I crashed into the barrier with a hefty thump. Out of consideration for my accident, she came rushing over to see if I was OK. In fact, I was perfectly all right; but with a sudden rush of courage, I actually invited her to join me for a coffee. No doubt again feeling guilty at projecting me into the barrier, she agreed; and for the very first time I had the chance to talk to her face to face. So I began to find out where she came from and why she was lodging with the Warnefords. Having exhausted our cups of coffee, we returned to the rink; and at last we left the stadium and caught the bus back to Chiswick and Hammersmith.

Somehow I managed to get a seat next to her, and grandiloquently insisted on paying her bus-fare home. What with a threepenny cup of coffee and a fourpenny bus ticket, you can see I was a lavish entertainer! Still no date; but I did discover that she would be at the Scouts dance the following week. Armed with my new-found dancing expertise from the Gunnersbury school, there was no way I was going to miss that dance. However, when I turned up, it was to discover that she had been escorted there by Reg Hunter. This time, though, my luck was in, as Reg was also the Master of Ceremonies at the dance, and his duties occupied most of his time, while I hogged all the dances. Now, I suppose, my abilities at dancing began at last to make an impression. I explained my attendance at the dancing school; and my heart leapt when she said she might be interested in coming with Cynthia. At the end of what must be the most marvellous dance I ever attended, I had a setback. I asked if I could take her home; but she politely declined, saying that, as Reg had brought her, she ought to go home with him. Still, on my proposing a trip to the pictures as an alternative, she accepted. On 7 February, therefore, one month after first seeing her, I had my first genuine date with her. It was to the Gaumont Cinema, Hammersmith, and we saw the Crazy Gang in *Alf's Button Afloat*. On returning her to Sterndale Road, I managed to pluck up courage to get my very first kiss goodnight.

BEFORE I FORGET

ONE

Cardington

George Phelps in 1941

The day war broke out - to use a line that really belongs to Robb Wilton, a very successful comedian of the day - there was a very poor turnout for the Bayswater Wobblers' Sunday cycle ride. Three, to be precise, of whom I was one; and our trip to the old Roman road called the Nine Mile Ride near Wokingham meant that we missed Neville Chamberlain's solemn announcement of War, and also the air raid (a false alarm) that immediately followed it.

I was only 18 at the time; and, since I was singularly lacking in patriotic fervour, the idea of rushing out to volunteer to serve King and Country simply did not cross my mind. This was mainly preoccupied with the fact that the Wobblers' 25-mile Time Trial scheduled for 25 September had

BEFORE I FORGET

been cancelled. It had been my intention to try my luck for the first time in this, the last Time Trial of the season, and, if the resulting time had been in any way promising, to tackle serious training during the winter, and then to launch myself on the unsuspecting cycling world the following spring. Sober reflection at a later date convinced me that this cancellation was a blessing in disguise and saved me a lot of hard work for little achievement. I always had the legs for it but never the stomach, I fear.

In fact, it would be July 1941 before I received my call to the colours. The intervening period, which included my unenthusiastic participation in the London blitz and my distinctly more enthusiastic meeting with, and subsequent courtship of, the lady who later became my wife, is a different story. During that time, some of my friends and acquaintances actually did volunteer; but alas, their motives in so doing were generally to get themselves into something they fancied, rather than waiting to be conscripted into anything that happened to be recruiting at the time. I did wonder whether I should do the same, as I had a somewhat illogical fancy to join the Navy. But then again another voice would condemn this as cheating, and considered that I should take my chance in the lottery. In the end, it being simpler to do nothing than to do something, that was what I did.

Eventually the dreaded letter arrived, requiring me to report for medical examination to a centre in Ealing and offering me, to my surprise, a chance to opt for the particular service, Army, Air Force or Navy, that I preferred. Once again my inclination was to prefer the Navy; but as my deficient eyesight made it unlikely that I should be accepted, I reasoned that the result would be that I would be dumped in the Army. It seemed essential that I should avoid that fate; and so I eventually nominated the RAF.

The Medical Centre check-up duly took place, and was obviously so arbitrary in character that I remember little of it, except for one thing, and that was that the doctors expressed astonishment that the hearing in my right ear had been so little affected by the mastoid operation I had had at the age of seven. In the end my classification was A1 except for my eyesight, and this seemed to preclude my undertaking any clerical job, similar to that for which I was currently employed in Civvy Street. So without any real knowledge of what to select I put my name down as a Wireless Operator. By this time, the recruiting machine was really functioning smoothly, and it was not long before the summons to report appeared: "At noon on 18 July 1941 you are requested to report to RAF Cardington. Your railway warrant from London to Bedford is enclosed and transport will be provided from the station to the camp."

I can't say my departure was a tearful one. Naturally my girlfriend and I were sorry to leave each other, as we had become very close by this time. As I was their only son, my parents also felt some anxiety; but as none of us were of the over-emotional type and we had been conditioned to the event for quite a long time, the parting was fairly subdued.

My own feelings on the train to Bedford were more of excited anticipation than anything else. After all, a new and different kind of life confronted me. The change from routine auditing to what I believed to be wireless operating sounded both interesting and challenging. The war seemed far away at the time, as Hitler had turned his attention to Russia.

On the train, I tried to steal an advantage over my fellow recruits, as I had acquired a copy of the Morse Code and spent my time trying to learn it. On arrival at Bedford we were hurried outside into waiting buses that set off for the Cardington camp, situated some three miles outside Bedford. We were soon there and, on filing out of the bus, the welcoming RAF Sergeant gave us our first introduction to the service: "Righto, you lot, get fell in in threes." Some five minutes and an awful amount of shuffling later, we finally appeared as a column of threes. A short march took us through the camp gates, which clanged ominously shut behind us. We were in!

Cardington was a very well-established RAF base at this time, notable primarily for its earlier association with the famous airships R101 and R100, both of which set out on their fatal journeys from this base. The huge twin hangars that had formerly housed these dirigibles still dominated the camp, and at this time were used for the training of barrage-balloon operators. However, our concern was not with this part of the camp but with the main body of the camp, which was used as a kitting-out centre for new recruits.

Cardington airship hangars © Ben Brookshaw (Creative Commons)

Our group was soon allocated to the various huts and we were left to seize for ourselves a bed and the appropriate "biscuits" (i.e. sections of mattress). The beds were of good, sturdy metal construction, and the "springing", if such it can be called, was of good British steel strips, which, even when jumped up and down on, refused to give even a fraction of an inch. An even more welcoming note was the fact that the "biscuits", of which each man had three, were soaking wet. However, before we had time to digest this news, we were summoned outside to parade for our first luncheon with the RAF.

The intake to the RAF through Cardington was at the rate of 5000 a week, so the dining halls were extremely large and the queues extremely long. When I eventually presented my plate, it received a half slice of spam, a tablespoonful of peas and four very small new potatoes. This meal did not augur very well for the future; but to be fair to Cardington, it was the only meal that I actually recall. This first meal also introduced me to an old RAF custom, and gave me one of my first lessons on how to keep my nose clean in the Air Force. As we pushed our plates aside, the clatter of plates and crosstalk was penetrated by the stentorian tones of the Duty Sergeant. "Orderly Officer - any complaints"? And there, standing by the door, was the sergeant himself, and the Officer whose duty it was to ensure that we were all replete and satisfied. Up stood bold Horatius:

"Yes, sergeant", he said, "the potatoes were green." And immediately came the reply from the Sergeant: " Outside you, and scrub the buggers till they're white." I've often wondered since whether this little scene was skilfully produced; but it certainly taught us a useful lesson.

On returning to our hut, one enterprising member buttonholed the sergeant to complain that the biscuits were wet. Perfectly logical, if you think about it! So the evening was spent trying to get your biscuits into a favourable position around the hut stove, and with clouds of steam rising to the ceiling. As an encore, the sergeant drew our attention to the duty list for cleaning and tidying the hut ready for inspection at 9 a.m. the following morning. My task was blackleading the stove. A tentative enquiry as to how this was to be accomplished, as there appeared to be no blacklead, elicited the natural response: "Use elbow grease." Of course, the following morning the performance on a number of the tasks was rubbished, and the unlucky workers were required to do them all over again. Very little improvement seemed to result so far as I could see, but no doubt the recruits learned a little more about the Air Force.

By evening we had acquired blankets and a bolster to add to our partially dried biscuits. No sheets of course, and the blankets felt a bit rough to the tender recruits' skin. The bolster was I suppose filled with straw, but felt more like rocks. Once free of the Air Force's clutches for the day, we lay on our bunks and tried to get to know each other. The only individual who stands out in my memory was a Scottish commercial traveller who proceeded to regale us from his enormous stockpile of jokes. For every one produced by the rest of the hut combined, he could produce three, and they varied from the slightly smutty to the downright filthy. Although fairly innocent at the time, I had at least knocked around in the business world for a few years, and so my reaction was more amazement than horror. However, there was no doubt at all that, to some of the more tender violets scooped up by the recruiting net into that Cardington hut, the evening came as a terrible shock. Not only were they hearing freely used words that they had never heard before, but all sorts of topics, taboo in respectable society, were bandied about with brutal frankness, often accompanied with the appropriate actions as well. One could only feel sorry for such individuals, faced with the way the other half lived. I subsequently learned that the situation was as bad if not worse for girls thrown into the Services for the first time.

From all that stock of jokes only one remains in the mind, perhaps because of its aptness to our own situation: Joe Bloggs received his call-up papers and was required to report for medical examination, bringing with him in a bottle a specimen of his urine. Since he was not an enthusiastic recruit, he thought he would delay matters by complicating the issue, and he invited all the other members of his family to contribute to his sample. On his arrival at the Centre the Medical Officer came out from the examination of his urine to say: "This was a very complicated case, but I believe we have finally worked it out. Our conclusions are:

Your father has Bright's disease.
Your mother is in the change of life.
Your sister is in the family way.
And you're in the bleeding army!!"

The main task of Cardington Camp was "kitting-out", and so we trailed around from hut to hut gradually acquiring a kitbag and the items of kit to go inside. Air Force underwear, somewhat scratchy until you got used to it. Shirts, socks, boots, gym shoes, tunic, trousers, hat, greatcoat and the essentials of service life, such as "irons" (a set of knife, fork and spoon). Mess tins, hussif (sewing kit) and buttonstick, a plastic device to enable you to polish brass buttons and still keep the uniform clean. Here we learned the magic word "Nearest", meaning that, if they hadn't got your size, they would give you the nearest to it that they had. Fortunately, in my case, most items fitted, except for some over-large shirts. Included in the kit acquired was a gas mask and a gas cape. The latter was a very useful acquisition, as the instruction on how to fold it neatly has been invaluable subsequently when dealing with the ubiquitous plastic mac!

More interesting than the items we received, were those that we did not receive. We did not get our grey webbing equipment, which was no great loss. Nor did we get Wellington boots; and in fact my whole Air Force history was one of having wellies when I didn't need them and losing them when I did!

At this time we also had our first brushes with the RAF medical authorities. We were introduced to the FFI, that ignominious examination, which requires the recruit to drop his trousers and expose his nether regions to examination, presumably for disintegration of some kind.

Another test was for colour blindness, and I felt only great sympathy for a lad sitting next to me who simply could not read the hidden numbers and there learnt for the first time that he was colour blind.

One other development here was an interview with the Technical Officer, who was clearly under instructions to round up some potential Wireless and Radio Mechanics. Did I know anything about Radio?, said he. "No," said I. "What about your school subjects?" Yes, I admitted to Matriculation in Physics specializing in Electricity and Magnetism, and also in Mathematics. "How about changing from Operator to Mechanic", said he. "Well, I don't know," said I. "It's worth another 3d. per day." "Done," said I. And that's how I became a mechanic.

BEFORE I FORGET

TWO

Skegness

Eventually our kitting-out was complete, and we learnt that we were shortly to be transferred to Skegness, where we would undergo "Preliminary Training" - or Square-bashing, to the initiated.

The day of our transfer to Skegness dawned, a beautiful, hot July day, well into the 80s. So we garbed ourselves in full kit, including greatcoats buttoned to the chin, in the approved official manner. We shouldered our kitbags and stood ready to move off. The journey was by train and across country, so it seemed interminable. However, we finally arrived, by this time reduced to grease-spots, and were marched through the town and along the seafront to the commandeered boarding-houses that were to be our homes for the next five weeks. I was allocated with two others to a most desirable front room on the ground floor, overlooking the sea, from which I was to watch the sun rise between 5 and 6 a.m. for those 5 weeks.

I had no sooner distributed my belongings here and there and collapsed disconsolately on my bed, which miraculously did actually have springs in it, when a stentorian yell of "Stand to attention when I enter the room" greeted my ears. It came from Corporal Summerfield, a big tough and fit-looking PT Corporal[1], who proceeded to inform us that he was in charge of our squad and therefore of this billet, and of the process of turning us from raw recruits into smart, alert, well-disciplined airmen. This was accompanied by exhortations to "jump to it" when he appeared, and to keep our personal bedspace and kit clean, smart and tidy, with dire warnings of what we might expect for the slightest deviation from these

---

1 PT stands for Physical Training, more usually known today as Physical Education.

strict rules. Our attention was drawn to the approved official method of laying out kit and folding blankets, the duty list for domestic chores and the expectation of frequent check-ups by the more senior members of the hierarchy. Reveille was to be at 5.30 a.m., and we were expected to parade outside the billet, and to march to the Imperial Hotel for breakfast at, or before, 7.15 a.m. (Let me say at once, in case you are led astray by the words "Imperial Hotel", that the food served there was undoubtedly the worst I ever encountered in my service with the RAF or indeed in my whole life. In general it varied between nauseating and uneatable.)

This peroration sounded pretty horrifying, and I must admit my heart was in my boots when I heard it. In actual fact, however, Corporal Summerfield was a model of what a PT Corporal ought to be. Hard on his men, he required prompt obedience to orders and personal smartness; but he was always fair and reasonable, and, by the end of our time there, he had produced a squad that was smart, well turned out, and disciplined; and what's more, they knew it, took a pride in it, and considered themselves the best squad in Skegness, and of course thought Summerfield the best PT Corporal there. Next day we plunged straight into the routine, and the first thing we discovered was that we were by no means the only squad appearing for breakfast at 7.15 a.m., and we could expect to wait up to 30 minutes outside for our turn to enter. At least it was July, and the temperature warm. However, being England, it did rain, and that was never too pleasant. Fortunately, not often during our stay, though.

After breakfast, on parade for the real square-bashing, we learned that we would start with basic foot drill and move on to rifle drill later in the course. Each and every day, however, we would also get some genuine PT.

Immediately, we were advised that the rubber heels on our service boots should be replaced by metal bands shaped like horseshoes, the reason being that with these we could hear ourselves march along. Really a very useful tip, as we subsequently found. Many, many years later, I was reminded of this little trick as I stood watching a parade on Bastille Day in the Champ de Mars of what looked like the entire French Army. The parade finally terminated and the Army then stole silently away in their rubber boots. My heart was filled with contempt. "Foreigners!", I said. "How can you frighten the enemy when they can't even hear you coming (or going!)."

Another trick fed to us was to accompany our drill manoeuvres with the merry cry "One – pause – two – pause - three," which you could hear filling the streets of Skegness. Actually, if you try saying it several times, there's a sort of insidious seductive rhythm about it! One – pause – two – pause – three!

Next day we launched into our programme of "Quick march - About turn—Halt, etc.", and our only respite was the arrival of NAAFI or Church Army vans mid-morning and mid-afternoon to dispense the ubiquitous "Cuppa Char and a Wad". We were of course also introduced to the NAAFI for evening snacks and even entertainment, whereby we could repair some of the deficiencies of the Imperial Hotel.

The features of the PT sessions generally conducted in the local park were exactly those that have featured in any Keep-Fit class slimming exercises or FCAF booklets or anything else that you have ever seen since. There were really only two features that I particularly recall. One was a kind of free-for-all rugby played at the end of the session, by the combined squads and with about 60 a side. For those in the heart of the fray this could be a somewhat hazardous procedure. I recall one enthusiastic Scotsman who refused to part with the ball and was dragged through a barbed-wire fence for his pains. My own approach was to run up and down of the outskirts of the action trying to look a winger, and if anyone was foolish enough to pass to me, I hurled it across to the other side as fast as possible. Still, I got the exercise I suppose.

The other feature was associated with another treat that the authority had in store for us. This was inoculations: ATT, Anti-Tetanus and Typhoid; TAB - can't remember what that stands for; and of course, vaccination. I can't remember anyone passing out at the ceremony, as they are generally supposed to do, though some undoubtedly looked a bit green. However, I do remember that these were followed by games and PT. These games were versions of Piggy in the Middle, whereby the majority of the squad linked their swollen and sore inoculated arms and half a dozen worthies contained in the centre of the ring tried to break out by hurling themselves at it. This was alleged to get the inoculations circulating well, and thus to allow us to recover in the minimum time possible.

During this period we became familiar with a little more Air Force slang. We met the "Fizzer" - a charge sheet listing the airman's misdemeanours and bringing him before the CO. A few of these were dished out, as Voltaire says, "*Pour encourager les autres*." And one I recall is that of the airman charged with an untidy toothpaste tube, because he squeezed it in the middle and didn't roll it up neatly from the end. For this he received "Jankers" – being confined to barracks with extra domestic duties. After a time, we passed on to the rifle drill, and were issued with P40 rifles, which were slightly lighter than the Lee Enfield.

Gradually our drill technique improved, until, towards the end of our course, there took place a quite extraordinary incident, which remains indelibly printed on my mind to this day. If you listen carefully to any squad marching under drill conditions with their metal caps on their boots you will invariably hear a slight burring noise as their heels hit the ground. This is simply because they never get it exactly right. And it doesn't matter if you are watching the King's Troop or the Guards or whatever, the slight burr is there. Well, almost invariably, I should have said, because just once, and never again, but just once, from our drilling ground round to the billet, we got it absolutely right. The slight burr vanished, and the two dozen heels going at exactly the right fraction of a second produced a sound like a rifle shot. And continued to produce it for about half a mile.

Every man in that squad knew it, without speaking, and every man felt it and swung his arms higher and stuck his chest out. It was a most strange but exhilarating experience, and one never to be forgotten. When we finally halted everyone wanted to talk about it, because they were so excited by it. However, try as we might, we never did it again.

Some other new Air Force experiences came my way at this time. One was Pay Parade, where after marching smartly forward and saluting in my best style, I was presented with 11 shillings, representing my first fortnight's pay. To be fair to the RAF, I think they were withholding a few bob in case I was debited with Barrack Room Damages. Other delights of Skegness, beyond the NAAFI, I never did sample, as by 8.30 p.m. every evening I was so exhausted that I could only collapse into bed.

Towards the end of my stay I contracted impetigo, probably from infected blankets, and so I reported sick, or rather attended Sick Parade. At this, after a fairly lengthy wait to see the MO, I was introduced to M and D (Medicine and Duty), the standard RAF recipe for most ills. In my case this meant that I received some ointment to stick on it, and was told to carry on with training. Every morning I had to undergo the very painful process of trying to shave around the sores that now covered my face. I tried to get the blankets, which I had to leave behind, changed before the next intake arrived; but the Air Force wasn't having any. So the best I could do was to leave a note inside for the next man warning him what to expect! Not much of a welcome for him, I'm afraid.

Eventually the time came to depart from bracing Skegness and to move on to the commencement of our Technical Training. Here we should be split up all over the country. But when the news came through - joy of joys - I was posted to the Sir John Cass Institute, Aldgate, London: London again, and a chance to see my family and girlfriend.

BEFORE I FORGET

THREE

Sir John Cass, Aldgate

We were to spend sixteen weeks at Aldgate doing the basic Radio training necessary for our new vocation as Mechanics. At the end of the course, we would be divided between those who would become Wireless Mechanics, dealing with the telegraphy equipment, both on the ground and in aircraft, and the more successful trainees, who would become Radio Mechanics. It gradually began to filter through to us that this meant that we would be mechanics on the sites for Radio Location, or, as it was eventually to become known, Radar.

The Sir John Cass Institute was a Further Education establishment ("Polytechnic", in those days) situated in the City of London at the junction of Aldgate High Street and the Minories. It had an oldish building known as the Foundation Schools and also quite a new and well-equipped building on the opposite side of the High Street. This latter building was still intact, and was used as the instructional centre, while the Foundation Schools, which had been partially bombed, were used as dormitories. Also in use as a billet was a requisitioned office building in the Minories, and it was to this last building that I was first allocated.

The accommodation in this building left something to be desired. We were occupying the whole of the third floor in a fairly modern office building, which was well equipped with windows. Unfortunately, the RAF had neglected to provide blackouts, and the Air Raid Warden service was particularly sensitive at this time in London, so that strict darkness had to be maintained. The RAF managed this very well by removing not only the lamps, but the light fittings as well. So that beyond the stairwell no lighting existed anywhere or at any time.

BEFORE I FORGET

At this time I struck up a friendship with an airman from Diss in Norfolk, Jack Rook, and I am pleased and proud to say that friendship has lasted to this day, with each of us playing the role of Best Man at the other's wedding. Jack's quiet humour and easygoing attitude to life made my existence in the Air Force very much more acceptable, and often even enjoyable.

My first task at Sir John Cass was to get my impetigo settled. It was now looking much more serious, with the sores taking up increasingly circular forms, though as yet not complete circles. Sick Parade was at Air Ministry headquarters, then at 15 Portman Square. Here, to my great delight, I met a real doctor, who promptly installed me in the sick quarters, scrubbed my face clean with appropriate disinfectants, and then painted the whole of it with Gentian Violet. This immediately resulted in my being nicknamed Bluebeard; but, as I began to improve straight away, I didn't mind a bit. Shaving was out, as this type of interference with the sores had produced a cross-infection with streptococci, which, if left untreated so that the circles joined up, would have left me permanently scarred on the face. I have to admit, too, that before going into sick quarters I had rushed home to see the family and Mary, and, owing to her flat refusal to allow me to quarantine myself, had passed the impetigo on to her. Fortunately, she knew what it was, and so got over it as quickly as I did.

The Sick Quarters at Portman Square were in the building used as a dormitory by the staff of the Air Ministry in Whitehall - that is, by the other ranks of course, both airmen and girls of the WAAF[2]. These were segregated by sleeping on different floors, with I believe something approaching the Maginot Line separating the floors. One of the customers of the Sick Quarters while I was there was a corporal from within Portman Square itself. He appeared to be suffering from exhaustion, and required a rest for about a week. He explained that his job was that of Blackout Corporal, and his task was to ensure that all blackouts were in position every night, on all floors, WAAF as well as RAF. Whether his exhaustion came from lifting heavy blackouts or from

---

2 Women's Auxiliary Air Force

his officially authorized breaches of the Maginot Line, I'm not absolutely sure; but I fear the worst.

I claimed earlier to be a fairly innocent young man; but my education and experience of life was broadening very rapidly. In the Sick Quarters was a large wastepaper basket full of small packets. I suppose they might be classified under the name of preventive medicine: each contained one French letter, and a small tube of ointment to be used immediately after intercourse, the idea being to protect the seekers after London's night life from contracting VD. Airmen were invited to help themselves when going out for the evening. I was absolutely astounded at the rate at which the contents of this basket vanished.

Another temporary inmate of the Sick Quarters while I was there was the most foul-mouthed individual I have ever met in my entire life. The ubiquitous four-letter word appeared in every sentence he spoke. It replaced all the adjectives, and provided a fair sprinkling of the nouns as well. In frequency it averaged about one in every four or five words he spoke. The effect was boring and monotonous in the extreme, and I can't imagine what he did when he lost his temper and really wanted to swear.

Happily, however, my impetigo was on the mend, and I was soon discharged back to Sir John Cass. In the meantime my erstwhile colleagues had started their course, and I was therefore delayed to join the next course. This was a very important step as far as my time in the Air Force was concerned, as the next entry was predominately Canadian. I was thus thrust into the company of a variety of Canadians, which throughout my Air Force career gave me a tremendous amount of pleasure and a number of lifelong friendships. Also the somewhat irreverent attitude to authority taken by Canadians made Service life never seem quite the same again.

A few words concerning our domestic life in the Minories office building. The enforced darkness of the early mornings and evenings led to a fair amount of excitement. The unwary individual who collapsed on to his bed would find the bed collapse as well, as pranksters would have set the legs inwards. Also the unalert were frequently hit in the teeth by bolsters hurled from the darkness - these were, of course, the other fellow's bolster - never your own.

The principal victim of this type of assault was a meek and mild little Irishman by the name of Rafferty. At least he was normally meek and mild, and well liked by everyone. Unfortunately, a few beers taken during an evening, and the centuries of English oppression used to well up in his breast. Just after closing time he could be heard laboriously climbing the stairs cursing the English and describing vividly what he would like to do to them. Meantime the cowardly English would lie in wait; and the moment Rafferty pushed open the swing doors, a dozen or more bolsters would hit him squarely in the teeth. This did not improve his temper at all; but in the total darkness he had no chance of finding his attackers. However, by next morning we were *all* friends again.

Shaving represented a major problem in the dark mornings, and the general method was to take a small piece of candle to the washroom and there light it and shave by its flickering light. However, since almost everyone finishing his shave and blowing out his candle would obligingly blow out those of his comrades as well, there was a somewhat frenetic atmosphere every morning. The food was prepared and served in the school canteen; and what a treat it was after the Imperial! I suppose it was standard canteen food; but it felt like the Ritz to arrivals from Skegness.

Another hilarious domestic afternoon was spent at the Stepney Public Baths, where we were marched once per week to perform our ablutions. These cubicles had the rather peculiar arrangement that the water, both hot and cold, was controlled from outside the cubicle, so that for any adjustment it was necessary to hail the unfortunate attendant, who would provide the required supply. This individual was immediately christened the "Bath Steward", and always hailed as such. Our pranksters were in their element here, with merry cries of "Bath Steward, cold in number 18"; "Hot in 24", these numbers of course being any numbers you please but the caller's own. So your comfortable soak would suddenly be interrupted by a stream of cold (or, worse, hot) water. Your endeavours to get the bath steward to reverse his decision were very poorly received; and, after 15-20 minutes, he would retire and leave the b-s to get on with it!! I suppose there must have been an officer i/c; but we had so little contact that I don't recall him at all. There was a Flight Sergeant in charge of discipline, who was pretty miserable and unpopular; but really he did not bother us much. Our main contacts, apart from the Technical Instructors, were the two PT Corporals, Brooks and Davis. They had a tough time of it, with difficult conditions to contend with, not helped by the irreverent attitudes of the Canadians.

Every so often we had the pleasure of a route march, taking us down to the Tower of London and back again. This was invariably a shambles, and not improved on one occasion by some of the Canucks spotting an old rusty chair on a bombed site - picking it up when the Corporal wasn't looking, and, by passing it from shoulder to shoulder, producing a fair imitation of a chain-gang, for the edification of office workers scurrying past, until finally being detected and roared at by the PT Corporal.

Another session of marching given by Corporal Brooks was enlivened by the fact that, after he had allowed the squad to march a fair distance away before giving them a stentorian "About Turn", on this occasion only the back half turned round, while the front half continued to step out very smartly in the direction of Bishopsgate! A few more cries were totally ignored by the front half, and Brooks was eventually compelled to run after them to bring them to a halt. However, Brooks got his own back a day or two later, by commenting, following a march around the block: "That's the smartest walk I've ever seen H Entry deliver. You couldn't call it a march, but it was a pretty good stroll."

Every Wednesday we were transported to a Sports Ground near Grove Park in Kent for a sports afternoon. The facilities were really quite good, and there were options open in various sports. Incidentally, one of the most enjoyable parts of RAF life for me was always the chance, for a sports duffer like me, to have a go at many different sports. Anyway, I opened at Grove Park by opting for cricket; and, having claimed to be a batsman rather than a bowler, neither skill being really within my grasp, I went in at No. 5 and succeeded in making 15 runs. This may not seem much to you; but it was actually the top score on my side, and the following week I found myself opening the innings. I added a further 11 runs to my aggregate, and, since this was the last week of the cricket season, I ended with the highest cricket average I ever achieved, 13!

As H Entry was predominantly Canadian, softball was widely played. This is a version of baseball with a slightly softer and larger ball, underarm pitching and some other variants in the rules, but one that provides a good, fast and skilful game. I became very interested in this, and played regularly. I would never claim to be a real expert; but I managed to put bat to ball now and again, and learnt to manipulate the fielder's mitts. As winter drew on and the ground got soggier and soggier, there was a certain falling off in interest in softball, and I noticed that cross-country running seemed to be very popular. So I joined this group, and we duly lined up for the start, and were away down the field and through the gap in the hedge - along the highway, around the first bend and into a convenient café, where cups of tea and buns enlivened the remainder of our afternoon's cross-country. At around 4.30 came the cry "Finish up, lads", and off we trotted back up the field, with suitable hard breathing to justify our afternoon's run!

Did we do anything here that actually contributed to the war effort? Why, yes we did; and I found it both interesting and enjoyable as well. Basically, the bulk of this work was Electrical and Radio Theory, Mathematics and Workshop Practice. The maths I found fairly easy, and I really enjoyed the opportunity to learn something about Radio. My Workshop Practice, as throughout the rest of my life, was somewhat shaky; but I did learn some wrinkles on wire-jointing, soldering, the use of tools and welding that have frequently been useful to me in later life.

The teaching was by civilian instructors; and as virtually all the airmen were keen to learn, we made a lot of progress. At the end of the course we had examinations; and though no official statement to this effect was ever made, it was widely rumoured that good results would mean allocation as Radio Mechanics rather than as Wireless Mechanics. This somewhat obscure distinction would mean that we would go to a Radar or, as it was then known, a Radio Location site. In the end my Workshop Practice held up and my theory was good enough to put me in the top quartile, and thus to allow me to pass out as a Radio Mechanic.

Altogether, this time at the Sir John Cass Institute was the most enjoyable of all my RAF career. Interesting work, lots of fun, and most enjoyable friends and company. The RAF seemed far away. Regular trips home after work, parties at the Hammersmith Palais de Danse. Those were the days when dancing together was still popular, and Harry Leader and Roy Marsh led the bands who gave the airmen of Sir John Cass and Mary's girlfriends from the Post Office Savings Bank some very good times.

My romance prospered, and during this time Mary and I became engaged. We had a marvellous engagement party, notable mainly for a long line of airmen trying to sleep on the floor of our front room, with the man nearest the fire being dehydrated while the outside man was frozen in the draught under the door! However, all good things come to an end, and in January 1942 we got our marching orders - to RAF Cranwell!

BEFORE I FORGET

FOUR

Cranwell

There could not be more of a contrast between the pleasant life of Sir John Cass and RAF Cranwell. Cranwell was of course a major peacetime RAF camp, as indeed it still is today. At this time Cranwell had well over 5,000 airmen in residence, and included also a number of WAAF.

There were two airfields on either side of the camp - the North and South Fields - and two main camps, the East Camp, virtually entirely given over to the training of Wireless Operators and Wireless Mechanics, and the West Camp, which contained the Radio School, training on the various forms of Radar equipment, and also the Officer Training School, which has always been the foundation of Cranwell's training programme. Cranwell is situated right on the top of the Lincolnshire wolds - high up, exposed - and some 7 miles from Seaford, the nearest town, if you can call it such; and Grantham is approximately 20 miles away.

We were housed in the usual RAF huts, as at Cardington, and were subjected to the whole gamut of RAF discipline - parades, Warrant Officers, PT, Flight Sergeants, fatigues, etc. We had the first fortnight of our stay to become adjusted to the RAF again, as our Radar courses could not start immediately; so we certainly came down to earth with a bang. Winter was very much on us; and, though it was not then snowing, it had snowed in the previous week, and the snow had been trodden down into ice. Of course the RAF had not thought about clearing it until it was thoroughly trodden down and could only be moved by chipping. So that was our primary introduction to Cranwell. The huts were issued with the very minimum of fuel, while the main supplies were locked away in a barbed-wire-guarded compound. However, I regret to say that this did not save them, and, as the cold became more intense, almost everything movable found its way on to the hut stove.

The Radio School had about 400 students and was run by a CO and an Adjutant, assisted by a Warrant Officer, a Flight Sergeant and three Regular Sergeants. The officers made no impact on me at all. The WO was a dyed-in-the-wool bastard whose main delight was in getting some airman to double round the square carrying a rifle at the high port (i.e. over his head). A somewhat agonizing process! The Flight was quite a reasonable bloke; but the three sergeants were, without doubt, the most despicable, degraded individuals I have ever encountered. One ran a thriving trade in pornographic material. All could be bribed to escape any type of duty. All were a very poor example of scruffiness to set the troops; and the only decent thing one of them did (after we had departed) was to hit the WO with a bottle.

Here it was that we really learned our lessons in scrounging. So many of the tasks we received were so manifestly unnecessary or, at best, a misguided direction of our enthusiasm that it seemed our bounden duty to try to dodge them if we could. It was here during this waiting period that the classical services joke came to life for me. You know the joke I mean: Sergeant: "Is there anyone here interested in music?" Recruit: "Yes, me, Sarge!" Sergeant: "Right, get out there and lift that piano." Only in our case it was a Radar Set. "Would anyone like to have a look over a Radar Set? Right, get out there and shift it!"

The food at this camp was atrocious, and only the NAAFIs kept us alive, as usual. Another grisly service was the Laundry - run I should suppose by neo-Nazis - which used always to run up all the clothes so that in two or three weeks you had nothing left that fitted you. It also had the greatest sock shrinker I have ever seen. In no time I was reduced to doing my own washing on a Sunday as the only way to survive. No complaints did any good; they were so overwhelmed by them.

Being a well-established camp, Cranwell did have some amenities. First was a cinema, actually in the East Camp, which I tried on a couple of occasions. The films were always accompanied by some raucous advice;

and as one of those I picked was a romantic film, this advice made my innocent little ears turn pink! Particularly so, as most of it seemed to come from the WAAF ranks (segregated, of course). I never thought that ladies would behave like that!

Also - and this actually had a profound effect on my subsequent life - there was a Music Society. At that time I listened to nothing but jazz - classical music was just a drag. However, I allowed myself to be persuaded go to a Music Society record recital, at which the main work was Dvorak's New World Symphony. I listened, and my ears were opened to the world of classical music, which has given me so many hours of blissful enjoyment. And it all started at Cranwell's Music Society.

Cranwell also had a Swimming Pool (indoor), and at least some of the PT periods could be spent in the pool. I broke the heart of yet another swimming instructor by failing to learn to swim yet again! This pool was situated at the bottom of the West Camp, while our huts were at the top end. To get there, the Sergeant in charge had to parade 90 men and march them in a long column, winding their way through the huts and down to the pool and the gym alongside it. If the sergeant marched behind the column, as it went round the corner, the front ranks would dive into the huts; whereas if the sergeant marched at the front, the back ranks would similarly disappear. When the column arrived at the gym, the first in would run like hares across the gym and through into the pool and out the other side. That sergeant never had more than two-thirds of his men for PT.

Another interesting aspect of life in that hut was Reveille. Normally the duty corporal would stick his head in at 6.30 a.m. and shout "Everybody Up, Wakey-Wakey." No one took much notice of this until the Flight appeared about 20 minutes later and read the Riot Act.

One morning, a drive was laid on to get Reveille really recognized. Ours was the first hut, and when the Flight appeared it was with the Duty Officer in tow. "Right," said the Officer to the Flight, looking round the room at the bodies still in bed. "Take the names of all the men still in bed." Then, realizing that 3 were up and 27 in bed, he changed it to:

BEFORE I FORGET

"Take the names of all those up." The party then proceeded to the next hut, where, sad to say, all 30 were still in bed. At that, the drive was discreetly abandoned, and our sleeping habits thereafter were left undisturbed.

During the early part of our stay the snow continued to fall intermittently, and one evening at around 6 p.m. we were paraded outside our hut in greatcoats with about 9 inches of snow lying on the ground. As we did not have wellingtons at this time, this was an unfortunate height, just enough to lap over the tops of RAF boots. Anyway, we were marched off across the camp, down past the gym and out on to the South Field. By now darkness had fallen, and we proceeded out to the centre of the field in the direction of a group of trucks with headlights ablaze. On arrival there, it was apparent that we were now on the runway of the airfield, which had been cleared of snow, which however had been hurled into banks about four or five feet high on either side of the runway. This made a wide shallow trench along the runway itself, and seemed very far from conducive to safe landings. A line of eight or so trucks appeared, carrying every spade or shovel the camp possessed. These were quickly distributed amongst us, and we were ordered to shovel the piles of snow from the edges of the runway on to the waiting trucks. These were ordinary-type trucks, and so every shovelful had to be raised to shoulder level to fling it over the tailgate. There were about half a dozen men to a truck; and, as the truck finally filled, we had to leap on board complete with shovels, and the truck would drive down the runway, where we would then shovel it all off again!

Though we didn't know it at the time, what had apparently happened was that a large raid had been dispatched out to Germany, and fog had then closed in over the operational fields. A desperate search had then begun for any airfield free from fog to receive the returning planes, and Cranwell, being on top of the Wolds, was the lucky choice.

The authorities turned out their one snowplough, which consisted of an ordinary three-ton truck with two large pieces of sheet steel welded at a suitable angle. This, when driven along the runway, had cleared it successfully, but only at the cost of building these ramparts on either side.

They themselves were too high to be tackled by the plough, so, after a few seconds' deliberation, the powers that be came up with the services' ultimate solution – "Manpower". So there we were on the airfield with shovels in our hands.

I looked around for a chance to get lost; but it was by now pitch-black, and the camp had disappeared from sight. I was disorientated by now - which way was it? In the end I could not face the prospect of wandering off into a snowdrift on top of the Lincolnshire Wolds, so I resigned myself to an unpleasant evening. The party was encouraged by the appearance of the Air Commodore commanding the whole station (a very big noise indeed), and his exhortations to extra efforts were not too well received by the toiling airmen, who, emboldened by the dark, gave the Air Commodore a selection of their views concerning his undoubted ancestry and his future prospects!

So the evening wore on - truck after truck - fill up, leap on board, empty out, with the snow lapping over the boots so that feet and socks were in puddles of water. I had on a nice pair of knitted woollen gloves, which were gradually shredded until quite useless. Finally it was all over and as a final flourish, the snowplough drove to the end of the runway, tried to turn round and 'sank' up to the axles in mud. So there was the plough broadside across the runway as a welcoming hazard to the returning bombers. Immediate recourse to the shovels - revving the engine and trying to force lumps of wood, sacks, anything under the wheels. All to no avail! The situation was deteriorating rapidly when the unbelievable happened. Every man jack who could get there surrounded the plough, getting two hands, one hand or even a finger on it and with the strength of sheer desperation actually lifted the truck into the air, sufficient to push the blocks under the wheels. So at last we were released and wearily shouldering shovels straggled back to the camp where, to give him his due, the Air Commodore had rousted out the cooks and made them serve a hot supper with plenty of tea. So ended what I have always referred to as the most unpleasant and uncomfortable night of my life. Just as an afterthought, the wind sprang up, the fog blew away and the returning bombers landed safely at their own fields.

BEFORE I FORGET

Once again, the reader will begin to ask. "Did they never get down to radar training on this camp"? Well, yes, they did after about a fortnight's delay. I should explain here that despite all the snow clearing and the general bull surrounding the camp, we were all as keen as mustard. We anticipated something new, advanced and really worthwhile and all were determined to do our best and master the complexities of the new medium. The course consisted of a series of machines - transmitters and receivers from the CH[3] chain and then from the CHL[4] chain. Each man received about a fortnight of theoretical lectures on the circuits and philosophy of the sets, followed by practical classes and instruction, fault finding and testing. While the classrooms (all Nissen huts) were in the main camp, all the equipment (being secret) was housed in an enclosure entirely surrounded by a steel fence some 8 feet high. After each day's tuition our notebooks were taken away and locked up in this compound. We were allowed to return to the compound after dinner, to collect our books and put in some private study. One (yes one) Nissen hut was set aside for our study. Our entry was about 90 strong and altogether some 400 men were in the middle of their course. So 400 men and one Nissen hut! Of course the other courses had already given up on any additional studying, but even 90 is a bit of a crowd. And so after about three nights, everyone gave up; so typical of the Cranwell approach to the task of creating new Radar mechanics. We shall hear more of that attitude later.

Our group got off on the wrong foot in our practical class. We were tackling a large transmitter used on the CH chain and on our first fault finding session, we discovered that the switching-on procedure would not even start. Every group has their know-it-alls and ours was no exception. These grabbed the AVOMETER, claiming that there was no input supply. Down behind the transmitter they go and instead of testing from each of the three phase inputs to ground, they smack the AVO across the phases. Fortunately they were holding the insulated part of the clips, because in a shower of sparks, the AVO clips promptly welded themselves to the terminals. The instructor hit the roof, but at least the know-it-alls

---

3   Chain Home – the string of large radar stations built along the east coast of the UK in 1939 to detect incoming bombers.
4   Chain Home Low – a later adaptation of Chain Home, designed to detect low-flying aircraft

were more circumspect in future. In general the instruction was quite good though somewhat stereo-typed in form and I believe most of us finished with a good grasp of each of the machines.

A certain amount of excitement was caused one day when an instructor, who had managed to evade the RAF regulations and grow his hair to a more artistic length, was leaning negligently against a receiver whilst lecturing. The class could see clearly that his long hair was entering the jack sockets on the front of the receiver. We watched with bated breath and finally, one lean too many and the hairs touched the live part of the socket. The resulting jump into the air of a couple of feet enlivened the callous crowd of students!

On another evening, we were suddenly visited by the Flight Sergeant and ordered to stand by our beds while a thorough search of our belongings was carried out. This was apparently to locate large quantities of valves that had been disappearing from the secret compound despite the 8-foot fences and a regular guard mounted night and day on the gate. I could easily see how the smaller valves could disappear with squads moving in and out, but apparently the big transmitter valves - 2 feet high and 1 foot high and deep were also going. How anyone could spirit these away I don't know. Certainly nothing was found in our hut.

The cold weather continued during this time and seemed, surprisingly to affect the Canadians more than the British. Something to do with Wet Cold rather than the Dry Cold they claimed to be used to in Canada. None was affected more than one Micky Barnett whose counter-measures involved covering himself with ten thicknesses of blanket and moving totally inside this tent so that no part was left in contact with the icy English winter. Sunday was a free day for us apart from an occasional Church parade and one Sunday when the weather was typically English i.e. a constant steady drizzle, Barnett was enjoying an extra lie-in somewhere underneath his pile of blankets. Four stalwart lads raised his bed very slowly and very gently and transferred it outside to the middle of the field. Some 3/4 hour later, the drizzle finally penetrated the last of the blankets and Barnett awoke. He was not amused!

BEFORE I FORGET

As our training proceeded, the new entries coming into the Radio School increased the pressure on accommodation particularly within the secret compound so that eventually they had to move to double shifts and our entry found itself working up until 1.30 am at night. We accepted the necessity for unconventional hours though no adjustment was made to times for breakfast etc. and no one really complained. However very shortly after this change over occurred, another alteration was introduced which did cause a great deal of indignation. The CO of the Radio School made an inspection tour of his domain and was appalled by the untidy character of the area particularly around his own headquarters. So instructional time was reduced by 2 hours per week and given over to "Domestic Economy" during which time we were instructed to tour the camp picking up all waste paper and delivering same to the HQ dustbins. This, in April 1942, at what must have been the absolute nadir of the country's fortunes during the war with Rommel at the gates of Cairo and the Japanese dominating the Pacific. While we, the embryo Radar Mechanics sacrificed our Radar instruction to pick up waste paper for the CO. Of course, we did nothing of the sort during this 2 hour period, but returned and lay on our beds, the whole time bitterly complaining about the obtuse behaviour of the RAF regular administration and, at the end of the period, grabbed the sacks of rubbish hanging on the billet wall and turned up at HQ with virtuous expressions. I hope the CO was satisfied with the improvement.

Every day we had to start the day with a parade of the whole school and it was the practice for the Officers Training School to provide a trainee officer to take this parade, no doubt his only experience of such an ordeal. The method employed was for the WO to bring the parade to attention and to march across to the officer and hand the parade over to him. He would march smartly to the centre of the parade ground and issue the orders to left turn and march off in column of route. One day, an unfortunate young man confronted with this nerve wracking task, arrived smartly in the centre of the parade ground and cried, "Parade will move off in column of route", but forgot to add the magic words "Right turn - quick march." As a result no move whatsoever was made. One could only feel the greatest sympathy with the young man as across his face visibly passed the agonising thought, "Why did they have to choose today to mutiny?" Eventually the WO had to whisper in a voice that carried for miles ,"Right turn" and suddenly it worked.

So our three months stay at Cranwell wore on and despite the efforts of the RAF Establishment we still retained a fair amount of our initial enthusiasm and became generally pretty useful Radar Mechanics. However, the whole process generally left me so exhausted that never once did I take the regular Liberty Runs to sample the delights of Grantham or even Seaford. As the course ended, our interest centred on the forthcoming postings which were going to be, as so often the case in the RAF, on an individual basis, and the good friends we had made both at Sir John Cass and at Cranwell would be spread all over the U.K. Our main concern was not to get sent to one of the remote sites up in the Shetlands or Western Isles. As exemplified in the parody of the old Irish folk song - "A little bit of heaven fell from out the sky one day - and when the Air Force saw it, why it looked so bleak and bare, they said that's what we're looking for, we'll send our airmen there!"

In the event, I was pretty fortunate and together with another English lad, by name Tony Dell, I was posted to RAF Happisburgh, pronounced Haysboro, a CHL station on the Norfolk coast between Cromer and Yarmouth. And on May 6th 1942, Tony and I took a train from Cranwell for the Norfolk coast.

BEFORE I FORGET

FIVE

Happisburgh

Happisburgh is a tiny Norfolk village right on the coast equidistant between Cromer and Yarmouth. Its main claim to fame was the lighthouse, which advertised the presence of the notorious Haisborough Sands - why the spelling is different, I never did find out. In those pre-Beeching days, there was a single-track railway that diverged from the Norwich to Cromer line at North Walsham and wandered out to the coast at Mundesley and then via Trimingham and Overstrand to Cromer, but this did not remotely approach Happisburgh. There was a bus service to North Walsham, but this only ran twice a week. So Happisburgh was pretty well cut off from civilisation, which had both advantages and disadvantages. Disadvantages in that any chance of escaping to enjoy the night life of Walsham or even Norwich was practically non existent, the bus being useless in this respect, and advantages in that as the local bobby appeared about as frequently as the bus, the licensing hours at the local Hill House Hotel (the only pub in the village) were flexible to say the least.

RAF Happisburgh was a small CHL Station with a Pilot Officer as CO and run by a Flight Sergeant Slack in charge of the Mechanics and Sergeant Dodgson in charge of the Operators. At this time a CHL station consisted of an Ops block of two Nissen huts side by side with the Transmitter in one and the Receiver plus any additional plotting gear in the next. The whole being surmounted by a 40-foot gantry containing an antenna array of stacked dipoles, the whole array being rotated manually by a wheel in the receiver cabin below. The receiver had two Display Tubes - the first being a Height/Range display allegedly tracking up to 200 miles but in reality only detecting high-flying aircraft over about 100

BEFORE I FORGET

miles and a PP1 tube (Plan Position Indicator) on which the trace rotated synchronously with the antenna scanning an area of 60 miles around.

However the most interesting part of the activities of RAF Happisburgh was that it was also called upon to simulate a GCI Station (Ground Controlled Interception). There was actually a genuine GCI Station not far away at Neatishead, and this station together with Happisburgh constituted the main defence of East Anglia and the East Midlands against the Nazi night bombers. These two stations both controlled Beaufighter night-fighters from RAF Coltishall station, a squadron commanded by Wing Commander Max Aitken.

Neatishead had the advantage in that it had technical means of estimating the height of the hostile bomber, whereas at Happisburgh this had to be estimated by looking at the lobe diagrams of the station's propagation. Fortunately Sgt. Dodgson a very experienced NCO with flight observer experience in the first World War, was really expert at this and could unerringly determine the important factor of the hostile's height. The Controller working at the station was Ft. Lt. Everett who was very experienced and expert at directing these interceptions.

The personnel at Happisburgh when Tony and I first arrived was entirely male and they included four sailors whose primary task was to send information to the Naval Control Centre at Yarmouth but in fact they were totally integrated with the operators team and participated in all the interceptions. Very often too, the Mechanics were called in to make up the operating team and did so with great enthusiasm. The Interception team consisted of two operators on the Receiver, one on the H/R tube and sweeping the aerial and plotting where necessary outside the 60-mile limit of the PPI. The main plotting, however, came from the PPI tube and was recorded by another operator on a large plotting board from which the Controller operated. Liaison operations also connected the site with the Sector control at Coltishall, the central plotting board at the nearest CH station West Beckham and the GCI at Neatishead.

The West Beckham site could be expected to detect hostiles coming in at greater distances and so would provide advanced contacts for future interceptions. The Coltishall Sector would provide contacts with night-fighters already in the air and waiting to be used on an interception. The Neatishead contact was necessary to keep track of their interceptions to avoid overlap and, even worse, chasing their own fighter. At the same Sgt. Dodgson would be estimating heights for the benefit of the Beaufighter pilot.

The pattern of an interception went thus. West Beckham would detect an aircraft coming in towards a UK target. It would first be labelled Unidentified until its IFF signal (Identification Friend Or Foe) had been tested. Failure to respond would classify the aircraft as hostile and number it. At Happisburgh the H/R operator would be sweeping that area to try and pick up the aircraft - early detection being necessary to give accurate height readings. Meantime the Controller would be scanning the positions of several fighters aloft received from Coltishall and selecting that most suitable to fly an interception path. At the same time he would be checking that Neatishead had not collared either the hostile or the fighter selected. Once the interception was launched the plotting would sweep back and forth between hostile and fighter as the Controller gave vector, speed, and height instructions to the pilot over the WT links. Within a certain range the fighter would switch on his AI set (Air Interception) and hopefully pick up the hostile. Often of course they would actually see it. At the cry of "Tally Ho" the job of Happisburgh was finished and they turned immediately to the next hostile and an appropriate fighter. Later of course, they would hopefully receive confirmation of destruction from Coltishall Sector.

The enthusiasm of the teams at this time was whole-hearted and the watches vied with each other to participate in successful interceptions. I have as yet not explained that in order to provide round the clock cover, both operators and mechanics were working on a three-watch system 8-1, 1-6, 6-11 and 11-8.

Although things were fairly quiet when we first arrived, they soon warmed up as Hitler chose during the June moon to launch the second series of so-called Baedeker raids, intended to strike at British cathedral cities presumably in retaliation for RAF raids on Germany. A number

BEFORE I FORGET

of these were on East Anglian and East Midlands targets and were generally around 50 aircraft in strength. During this fortnight, RAF Happisburgh ran 15 successful interceptions and on one night when I was privileged to be a minor part of the team, we intercepted three bombers while Neatishead scored 4. Seven out of 50 proved too much for Hitler and he soon gave this up.

One other interesting little quirk of the interception game occurred during a Calibration run. Because of the necessity of height-checking by means of lobe diagrams at Happisburgh, it was necessary to run Calibration flights regularly and, as these needed to be towards the coast of occupied Europe, the aircraft doing the run were always fully armed. On one occasion during such a run, a German Junkers 88 was detected flying down the Dutch coast obviously on a training run himself. Imagine his surprise when a fully armed Beaufighter 140 miles from its controlling station, intercepted and shot him down.

My first preoccupation of arriving at Happisburgh was to get leave (now very much overdue thanks to the lengthy training). Very important to me as I was anxious to get married. Mary and I had been engaged for six months and knew our own minds. The Flight Sergeant proved surprisingly cooperative and so within three weeks I was off on seven days leave and planning our marriage for the middle of that period. We had decided to marry from home and to defer a honeymoon (such as it was in wartime) till my next leave. And so on May 23rd 1942 at

Turnham Green Church before the Rev. Osborne Goodchild, Mary Houghton and I became man and wife.

Tony and I had been allocated a civilian billet in Happisburgh village with a certain Mrs. Clarke and on the station everyone commiserated with us as Mrs. Clarke's was known to be a lousy billet. When we first arrived there, she lived up to her reputation and we had a fairly miserable time. I particularly remember the breakfasts. A slice of white bread untoasted covered with a kind of Brown Windsor type gruel drawn from a pot constantly on the fire. The house was very much in the country and water was drawn from the well operated by a long lever type plunger with defective valves, so that the pump needed priming before it would work at all. Waste disposal was also somewhat primitive and consisted of a wooden contraption in the garden which had to be accommodated from time to time by Tony and I digging a large hole in the back garden and hurling the contents of the contraption into it.

Mrs Clarke's family was an interesting one. She had two sons and one daughter. The eldest son Ron was a Staff Sergeant in some Army Corps and I guess a fairly typical Staff. He was married and his wife, whose name escapes me, lived with Mrs Clarke. She didn't hit it off very well with Mrs Clarke and so was somewhat sympathetic to us. The second son Jimmy was a submariner aboard the HMS Ursula and Mrs Clarke used to bewail the fact that poor Jimmy had been forced into the submarines against his will but as whenever she said this to us when he was there, it was always accompanied by winks and thumbs up from the redoubtable Jim himself, I rather doubt it.

The daughter was engaged on war work at the Pye Ltd factory in Cambridge and I don't recall seeing her at all. However at an early age she had had an unfortunate experience and the result was a small girl of about six who resided with her grandmother. This young lady used to switch her affections from Tony to me and back again quite regularly and her favourite practice was to sidle up to you while perhaps you were writing a letter with a beatific smile on her face and then suddenly would deal you a smart kick on the shins and retreat hastily to the door where she would shout " I love Tony but I hate you—Yah!"

BEFORE I FORGET

One spectacular event during our stay was Jimmy's leave of fourteen days duration. He arrived with £25 and borrowed a further £7 from his mother and succeeded in blueing the lot at the Hill House Hotel every night. Though the hotel was no more than 300 yards distant, he used to ride there on his bicycle and as the entrance to the house was a five-barred gate, usually left unlatched, he would ride the bike straight at the gate and make it swing open to allow him to pass. Unfortunately one night about 1.30am with a real skinful on board he tried this manoeuvre when some swine had latched the gate and as a result he fell smartly in the ditch where he was discovered at 5.30 a.m. sleeping peacefully by his doting mother. Fortunately the inner fires burning within him kept the chill night air at bay.

Later that summer I managed to get another seven days and Mary and I went to Torquay to stay with two friends for our honeymoon and delightful it was too.

Coming back both Tony and I picked up our bicycles and were thus able to explore the neighbourhood much more. Also we volunteered to do a little shopping from time to time for Mrs Clarke and gradually the old termagant softened up and began to treat us very well. The chickens in the garden began to lay eggs, and breakfasts turned into much nicer meals. As well as the chickens, Mrs Clarke kept rabbits and the rations began to be supplemented very nicely.

We could also add to our rations by patronising the village fish and chip shop a little outside the main village area. This was run by a nice woman, who worked hard, and produced some tasty fish and chips. She was however cursed by a lazy good-for-nothing husband who as far as I could see never did a stroke of work. They had a small child and the husband used to pall a pleasant evening by tipping this child a half-penny or a penny to burst into the fish and chip shop and offer some foul language to its unfortunate mother who was slaving over the hot fish fryer. Somewhat disconcerting when your mind was on a 4d and a pennorth[5] only to have this kid sounding off.

---

5 Four (old) pence worth of fish, and a penny's worth of chips

The Naval personnel were all billeted down a small side road in two semi-detached houses in a common yard. The two houses were occupied, one by a middle aged couple and the other by their daughter of about twenty two and her husband, much older than herself. The daughter was named (if you can believe it) Audrey and so was universally known as Little Audrey. Her sex life with her husband must have been somewhat frustrating but she certainly made up for it with the Navy. Her mother frequently had to yank Audrey out of bed so that the matelots could make the Duty Truck. As one of them once said to me "I believe Audrey is the only girl I know who could make violent love and read the Daily Mirror at the same time." I don't know whether it was caused by living in such an isolated community, but I found the Norfolk people a pretty amoral lot.

Up at the station plans were afoot to separate the CHL station from the ACI component and a new Ops Block was created and a 200-foot wooden mast began to be erected. The operators were rewarded for their enthusiasm by being steadily posted to Burma together with some mechanics and the Ops were replaced by a contingent of WAAF Radio Operators. I must say that these were all charming, well brought up girls – though I regret to say that I remember only one of them, a Scots lassie by the name of Margaret Monteith (Ops). I remember her particularly for an astonishing feat of nerve. At that time the wooden mast had almost reached its full height but the erectors made their way from stage to stage by building ladders lashed to the cross members. Some badinage took place one evening about climbing the mast whereupon Maggie Monteith said, "I'll climb the mast" and promptly did so, as far as she could go, practically to the top and all the way up the builders' ladders. At the first stage about 40 feet up she walked from one ladder to the next, only a couple of yards but standing on two beams about two inches wide and about six inches apart. My knees went to jelly just thinking about it.

Technically Tony and I made slow progress. We started by cleaning out the new Ops block and then penetrated as far as the daily maintenance but all fault finding was seized upon by the Flight and his sidekick Cpl

BEFORE I FORGET

Morley and the erks[6] seldom got to the set in earnest. By the way I should say that both Tony and I had qualified sufficiently well before coming to Happisburgh to be made up to AC1 Radar Mechanics and our pay went from 2 shillings and 6 pence per day to 6 shillings a day. I probably got married on the strength of this affluence.

One subject that we did begin to master was maintenance of the Diesel standby, in a separate truck alongside the Ops block. If there was little or no hostile activity on a night watch the mechanics were accustomed to stretch themselves out on a mattress in the Transmitter Room and get a few hours sleep. One night, I was well away in the early hours of the morning when the mains supply failed. The Operators immediately rushed in and woke me – shouting, "Get the Standby going". I leapt up and into my boots, tightened my belt and pulled on my jacket and rushed forth into the night. Unfortunately the rain had been coming down in buckets and outside was an absolute quagmire. As soon as I emerged my feet slid from under me and I went full length into a mud bath. Well, I got the Diesel going but I was covered in mud from head to foot.

Tony and I were now on different watches and one afternoon when he was on duty the Wing Dental Officer arrived driving his natty little caravan in which all the instruments of torture were laid out. The caravan stood on two wheels, rubber tyred of course. The Dental Officer leapt out and leaning under the van brought out a long wire with a plug on the end. He said to Tony, "This is my power supply, you'll have to take the plug off and feed it through that ventilator into the Ops block and then reconnect the plug." With that he cleared off. Tony did as asked but when replacing the plug was a little more careless than he should have been, reversing the earth and live wires. As a result the Dental Officer arriving next morning, put his hand on the door handle and leapt a yard of so into the air with 240 volts up his arm. Was it really an accident, I wonder?

---

6   RAF slang for Aircraftman, the lowest rank in the British Royal Air Force.

One Man's Radar War

Part of the daily maintenance was to polish the dipoles on the aerial and this was normally left until after the station was on the air, when the mechanics could be seen floating round polishing the aerial as it rotated at the expense of some unfortunate operator struggling to drive the rotation. Now that the separation of the CHL and the GCI site was complete, we were transferred to the CHL site where, at 200 feet high, the new aerial mast somewhat curtailed our enthusiasm for sailing around. The mast itself was quite scary to climb and had some protection from falling off. However the last twenty five feet I always found somewhat trying as the ladder rose absolutely vertically to the last platform and all the strain was placed on the arms. Tony and I did force ourselves to climb out to the end of the dipole array and thus right out over the 200 foot drop just to prove we could do it, but I must say I clung on like a limpet and I can still clearly see the ground 200 feet below me in my mind's eye.

Another technical advance which came in with the CHL site was power operation of the aerial rotation and to achieve this a huge box appeared in the Transmitter room containing both motors and the Contactor used for starting, stopping and reversing. Normally this gave off a low hum when the aerials were rotating normally and since it also had a wide flat top this formed an ideal bed where the Mechs could be soothed off to sleep during a night shift. However if suspicious echoes arose then if would be necessary to stop, reverse and sweep back for identification. This was achieved by the contactors which gave forth cracks like rifle shots. However after a time the seasoned sleepers on our squad could take this in their stride and never wake.

Another staff reshuffle took place following the splitting of the sites. The WAAF Radio Operators all moved to the CHL site and on the GCI they were replaced by another set of female Clerks (Special Duties). These were the girls most often seen pushing the counters around with croupier's rakes in Sector Rooms. They were a very different type of girl to the Radio Ops. Tougher, older and perhaps not so nicely brought up. They obviously knew the score and lost no time in getting "bedded in". I remember particularly a Mrs Lily Paget,

49

BEFORE I FORGET

known affectionately amongst her chums as Tiger Lil. She could normally be found on off-duty evenings behind the bar of the Hill House Hotel and rumour had it that she provided extra-mural entertainment for the proprietor.

Another I remember was a girl called Muriel. One evening Muriel and I were despatched to the stores hut to fetch some biscuits (those you lie on not eat). As we arrived at the blacked–out hut, it became obvious that Muriel was in no hurry and wanted to test out the biscuits there and then. I am forced to admit I was very young at the time – that I grabbed some biscuits and ran away!

We did have one technical mishap, which could have had a rather nasty outcome. The Transmitters operated with a very high voltage (25,000 volts) on the anodes of the main valves and for the purposes of the pulsed oscillations needed by a Radar transmitter a very large condenser was in the circuit. This received a big charge whilst in operation and when run down for maintenance had to be approached very gingerly with an Earth Stick (i.e. a connection to Ground). At some inches from the condenser (or the anode of the valve) a very large and menacing spark would leap across with a loud bang.

One day, in the middle of the maintenance period, one of the new mechanics was servicing this compartment on the transmitter and duly performed the earthing operation. He had to go outside for a few minutes and whilst he did so Cpl Morley arrived, closed the compartment and ran the Transmitter up to provide a pulse for tests he and the Flt Sgt were carrying out on the receiver. Having completed this test he then switched the Transmitter off again but failed to earth the condenser. In comes the mechanic, totally unaware of these activities and dives straight into the TX valve compartment. Well 25,000 volts will normally kill without hesitation but perhaps because of the short duration of the test or some leaking of the charge he received only a very severe shaking. But I should imagine it left his nervous system permanently damaged!

There were a few men among the Clerk SD operators for the GCI site. One of these was allocated to the Mrs Clarke billet and so Tony and I got to know him well. He passed by the unlikely name of Charlie Crump and was a lugubrious individual of about forty. He claimed to have been at one time a speedway rider, though anything less likely a daredevil of the track I've never seen! I'm afraid that he did not go over well with Mrs Clarke and so was subjected to blatantly unfair treatment as Tony and I were now well in with our landlady.

I don't really believe that Charlie ever really grasped what was going on at the GCI site. Someone must have told him what he was to do but I think the reason behind it escaped him. He used normally to handle the GCI Neatishead liaison and would listen to the plots of fighter and target over the phone. It did not seem to occur to him to link this with what was going on in the Happisburgh Ops block. One spectacular night our Controller did an excellent interception on the Neatishead fighter without any intervention from Charlie and only at the last minute did they discover the error. Poor Charlie bit the dust very rapidly.

Our CO Pilot Officer Nick Carter suffered from the same problem as Tony and I. That is the Flight wouldn't let any of us near the machinery. So his technical know-how never blossomed. However he was keen on cricket and managed to organise a match against a local Army Unit and a field to play in. I managed to get into the side but only to make the numbers up. However on the day, the experts turned out to have feet of clay and RAF Happisburgh were five wickets down for twelve runs when I came in, followed immediately by a young MT driver. We managed to stop the rot and put on thirty between us, 18 to him and 12 to me. The team actually got to just over 50 all out. Not a very impressive total; however the brown jobs turned out to be no better than we were and we actually won comfortably.

About this time the Air Ministry had a brilliant idea. They decided to have female Radar Mechanics. So they carefully selected a dozen clever young ladies with the right background and passed them through the course where they mostly did very well, particularly in theoretical

BEFORE I FORGET

studies. Three of the girls were posted to Happisburgh. They included the star of the course, the young lady who finished first, but also the one who finished bottom. This latter was put on my watch and as she was content to listen respectfully to me pontificating on the equipment, we got on very well. The star fared somewhat worse however. She was very confident of her abilities and did not hesitate to tell the Flight where he was going astray. As a hard-bitten experienced NCO with a long record of successfully keeping RAF Happisburgh on the air and working well, he did not take kindly to this advice and I'm afraid that the girl in question found herself specialising on the Diesel and any other mucky practical job that arose. No one I'm afraid had much sympathy for her as the extraordinary thing was that these three girls seemed to consider themselves a cut above the operators and refused to mix with the hoi–polloi. Oh the peculiar ways of the female sex.

By now, September 1942, we were beginning to really like the equipment, we enjoyed the job, and the billet was now comfortable. As you know, the RAF does not like that sort of thing, so Tony and I were suddenly uprooted and despatched from Happisburgh. We had constantly lived in fear of being despatched to Burma as many of our people were, but to our delight our posting was to Telecommunications Research Establishment, Malvern, where most of the research on Radar was carried on. So reluctantly we packed our bags and our bikes and set off for Worcestershire and the Malvern Hills.

SIX

TRE Malvern

TRE was ensconced in the buildings of Malvern School supplemented by a number of Nissen huts erected in the grounds. The airmen sent there on courses were billeted in civilian billets throughout the town for sleeping purposes only, and meals were served in RAF canteens at TRE.

Tony and I were allocated together with two other airmen to a large house some way away from TRE itself. It was owned by three maiden ladies and I remember being very impressed by the fact that it had no less than three bathrooms. We were allocated the third and I suspect we were resident in the servants' quarters. We had our own back entrance and a sitting room to ourselves and so were quite comfortable. We saw very little of the ladies themselves, but observed from the Sacred Hearts gracing the walls that they were keen Catholics. Almost the only contact I recall, was a conversation on one very bleak cold night, when one of these ladies explained to me that a severe cold wind blew across the North German plains directly from the Russian steppes, and that the first obstacle it encountered, on its way westward was the Malvern hills. That was how it came to be so cold. I also formed the impression that in the minds of these ladies, Joe Stalin was directly responsible for this, despite being an ally at the time.

I was always surprised at the ease with which entry could be obtained to TRE. Turning up in the Air Force uniform armed with a proper Identity Card seemed to be all that was necessary and I would have thought that any self-respecting German agent could have fixed himself up with that. Once inside, one was free to walk around the various compounds and the scientists, being like scientists everywhere, were only too delighted to talk about their pet baby. Tony and I had several interesting conversations by putting our heads in some door and saying, "Hallo, what's this then?" We learned some interesting facts about Gun-laying equipment and radar-controlled searchlights *inter alia*.

As far as our own operations were concerned we learned that we were to learn about and be posted to sites for OBOE stations. OBOE was a blind bombing system, which at the time was very much under development. The men in charge of this project were Mr. A H Reeves and Dr. F E Jones. Another man on the team that I remember was Mr Blanchard and there were two other civilians, Mr Rollinson and Mr Boshier who were ultimately drafted into the RAF and made officers.

OBOE as presented to us at the time was a development out of a German system which had been used in the raid on Coventry and detected as a result of that raid. The basic premise of the German system was that an aircraft flew down a beam from one station directed over the target and that a second station situated at an angle to the first would measure the distance down the beam and from the target and send signals requiring the release of the bomb.

The OBOE system was a substantial modification on this in that one station known as the CAT station would fly the aircraft down the arc of a circle passing over the target. It would do this by tracking the aircraft by radar and sending a constant stream of Morse Code signals which became dots if the aircraft was inside his circular track and dashes if he was outside it, but became a continuous note if he were on course. These signals of course being sent to the pilot. A second station known as the MOUSE was also tracking the aircraft as it approached the target and when it reached the calculated release point would send release signals to the bomb aimer. Of course, there were a lot of factors to this calculation. First the aircraft track at the MOUSE station was not head on but at an angle which need be allowed for. The time of bomb fall and the wind effect on the bomb once released also had to be taken into account. Nevertheless targets appeared with four decimal points of a mile accuracy.

The two main stations were to be sited at Trimingham in Norfolk (generally the CAT) and Walmer, near Deal in Kent (generally but not invariably the MOUSE). There were also plans for two other stations at Worth Matravers in Dorset and Sennen Cove in Cornwall but these were to be developed later.

Some technical points concerning the system. Ordinary CHL type transmitters would be used. These normally ran at approximately 200 kilocycles frequency but the OBOE transmitters would be slightly higher than this at 220 kcs. The result of using these frequencies meant that there was little curvature and so the beam had to be measured directly. That meant that tall transmitting and receiving towers were required at the stations and that the aircraft would need to fly as high as possible, generally around 30,000 feet. Even so the maximum achievable range was about 275 miles. Fortunately the nearest part of Germany to the UK was the key Industrial and Manufacturing area of the Ruhr, which is at a range of between 250 and 275 miles. Beyond this range OBOE would be useless.

Some other cardinal points of the system were that only one aircraft could be handled at a time, so that for any big raid the OBOE aircraft would need to drop markers, which would then be bombed by the main force. Whilst under OBOE control and flying down the beam the aircraft had to keep a steady course and therefore was more vulnerable to attack.

It was decided to use the Mosquitoes of 109 Squadron stationed at Marham. The Mosquito was a unique aircraft. Highly-powered, but with a light wooden airframe, it could reach great altitudes. The extreme height they were required to fly gave them some protection from attack. Each aircraft would be flying down the beam for about six minutes, unable to deviate. Probably no more than five of six were to be employed per raid.

BEFORE I FORGET

The whole business of blind bombing had been given an impetus in the spring of 1942 as the first 1000 bomber raids took place then. The third of these was on Essen, the site of the immense Krupps munitions works then said to be employing 175,000 people. This was of course heavily defended particularly by smoke screens and dummy fires, which were so successful that this first raid had completely missed its major target.

The OBOE system of course completely discounted any ground defences and trials had indicated that good pilots could guarantee a bomb within 100 yards of its target. The feeling was that OBOE could be set up for this one major strike at Krupps and then that the Germans would consider it so serious that they would jam it out of existence. However one huge strike at the most important target would be very damaging to the Hun.

The receiver systems for the OBOE stations were adaptations of the normal CHL receivers using an H/R tube calibrated in five-mile steps. However the PPI tube would be replaced by another H/R tube magnifying the critical area so that about 20 miles would be displayed as against the 300 miles on the first tube. The area displayed on the second tube was selected by a strobe which could be moved also in five-mile steps on the first tube. Once selected, the actual target range in the CAT station would be located by moving another strobe signal consisting of two brightness signals separated by a tiny dark area, along the trace until the actual target distance coincided with the dark area. When the aircraft signal appeared also on the trace, it would obviously move from side to side, but when straying to the inside strobe, would generate dot signals and when straying to the outside strobe, generate dash signals.

When the station operated as a MOUSE, the display on this second tube changed. The aircraft would not remain in a relatively stable position but would be moving along the trace, either coming in or going out. Once again a signal would be positioned over the target points but of course to hit the target the bomb would need to be released at an earlier point in time and thus in distance. The bomb would descend in a parabolic curve dependent on the height and the speed of the plane and release time. Thus prior to release point yet another signal had to appear so as to enable the effective apparent speed of the aircraft to be estimated at the time. Since the aircraft is travelling at an angle to the station its apparent speed is not the same as its registered airspeed. Technically the crucial points were these strobe circuits which were delicately balanced - so much so in fact that in the circuits produced by TRE, the resistances used were adjusted by delicately filing away some of the carbon body. This was to lead to trouble later.

We were at Malvern for about a month altogether, and although we were learning about the circuits, and the design of the system, it was apparent that the TRE people thought it all so delicately balanced, that they were going to be very reluctant to release the gear to the RAF.

A couple of incidents of the domestic front still remain in my memory. The four of us in our billet were playing Bridge one evening and Tony picked up a blockbuster of a hand. However he was by nature a very cautious individual and decided to 'pass' to see what the others would do. They of course all passed as well and the hand was thrown in ,much to Tony's chagrin and everyone else's hysterical delight.

There must also have been something of a dance hall in town and we repaired there one evening. At closing time, I was walking a young lady home and was about to exact a small peck before leaving her, when no doubt influenced by the romantic cinema of the time, she flung herself backwards in my arms. Only by making a desperate grab did I prevent her from falling flat on her back on the ground. As soon as I had hauled her back to her feet, I beat a hasty retreat.

So eventually our short but pleasant and interesting stay at Malvern came to an end and we learnt that I was posted to Trimingham on the Norfolk coast and really not very far away from our previous location at Happisburgh.

BEFORE I FORGET

SEVEN

Trimingham

Our journey to Trimingham was a typical cross-country rail trip with an overnight stopover in Cambridge where 60 Group - that group responsible for all Radar installations in the RAF - had established themselves in the Colleges of the University. We had no time to tour the town however and next day were on our way via Norwich and North Walsham to Trimingham.

It could be said that Trimingham was not such an out of the way place as Happisburgh, as it was actually on a railway line and there was a daily service. However from North Walsham, this was a single–track railway that hit the coast at Mundesley and then worked its way along through Trimingham, Sidestrand, and Overstrand to Cromer. By the time we picked up this train at Walsham, it was dark and we rapidly discovered another defect of the line. The guard came along to check our warrants and also to sell tickets to the civilian travellers. Very shortly we were at Trimingham and we all filed out on to the platform which was in total darkness and our kitbags and other items of kit were piled out of the train in a heap. As the train pulled away we realised that the station was deserted – no lights—no one in sight. Eventually we got our kit sorted out and we realised that we had no idea where RAF Trimingham was. Anyway, we oriented ourselves towards the coast and set out along the road. Before long we came to a house and from there got directions to the nearest phone box. The telephone operator insisted that RAF Trimingham was ex-directory and she didn't feel inclined to issue directions to what might easily have been Nazi paratroopers ringing up to ask the way. Eventually she decided that she would connect us to the CO of the station, who directed us to the nearest pub and said he would fix accommodation there overnight.

Next day a truck arrived to pick us up and we were introduced to Trimingham and also advised that our billets would be in civilian houses located in the village of Overstrand. This was distinctly more promising as Overstrand was a mere three and a half miles from Cromer, where there seemed at least to be the prospect of a little life. My billet in Overstrand was in a house on the cliff top, in fact almost over the cliff top, called Poppy Lodge[7]. It was owned by Reggie and Hettie Balls and there were already some five airmen in residence. Hettie was known to all of them as Ma Balls and they had a teenage daughter whose name I must have known at the time but was universally called Dumps. They were delightful people and Ma, though sometimes rough and ready, had a heart of gold and treated all her airmen as if they were a part of the family.

I was to spend from October 1942 to January 1944 at this billet so we should get to know the inmates. Senior amongst them was the Technical Flight Sergeant by the name Cyril Ewing, known to all as Chiefy and by far the nicest Flight Sergeant I ever met in the RAF. A West Country man with a very pleasant Devon burr in his voice, he came from Brixham and had been in the radio business in Civvy Street. Then there were three Corporals. Corporals Crossley, Limpus and Brown. The first two were Air Force regulars - old sweats in every way - and telephone operators. They answered to the nicknames of Yorky and Limpy. The third was a Corporal in the Special Police and his main claim to fame was that he was on the Kent CC ground staff as a spin bowler. Of course the RAF SP is on to a pretty cushy number as his job is generally just to guard the site gates. Brownie used this time to perform his duties as the most devoted husband I have ever met. He and his wife used to write to each other every single day and not brief notes either but lengthy missives. What on earth they found to say, I don't know! The only other erk in the billet was a gaunt lanky Scot by

---

7 Poppy Lodge has long since disappeared into the North Sea as the coastline has eroded.

the name of Jock (wouldn't you know) Allen. He was also a Radar Mech.

The Trimingham site was well chosen as it was on the top of the highest cliff on the Norfolk coast, some 300 feet up. Our Ops block was already well established as it had formerly been used by the Army for Gun-laying equipment. Also on the site, they were in the final stages of completing a 200 foot mast, of which more anon, which would provide a tracking station for the Navy reporting to their Operations Room at Great Yarmouth. In due time we were going to find ourselves exposed to some pretty rough weather on this site.

The Commanding Officer, already on site was a Flt Lt Conway, a Canadian Jew, who was technically probably the best officer I ever met. However, I didn't like him and he didn't like me. His views were probably more justified than mine, as I must confess that as time wore on here, I concentrated more on the social aspects of the station rather than the technical ones. We were rapidly joined at Trimingham by the two TRE men Rollinson and Boshier whose task was to get the gear set up and operational. Naturally they did not encourage any interference from the mechanics so our tasks were confined to the general construction and repair jobs around the site. Also within a short time, the Controller arrived, one W/Comndr Metcalf. His was the responsibility to command the operations, to ensure that targets were identified and set up correctly and that the marker aircraft were picked up successfully and brought over the target. He was followed by the first consignment of WAAF operators. They included Sergeant Margaret Macdonald, and LACW's Vicky Winks, Elizabeth Shaw and Jill Harpur. Let me say at once that the WAAF operators on OBOE at Trimingham were the nicest bunch of girls I ever met in the Services or since for that matter. All very intelligent, cheerful, good at their job and friendly to all - thoroughly nice girls in fact. All this first four became officers subsequently.

By December 1942 the stations were on the air and TRE were anxious to test out the accuracy of the system. At the same time, it would appear that it was also necessary to check the surveys and maps on

BEFORE I FORGET

which accurate ranging would be done. So that a raid was arranged on a Nightfighter HQ near Florennes in Belgium. According to R V Jones' "Most Secret War", the effects of this raid were to be reported back by the Belgian resistance. The raid was carried out by Mosquitoes only dropping bombs themselves and without the supplementary force. The location of every bomb strike was reported back to the precise yard, by the Belgians and we were delighted to hear, that they included a direct hit on the actual building housing the HQ.

Following this success, everything was now ready for the major attack on Essen. My recollection was that this took place on March 5/6th 1943 but elsewhere I see earlier dates quoted. I believe the raid was made with some 600 bombers in the supporting force. Bearing in mind the previous failures to hit this very extensive and important target, it must have been a very nasty surprise for the Germans to find the bulk of the main force actually hitting the target. Again as I remember, further raids did not take place on the very next night but further raids on Essen did take place at fairly rapid intervals. In the light of subsequent knowledge gained in the raids on Hamburg these raids could well have created the firestorm effect which was so damaging to that city.

In the intervening period between these raids, we had begun to simulate ordinary CHL stations by maintaining operators on duty twenty four hours a day and keeping up constant sweeping of the aerial systems without of course doing any plotting. A further supply of WAAF operators appeared and included a Corporal Elspeth Kenward who was really one of the sunniest personality girls I ever encountered. Cyril Ewing, the Flt Sgt was very keen on her and pursued her remorselessly but I fear unsuccessfully. Also in this group was I recall Irene Taylor and Marjorie Hill delightful girls with sparkling personalities. However the girls did not undertake the night shifts which were left to the hapless mechanics.

Operating was assisted to some extent by a device, which detected the arrival of the aerial array at the Circuit of its rotational cycle and then automatically reversed it. You may ask why this was necessary but I must tell you that the feed to the aerial system was a twin copper wire

One Man's Radar War

which twisted about as far as it would go one way and then the same distance in the opposite direction. A mechanics dream, you might think, which could be safely left to rotate back and forth by itself while the mechanic closed his eyes in restful contemplation. However, the device was one of those vicious-minded gadgets which only waited for you to take your eyes off it, to crash through the reversing device, to knock off the mechanical stops and to twine the twin aerial feeders like a knitting pattern.

After about five or six shots at Essen and a belief that very serious damage had been done to Krupps, there was a feeling of surprise that the Germans appeared to have done nothing to detect or destroy the obvious radio-assisted raids. So the attention was turned to other targets and in the weeks to come Düsseldorf, Duisberg, Köln, Bochum, Wuppertal, Aachen, Gelsenkirchen and Dortmund all suffered the weight of RAF bombardment accurately placed by markers dropped by OBOE Mosquitos.

On the technical side TRE was already working on answers to the anticipated German jamming and they very soon produced a simple but clever idea which must have caused the Germans many headaches. It would appear that the German jamming devices swept steadily through the whole of the frequency ranges around 200 kcs swamping the receivers. But the emphasis was on sweeping. So a second transmitter at 228 kcs was installed alongside the first and the trigger pulse fed simultaneously to both transmitters. In the aircraft a gate circuit only filtered a signal through when both the 220 and 228 kcs gates were open together. So the sweeping action of German jammers arrived at 228 a fraction after 220 and thus were filtered out, whereas the true signals arriving simultaneously went through. Of course the ultimate in overcoming jamming was to move onto the centimetric wavelengths and this development, which was of course a radical change, was going on in the background. But for the time being this worked very well and the Germans remained apparently baffled.

I recently read Len Deighton's book 'Bomber' which creates very graphic accounts of an OBOE directed Ruhr raid from both the

BEFORE I FORGET

English and German side. It gives a terrible impression of what it must have been like to see the remorseless red markers descending and to know that a relentless rain of high explosive and incendiaries would follow. In fact, he claims in the book that an error in set-up means that the raid missed its target and the whole business was a waste of life and money. Good literature but not very likely as OBOE practice. Not impossible, though, as I recall two occasions where something went astray. The second belongs in the next but the first happened while I was at Trimingham. The raid was set up on Bochum and everything apparently went well. Next day however the newspapers identified a raid on Gelsenkirchen! Worse than that though, reconnaissance aircraft checking on damage following a raid had been quite unable to find the damage at all and one could only conclude that the entire raid had been dumped in some unfortunate farmer's backyard!

Another book which touched on the Norfolk OBOE situation was Jack Higgins' 'The Eagle has Landed' where a German spy in Norfolk was supposed to have obtained information by posing as a Salvation Army woman delivering cups of tea to the sites. I can only say that operational information never appeared until the afternoon of a raid and sometimes not till evening on site. Technical information I suppose could have been picked up but if so Jerry was extraordinarily inept at doing anything about it. And in any case, it was the Church Army that used to come to our site!

As the summer wore on, the destruction of the Ruhr continued night after night and the affected towns widened, München-Gladbach, Ramschied, where one single raid wrecked the whole town, and Krefeld. This last town I will return to in a moment.

By now the equipment had been handed over to the RAF by TRE and that had immediately caused problems. The first thing the RAF wanted to do was to clean it. But TRE said the circuits were so finely balanced that even to disturb the dust would upset them. Needless to say, cleanliness triumphed over winning the war, and the sets were cleaned. However it didn't appear to affect them at all and the raids went on as usual.

On another occasion, two officers from 60 Group, RAF's Radar technical HQ, arrived down with an extensive modification which they put in on one night shift on which I was compelled to act as their stooge, desperately keeping myself (and them) awake with cups of coffee. However Ft Lt Conway the CO was a rather forceful character and apparently did not agree with this modification. So next morning he ripped it all out again!

To return to Krefeld. You will have appreciated by now that Mechs were really seldom caught up in fault finding. Most faults that appeared turned up during set–up and were dealt with by the CO or the senior NCO's. Others might occur after maintenance when one had plenty of time to track them down. However, the one occasion on which I personally dealt with an operational fault occurred during the raid on Krefeld. I may say that on subsequent visits to Krefeld I haven't found it necessary to mention this. It happened this way.

When an operation was on, the Receiver Room where all the action took place was always pretty full. There would be the Controller, his deputy or assistant, an operator NCO in charge of the set-up, her sidekick alongside, the CO in charge of the technical side, the Flt Sgt Mechanic, probably another operator on the plotting table and maybe some visitors as well. As against this in the Transmitter Room apart from the hum of the sets, all was calm and peaceful. The night of the Krefeld raid, I was quietly sitting there reading the newspaper when the sliding door to the Receiver Room opened with a crash and twenty-five people burst through it simultaneously all dancing around like dervishes waving their arms in the air and shouting "The set's off the air," "It's all gone wrong," "There's hundreds of guys dying out there," "Fix it, fix it," and sundry other cries. Trying my desperate best to stem this tide and to get some sense out of the pandemonium – I finally managed to latch on to: "There's no signal," and I concluded that the trigger pulse coming through from the Receiver to fire the Transmitter was at fault. On checking the plug entering the Transmitter I discovered that it was loose. So back came the signal and on went the raid with really no interruption.

BEFORE I FORGET

By this time a number of extra Mechs had appeared on site. Gordon Eagle had joined us in Poppy Lodge and Corporal Len Tweedie from Canada, Cpl Nobby Collins from New Zealand and Cpl Cec (Sees) McConnell from Canada were also notable additions. Len was a particular pal of mine and a very nice chap indeed. He was also a great favourite with Mary too. He was formerly a bank official in the Maritimes and though a non-smoker received regular supplies of cigarettes, which he always gave away to other lads on the station.

Perhaps we should turn away from the operational side of RAF Trimingham and look for a little at the social side and perhaps surprisingly this was a very active area. We had initially six airmen at Poppy Lodge and later on this rose to eight and even nine for a short time. Most of us were working a watch system so hours were generally erratic. Most evenings there was a card school in operation - so much so that the billet came generally to be known as Gamblers' Paradise. Mainly Solo was played and also quite a lot of Bridge with the occasional riotous games of pontoon or shoot.

There was one pub in the village of Overstrand, the White Horse but it was not popular, as the landlord was a bit of a surly customer. The favourite evening promenade was over the hill to the inland village of Northrepps where the publican was much more congenial. Here the Norfolk accent could be heard in its purest form and I recall putting my foot in it one evening. I had gone over to Northrepps with Ma Balls and one of her cronies and when asking these ladies what they would like, the crony replied "Half o' bitter" - or so I thought. Turning up with the goods it transpired that what she had actually said was "Had I better?"

Also stationed in the village was a training battalion of Seaforth Highlanders who were something of a mixed blessing. They had regular dances, which we were invited to attend but I was less enthusiastic when I returned from night shift to find the Bren Gun carrier platoon practising outside my bedroom window. Merry cries of "Mount," "Dismount" followed by hobnailed boots clattering on the ironwork were not conducive to sleep. The Seaforths were in the Overstrand

Hotel, which was poised right on the cliff edge and was expected to disappear over any time.

Two stories about the Seaforths that I cherished were about the mutiny and our New Zealand corporal Nobby Collins. Nobby was strolling along the village street one morning, when a Seaforths Lieutenant passed on the other side of the road. Nobby was somewhat surprised to be hailed by this officer and taken to task for failing to salute. I suppose that the Lieut. expected this to be received smartly at attention. However Nobby came from independent colonial stock and proceeded to argue his case vehemently. The Lieut. eventually complained to the CO who as you remember was a colonial also and threw his complaint in the waste-paper basket.

The mutiny was a hilarious episode. The Seaforths were real genuine Scots and proud of it and their dances consisted of reels and strathspeys etc. which went on and on till the participants collapsed. However the Army in their usual hamfisted way posted a set of English cooks who insisted on making the breakfast porridge with SUGAR. This was anathema to the Scots who insisted on salt and there was very nearly a riot!

The station personnel were now building up very substantially and I ought to mention a WAAF named Nancy Lewis with whom I became particularly friendly. Nancy came from a very good family in Stamford and was a very intelligent girl as well as being both attractive and vivacious. She did not want to get involved emotionally with anyone in the Forces and knowing that I was married and similarly wanted to stay free of involvement, we were able to have an excellent companionship which we could enjoy without any strong feelings appearing. I liked Nancy very much and I hope she found a good husband after her service and had a pleasant family life as I enjoyed too. Nancy was the victim of the one and only practical joke I ever played in my life. She was going on leave and had to catch the early train. Would I send a telegram to her parents as soon as the Post Office opened saying, "Arriving 12.30 train. Love Nancy." Certainly I said but when I got to the Post Office I made a slight amendment sending: "Nancy arriving

BEFORE I FORGET

12.30 train. Love George." This took her an awful lot of explaining away.

It was always possible to get down on to the beach at Overstrand though there was a lot of barbed wire and plenty of scattered mines around. So in the summer of 1943, the workings of the watch system allowed us quite a number of very pleasant beach parties though on the East Coast the wind was generally pretty chilly. Back up at the site, the 200-foot aerial mast was now completed and rather to our surprise this turned out to be for the 10cm Tracking radar used by the Royal Navy to track the coastal convoys very often on the move in these waters. Because this was centimetre radar, the operations block was put at the top of the mast just underneath the cheese parabola - I don't mean it was made of cheese, it was just called that.

This mast was a very peculiar contraption and warrants more extensive examination. Its ladders leading from stage to stage were the flimsiest construction and initially had no guards on at all. This made climbing the tower a very hazardous proposition especially on a windy coast. However, the tower also had a very crude lift right in the centre, which was designated for goods only - no passengers allowed. This did not deter our lads though and the lift was generally illegally employed. There were however, some snags. First, the contraption was just like an open biscuit box made out of sheet iron and only providing protection up to about waist level. It ran between runners made out of angle iron held into position by a squared off horizontal bar at regular intervals. Second it had to be operated by a spring – loaded switch at the bottom which had to be held in position until the lift arrived at the top. This meant that if you wished to go up, you had to get someone else to hold the switch. This brings me to the third snag. Often the lift would arrive at the top but not quite far enough to open the safety lock to allow you to get out.

Now imagine a nice rainy, windy day - and there were many of them up there. Your reluctant mate stands below holding the switch while the rain runs down his neck. As soon as the lift appears to stop, he is off back into the hut. If the lift hasn't quite gone home, you are stuck at the top and can't get out. Inside the Ops block, the fans are running and plotting is going on, so the chances of your bellowing loud enough to get them out is very slim. If you did not cower down on your haunches inside the 'biscuit box' you were frozen to the marrow very rapidly indeed. I was myself trapped there for about 40 minutes one day and I really felt grim after that ordeal.

Now there was a tale current at the time which I can't swear to, but which I could easily believe knowing the design of that lift. Servicing the lift was done by REME and up in Lincolnshire, these two squaddies were greasing the runners, which they did by moving the lift up 6 feet at a time and smacking a dollop of grease on the runners. One in the lift, and the other operating the switch at the bottom. They had arrived almost at the top and the wind snatched the beret off the head of the top man. He bellowed down "My hat!" but the man below thought he said "Up a bit" and he operated the switch. The top of the biscuit tin rose up past one of the horizontal supports, and sliced the head of the soldier off, just like a guillotine! Imagine the surprise and horror of the man below when the head of his comrade landed with a thump alongside him!

The working arrangements for this centimetric radar were that the operating was done by Royal Artillery personnel, and the servicing done by the RAF OBOE mechanics. These RA operators were a funny bunch. They were allocated to this job because they were less than A1 in fitness. Virtually every one of them had got a chit relieving him from marching anywhere.

It must be recognised that watch-changing in adverse weather conditions was very unpleasant. The exit from the Ops block went straight down ten feet to the middle of the top platform. The next ladder went down from the edge of the platform and so on a pitch black night you had to move gingerly from the centre to the edge without being able to see your way. There's always a rail around the platform to stop you falling off but I always had a very funny feeling edging along over 200 feet up in the pitch dark!

BEFORE I FORGET

Also going up the steel ladders was hair-raising. On a wet and windy night, I would climb the ladder with my arms wrapped around the back, clinging like a limpet and with any spare parts I had to carry stuffed up my jumper. One night the oncoming watch at 11pm took one look at the wild winds and pouring rain and refused to go up. That meant that the 6-11 watch could not come down. The telephone line down the tower became red hot as the 6-11 watch told the 11-8 watch what they thought of them, their antecedents and their prospects for the future. To no avail, they wouldn't go up!

Just to give you some idea of the winds on that coast, remember the site was on top of a 300-foot cliff and so the top of the tower was 500 feet up. At one time we had some builders erecting a new Nissen hut and they had erected the two end walls of brick and were then filling in between the two with asbestos tiles. They had got half way along and knocked off for the evening. During the evening a storm got up and the wind was trapped in the Nissen hut with the pressure building up until with a bang like a bomb, the whole thing blew into fragments. On another occasion the wind picked up a 50-gallon drum which was half-full of diesel fuel and threw it on to the roof of one of the administration huts. That again was just like a bomb blast. So one has to have some sympathy for the mutineers.

To return to Poppy Lodge. I have already mentioned how well Ma Balls looked after us, but there were some specialities of the house, as they say. Reggie used to perform a remarkable feat in catching fish. At low tide he would go down to the beach with a long line with fishhooks about every ten feet. With the aid of one or two of the airmen, he would catch a number of sandworms. This was achieved by observing the worm casts appearing on the sand, and then digging away frantically before the worm disappeared. These worms would bait the hooks and Reggie would attach each end of the line to a large stone, and string the line out seawards on three sides of a square. Then he would retreat and let the sea roll in at high tide. When he returned at next low tide there would never be less than three or four big fat cod, and often six or more. Quite astounding really but we all enjoyed magnificent fresh fish.

The place was always full of fun. Ma and Reggie enjoyed a laugh and so there was always leg-pulling going on and a marvellous friendly atmosphere. Ma had a soft spot for Chiefy and Yorky. Limpy would pull her leg unmercifully about favouritism. This reached an absolute height when they discovered that his "gazunda" had flowers on while theirs were only plain ones. Those two corporals were an amusing pair. Limpy was fascinated by the sea and loved to go down to the beach and stand at the edge watching the waves roll in. He would invariably stay just a bit too long and finish up with wet trousers.

Ma used to like to retire early to bed (and early to rise I might say) but would leave the door open to all hours for the airmen to return. The system was that the appropriate number of cups of cocoa would be made up with the kettle on the fire and the last cocoa drinker had to lock up. Woe betides the man who didn't down his cocoa!

It must be admitted that a certain amount of drinking took place now and then and one evening Yorky and Limpy arrived home much the worse for wear and succeeded in rousing the whole house as they endeavoured to get to bed without waking Ma. This process was to be achieved by very noisily counting the steps as they climbed the stairs and since they were doing two forward and one back this got very confused. However in mitigation of this, I must say that the fresh night air up there on the coast was very intoxicating by itself and mixed with two of three pints of bitter produced quite startling effects. I remember one occasion going down with some of the lads to Cromer about three and a half miles away and having a nice quiet evening's chat over a couple of pints, followed by a stroll back along the cliff top. I walked out of the pub in Cromer perfectly sober but by the time I got to Overstrand I was well and truly sloshed. I was due on duty at eleven and had to be pushed on board the truck. Fortunately however there was no action that night and Len covered for me.

This little excursion to Cromer was a favourite for a night out and the Cromer Conservative Club was kind enough to invite servicemen in to use the facilities of the club. As this included a full size snooker table, it was very popular. Unfortunately, they also served Watneys Brown Ale and a very light rough cider served from the barrel. These administered alternately throughout the evening used to induce a state where it was difficult to tell one colour from the other but some hilarious snooker resulted. On one memorable occasion a sizeable party were making their way back along the cliff top road which of course was totally blacked out and on a moonless night. They were in cheerful mood and were rendering some Air Force ditties at the tops of their voices, when suddenly Limpy opened his mouth too wide and his false teeth fell out. They must have bounced on hitting the tarmac because they simply could not be found until finally the whole party got down on hands and knees and crawled the length of road inch by inch!

Another of Ma's attempts to improve the rations of the airmen was by keeping a pig, which had a little pen of its own in the garden. It was acquired as a piglet but of course became rapidly a fairly strong and active animal. On one occasion, it managed to break out of its pen and get into the main garden. The cry for help went up and all airmen not on duty filed into the garden to aid in the hunt. At least 50% were aiding the hunt - the other 50% I fear were keeping the pig going and a merry hour was spent by all, going round and round the garden at high speed before the pig was safely restored to his sty.

I have already mentioned the Seaforth Highlanders and their rather strenuous dances. This was particularly noticeable in the unit located at Sidestrand and the piper played a very prominent part at any dance there. I remember two incidents from Sidestrand dance. Once when walking a WAAF called Billie Williams home to the WAAFERY from Sidestrand and having I suppose not quite come up to her expectations - she turned to me and said "Your trouble, George, is that you're a sheep in wolf's clothing".

However a much more spectacular conclusion to the evening coincided with the visit of one of the TRE boffins, a Mr Blanchard who had a small van which he used to cart about a dozen airmen and WAAFs to the Sidestrand dance. At the conclusion of the evening with every one tanked up, Blanchard was blindfolded and placed in the driver's seat of his van. Now you will recall we were doing blind bombing and the

One Man's Radar War

CAT station sends dots and dashes to keep the pilot on course. So the car was driven back from Sidestrand to Overstrand with the driver blindfolded and the passengers screaming DIT-DIT-DIT and DAH-DAH-DAH to keep him on course down the road. Fortunately no other traffic was coming the other way, as his course was distinctly erratic.

Another social occasion which occurred fairly regularly was the Liberty Run to West Runton where a local army unit used to put on a fairly formal dance in a large room with a full band. Some fairly serious drinking used to take place at West Runton and the returning Liberty Run used to be pretty riotous. I remember one unfortunate boozer who tripped as he climbed over the back and fell flat in the truck. Everyone was scrambling aboard at this time and every time he struggled to his feet he was knocked flat again by the next arrival. After two or three efforts he gave up and could be heard groaning from time to time as the tide passed over him. Another incident I recall from West Runton was, when nominated as the kittyman, I had the pleasure of fighting my way to the counter and saying to the barman, "Twenty six pints of bitter please."

To return to the technical side of life at Trimingham. There were a number of small incidents in the Mechs room worth recalling. Three involved the Canadian corporal Cec (Sees) McConnell, a very serious minded and conscientious lad. The first was a typical unthinking type of request from the Controllers. The target for the night was plotted and displayed on a large board about five feet square covered with a sheet of glass. They suddenly demanded a rotating ruler fixed on the board, located at Trimingham. This necessitated drilling a hole right through this large sheet of glass without shattering it. Cec undertook the task and with infinite patience and the end of a triangular file, he gently and carefully drilled away until finally he got through. It took him the whole of a night shift, eight hours solid work to get through about three eighths of an inch of glass. He wouldn't let me help in case I went too fast and shattered it and so I kept him supplied with numerous cups of coffee. And I don't suppose the Controllers had the slightest idea of how difficult and arduous a task had been completed for them. Another tale concerning Cec demonstrated the awesome power of electricity when mishandled. One day Cec was making a small adjustment to the transmitter using a long bladed screwdriver, 10 inches in length with a thickness of about quarter of an inch. Suddenly he managed to short the screwdriver across the main supply. The blade immediately glowed bright red, curled up and fell off!

Cec's relations with the transmitter were not good. It had on its side panel a series of contactors which were a part of the circuitry building up the operational voltage to 25,000 volts. These contactors were spring loaded so that they snapped home smartly after the time delays had operated and thus avoided pitting of the terminals. However if the spring was not correctly adjusted, the contactor did not snap home but chattered instead. Cec and Gordon Eagle were on duty one night when one of these developed a chatter. Cec decided that the cure was to change two of the contactors over. This of course resulted in two chattering instead of one. And so they went on, at one stage having all five chattering. I can still see Gordon's face as we relieved him at eight o'clock next morning, bleary-eyed and in a foul temper having spent the whole of the night watch dismantling and reassembling contactor units.

Another triumph of ingenuity developed in the Mechs room was the Nobby Collins instant kettle boiler. Nobby had the idea that the kettle would boil quicker if a contraption consisting of two copper plates about two inches apart was inserted and a current passed directly through the water. The kettle of course became as lethal as a bomb while this procedure took place. The first effect was of course to blow the fuses. This was cured by strapping aerial feeder wire across the terminals. Then the first few kettles full turned green from the copper plates. Gradually however a patina developed and the water became palatable. Eventually we used to boil a large six-pint kettle in forty seconds, but I'm afraid the lights went down all over Norfolk when the kettle was on. We used to use some heavy soldering irons with the body of the iron about one and a quarter inches square. They developed a fair old heat, which was not immediately visible, as I discovered to my cost. One day I leant across the bench to reach a tool and, for a fraction of a second, the scent of frying steak reached my nostrils. Then Yow! I had leant my forearm on one of these irons and the steak frying was my arm!

Another afternoon of fun was enjoyed when the aerial feeder wires got knotted up and needed to be replaced. This required the dipoles of the aerial array to be re-soldered to the feeders and since this had to be done on the gantry itself, out in the open air, then it could only be achieved by using a blowtorch. In those days we were using paraffin blowtorches not the butane driven aerosols available now. The blowtorch always was a temperamental beast anyway, needing careful adjustment of the spray to get the best heat and also frequent use of a device called a pricker to keep the nozzle free of gunge. While this manoeuvre took place, the thing frequently went out anyway.

So the procedure for this repair went as follows. First we discovered the impossibility of getting a match to ignite the blowtorch on top of the gantry. Then having got it going down below and hurtled up the iron ladder leading to the gantry, the capricious Norfolk wind promptly blew it out. Several attempts at this finally convinced us of the futility of this. Next, the bright idea of a biscuit tin to shield the blowtorch from the wind. This really required a man with three arms. One to hold the torch, the second the tin and the third to hold the ladder as you went up. Next we discovered that the tin became red hot as we climbed the ladder and the climber had to drop it halfway up with burnt fingers. Then we tried erecting a screen of Service blankets on the gantry to keep the wind off. Naturally the blowtorch would turn itself into a flamethrower and ignite the blankets. It was here I think that I discovered the principle that welding can be carried out easily if only you curse long and hard enough.

Somewhere along the line I was recommended for promotion to Leading Aircraftman. This was worth another bob a day raising my income to six shillings a day. However the CO wouldn't hand these out on a plate and wanted a proper Trade Test. So I performed, and rather badly at that, so that Conway refused to promote me. However Chiefy

BEFORE I FORGET

Ewing persuaded him to give me another shot, and this time I made it satisfactorily.

From time to time, the RAF used to worry about security. The site was by now protected by a detachment of the RAF Regiment who seemed to be recruited from the same decrepit sources used by the RA for their operators as previously described. Not good enough said the RAF. These Radar Mechanics must be turned into soldiers. So I was despatched to Great Bromley near Colchester on a seven day Assault Course. Here we banged off a few rounds, hurled the odd grenade and particularly put the bayonet in to some unfortunate dummies both standing and lying, with great enthusiasm. The most difficult part of the course itself was to get out of the starting trench – made slippery by recent rains. However, it was generally quite fun and most enjoyed it as a change. So much so, in fact, that one enthusiastic Irishman drove his bayonet in so fast that it was actually bent. This particular chap was a devotee of Liquid paraffin – he kept his bowels open with it, he used it on his hair instead of Brylcreem and he used it to pull through his rifle!

Once everyone had been through this exercise, it was time to test it out in practice and a platoon of Belgian paratroopers were borrowed to act as the enemy and to make an assault on the site. Their object was to penetrate the defences and to chalk a cross on the Ops block indicating that it had been blown sky-high. The main defence was the RAF Regiment but as the CO came and explained to us, we mechanics were to be stationed outside the Ops Block as the last line of defence. None of us exactly relished the idea of grappling with a Belgian paratrooper intent on chalking his cross on the wall, so we developed a defence of our own. These consisted of large notices saying, "This site is protected by 25000 volts." And, to give verisimilitude to this statement we strung a tripwire of new barbed wire about 18 inches high around the site. New so that it was visible to the onrushing paratrooper who would jump over it. However, this would be straight onto an old and invisible wire stretched about 4 feet above ground. This was the wire alleged to be carrying the 25000 volts and we actually connected the mains to it so as to dish out a real jolt to anyone actually touching it. We actually

One Man's Radar War

tested it out on ourselves to make sure that it didn't really kill anyone but there was enough there to know you had received it.

The referee of the exercise came round to inspect the defences and seemed to regard this as a foul and unfair tactic. A lot of argy bargy took place with us maintaining that as we had 25,000V available, it was senseless not to use it. Anyway when the attack actually took place, the word must have got around because they attacked the lower site but left us strictly alone.

Really, one had to admit that precautions were necessary and I was constantly surprised that the Germans did nothing to put the site out of action. They must eventually have discovered which one was the OBOE site but no attacks or even raids were ever made.

I did, however, get a fright one day. I had to climb the mast for some reason and as I passed the SP hut, Brownie advised me that an Air Raid Red Alert was on. I airily said, "They never come up here" and ascended the lower tower. It was a fairly misty day and when I reached the top and entered the little storeroom above the set, finally opening the hatch and popping my head out to the parabola aerial. Just at that instant, absolutely at the level of the mast, two single-engined fighters loomed out of the mist and peeled off, one each side of the tower. My head went back in pretty smartly, though I recognised them as Typhoons as they went past. But for a second or two they looked just like Focke Wulf 190s coming out of the mist.

The RAF was very keen on visits and it arranged that the pilots from 109 Squadron flying the Mosquitoes from RAF Marham should come down and see the Ground Stations in action. I'm afraid that they regarded the trip more as a day out than an educational trip and must have stopped at every pub between Marham and Trimingham. My first acquaintance with them was when the sliding door to the Receiver Room opened and the Ft Lt nose-dived on to the floor. He was picked up, dusted off and sent outside for some fresh air. Some time later I went outside on some errand and was seized by this chap and his observer. "Have a drink," he said, holding me by the lapels. Well I

77

thought, "He's a Ft Lt and I'm a LAC so I'd better obey orders." Out came the whisky bottle and handing it to me he said ,"What shall we drink to? I know" he said, "We'll drink to Queen Victoria!" So there in the middle of the afternoon, we drank a health to Queen Victoria and sang the National Anthem and one or two other less solemn ditties. Meantime the whisky bottle was passing round though I was sticking my tongue in the neck to minimise the intake. Eventually I managed to sneak off but I doubt whether they learnt much of the Ground Station operations that afternoon.

We in turn had our visit to Marham. I remember looking inside the Mosquitoes and seeing how absolutely crammed with electronic gear they were. The observer sat to the side and slightly behind the pilot but so jammed in together that I could easily believe how very difficult it was to eject from these aircraft. We also watched some take-offs and landings and as the plane came down, being so light, it bounced wildly up and down before coming to a halt. Quite terrifying even to an observer on the ground. Needless to say I clung on to my policy for my Air Force career of never going up in a plane.

Due to our having a number of Canadians in the unit (and a Canadian CO no doubt) we receive a supply of softball gear and so were able to resume playing that game. There were not enough people interested to play very much amongst ourselves but we were able to have several games against a nearby small US outfit and also eventually against a British Army team (not the whole army, just a bit of it). Due to my previous training with the Canadians at Sir John Cass I started with the advantage of knowing the game (at least reasonably well) and so was always in the team. We were generally beaten fairly easily by the Yanks but I do recall two instances very well – largely because they involved a minor success on my part. In one game played on the Yanks own terrain, their pitcher was achieving a great deal of success by interspersing a slower ball amongst some fairly fast pitches. When I came to bat, I rotated my feet slightly in the clockwise direction which I had found seemed to direct a hit (if I made one) between Centre and Right Fields and I waited for his slower ball. Sure enough it arrived and I put it beautifully between Centre and Right Field and put myself on third base with a Triple driving in two runs as I did so. The most successful hit I ever had! The other thing I remember about this particular game was the coffee they offered us afterwards. They made it in a large billycan and they made it with evaporated milk but it was real American coffee – a gorgeous golden brown colour and it tasted delicious.

I also remember the return game played in Overstrand. Let's face it my sporting career has largely consisted of playing a fairly wide variety of games pretty badly and I can't claim much success at anything. So these small highlights are cherished. This game was umpired by one of the older Yanks and I had had a few successful hits, mainly singles. He put his arm round my shoulders and said, "The Limey who always hits" which is actually quite a compliment to a Softball player.

The game against the Army was fixed up by Cec who umpired the game. He thought that the RAF ought to use an English pitcher so as to level the handicap and he picked on me! I was delighted at first to get a chance to pitch and we went into a good early lead with most of my pitches going across the plate. However, being unused to pitching, I rapidly began to tire and began walking a fair proportion of the batters. However, Cec wouldn't permit a change of pitcher and I was reduced to slow-balling the pitches and trying to put on topspin to play for the catches. Eventually we did hold on to win but as someone once said, "It was a damned close run thing." Still it was an experience to pitch a whole game.

Most of the time we were at Trimingham, we operated a three hour watch system i.e. 24 hours in every 3 days with shifts 8-1, 1-6, 6-11 and 11-8 but occasionally there would be a short spell on 4 watch, while one agonising fortnight we had to run a 2 watch system. We were really on our knees at the end of that short period. Of course there were also occasions when no operations took place and the evening watch 6-11 became an opportunity to argue out our views on life and society in general. I remember a particular argument with a WAAF called Pam Galloway who maintained that it was the responsibility of the potential husband to obtain explicit sexual knowledge and experience before marriage. On the other hand, she did not agree that this should be with his fiancée nor did she agree with the employment of prostitutes. I pointed out, somewhat vehemently, the logistical impossibility of this stance but she refused to see it.

After a substantial number of raids had taken place with outstanding success, the United States Air Force could no longer ignore the OBOE system. Of course they maintained that their usual Norden bombsight was infinitely superior for daylight raids but had to admit that cloud conditions were not always ideal in Northern Europe. So a test run was set up and the idea being that the master bombers would carry the OBOE sets and when master said "bomb", the whole wing would let go.

The raid was to consist of 3 successive wings of 60 Flying Fortresses each flying in a phalanx formation with the Master Bomber at the apex and each Wing following the other over the target. A fairly easy target was selected well within range but in the event one major problem was overlooked. This was that 60 aircraft flying in close formation screened out the radar signals and so as the Master Bombers switched on over the target, they got no response. The first Master Bomber thought "something has gone wrong. So I'll circle round and come in behind Wing 3 and use their explosions as a target." The second wing did exactly the same and so we had the interesting spectacle of 180 aircraft circling round over the target and doing nothing about it. I suppose eventually they cursed the black box and reverted to the Norden – anyway from that moment the USAAF lost interest in Mk I OBOE[8].

Aircrew flying OBOE Mosquitoes had a fairly comfortable time of it, as little of the flak or the night-fighters could reach them. In consequence the number of flights constituting a Tour was, I believe, doubled which did not please them. There were occasional accidents. One, a direct hit from some rare flak, resulted in the Mossy being reduced immediately to matchsticks (being made of wood) and the pilot and navigator suddenly finding themselves suspended in mid-air.

---

8   Mk I was the early, long-wave system in use before the advent of the improved Mk III microwave sets.

In some ways this was a blessing because the Mosquito was a notoriously difficult aircraft to get out of.

Night after night, the arrival of dusk saw the impressive flight of aircraft like migrating wild geese, setting out for their German targets and one had to feel a certain sympathy for the unfortunate recipients of so much death and destruction.

One little hiatus that occurred unfortunately quite often and visibly as far as we were concerned was when these aircraft crossed over a Coastal Convoy. The gunners on board the convoy often would not bother to find out whether the aircraft were British or German but would fire anyway. As the Lancasters were fairly low this was pretty uncomfortable for them and I heard that occasionally the Convoys got an egg or two back. This, however, I did not see, but the anti-aircraft fire was all too visible to us.

In addition to the operations, calibration bombing runs and training flights for new aircrew also had to be undertaken. For these the stations would reverse and look inland. I remember one particular flight where we were operating as CAT to a new crew and the pilot unfortunately had difficulty in distinguishing dots from dashes. So when he should have been stooging down the Welsh coast and as soon as he went out too far receiving dashes from us – he thought that these were still dots and continued to go further out. We even tried cutting the whole system off the air and back on again in a series of giant dashes. However, to no avail, and finally he disappeared off our screens further and further out into the Atlantic. Whether he ever came back I never did discover.

Of course, it should be remembered that OBOE was strictly limited in range and Cologne at 270 miles was about the limit. All targets further out such as Hamburg and Berlin had to be reached by H2S bombing. H2S was an airborne system displaying an instant radar map for the pilot and navigator. Its accuracy was very dependent on the skill of the operator and I think its results were never as accurate as OBOE. We did at the time bandy about ideas of increasing our range by dint of having a stooging aircraft at about 250 miles acting as a relay station onwards to the operational aircraft about 500 miles further on. Of course the physical problems of operating with a moving relay station were too difficult to solve at that time but I have wondered since whether aircraft like AWACS aided by the sophisticated computing now available could be operating this type of OBOE bombing in addition to their proclaimed role of airborne early warning.

I often feel that Air Force life must have come as a terrible shock to individuals with a sensitive character. I had found it pretty hair-raising myself but had a sufficient hardness of character to survive it. However, one often saw young men positively blanch at the bad language and the depravity of some others. Just as bad I suppose for a girl as I found out one night.

I had been across to Northrepps with Nancy Lewis to have a couple of jars and pass the evening. She came from a good family near Stamford, Lincolnshire and appeared to have a reasonably hard exterior manner. Whether the Northrepps beer had loosened her tongue or not I don't know, but suddenly half way back, the dam burst. She burst into tears and out poured all her disillusionment with the WAAF – the filthy language – the depraved talk of certain individuals – even the behaviour of some. She never believed that it would be like that when she volunteered. Well, I put my arm round her and did my best to comfort her - but what could I really say? Everything she said was true. Eventually she calmed down and next day was back to normal but it did show what was underneath the surface of people's feelings.

I had of course had several leaves at home and on one occasion Mary was able to come down and stay a long weekend with me in another house in the village. This visit and my prolonged stay at this one station, made us long for the possibility of being together. Also, although Mary was working at the Post Office Savings Bank she was at an age where she could be conscripted for factory work. Nor could we see any likely end to the war and so when Ma Balls. understanding in her usual kind way our feelings, offered to rearrange bedrooms so as to allow Mary to come and move in with me, we jumped at the chance and in November 1943, she came down to live at Poppy Lodge. At the same time, we decided to let nature take its course and have a baby if one should come along.

Now I know there is no way to prove it, but we have always been absolutely convinced that once our love for each other was given free rein, then its overwhelming power meant that David was conceived on the very night that she arrived in Overstrand. Certain it is that he arrived in the minimum time possible and his forecast arrival date was August 24th. However, we did have a few idyllic weeks together, until of course the RAF had to intervene and despatch me on a Mark III OBOE course at Malvern with the definite promise of a move elsewhere afterwards.

Anyway Mary did have a chance to join in the life of the unit – particularly in hockey which we were into at that time. A game I particularly recall was against an Army Signals Unit who had been stationed in India and who were really a very good hockey team. Mary and I played the two back positions side by side. We lost 7-0 but I like to think that but for our efforts it might have been a lot worse. Still, in the end the RAF ground remorselessly on and in mid January 1944 I was despatched to Malvern TRE once again. By this time, we were sure of David's arrival so at least Mary would escape call-up.

With my future parental responsibility in mind, I did get my nose really down to the grindstone and came out of the course knowing quite a lot about Mark III OBOE. And I found myself posted to Worth Matravers to the site which was being set up just above the Tillywhim Caves.

BEFORE I FORGET

EIGHT

Tillywhim

Worth Matravers was a very large station of the CH type which meant that it had a large administration staff and plenty of the RAF type of "bull". Fortunately, however, I did not encounter much of this, other than for pay and rations, as they say. Quite a large number of the airmen and WAAFs were stationed on site but others were in civilian billets down in the town of Swanage. I was one of the fortunate latter group and was quartered on a delightful couple called Phippard. Here I shared a room with an operator on the main site at Worth Matravers called Arthur Collier. He was a genial chap and we got on well together though our varying watch systems did not allow us much time together. Also in the house Mrs Phippard had a Sergeant who was part of the non-technical staff at Worth with his wife and small child. She also had another room which she let out on a daily basis (or should I say nightly basis) to a WAAF by the name of Sergeant Tucker. This latter room was on the first floor back. Mrs Phippard and her husband were a gentle innocent couple and I suppose totally unaware of the nightly clatter over the heads as Sergeant Tucker did her best for Allied relations by entertaining her American boyfriend.

Mrs Phippard was an excellent cook and managed to perform wonders with the wartime rations, so that our standard of living improved materially. She also had one other distinguishing characteristic that I remember and that was that she loved a flutter on the gee-gees and every day pottered down the road to the local bookie to plant 6d each way on a selection that she had produced by poring over the racing pages of the Daily Express. She was also extraordinarily successful as a

BEFORE I FORGET

punter and Arthur Collier was so impressed that for quite a time he doubled her stake as an additional side bet.

We got up to the Tillywhim site by picking up a truck from the main square at Swanage and we rapidly discovered that the site was still very much under construction. Tillywhim was destined to be a full Mark III OBOE site – that is to say that it would operate with eight times the capacity of the old Mark I sites. It also operated on the 10cm wavelength which ought to preclude interference which was now becoming a nuisance on the Mark I sites.

The site was a complex of 6 Nissen huts in two sets of three in parallel – all connected by a central corridor. The end pair of huts, each was to contain four consoles. The middle pair, the transmitters and receivers and the end pair were, on the right hand side, the Mechanics section with workshop and stores etc., and on the left hand side, the telephone exchange and what was to be a forerunner of the present day War Rooms where the Chief Controller could sit in front of a display which would allow him to electronically monitor the progress of all eight of his raiding forces. However, as we shall see, Tillywhim was overtaken by events and never achieved this grandiose idea.

Worth Matravers 1940

There were four airmen allocated to the site - originally two corporals, a Canadian named Bill Fritz and a New Zealander called Roy Walker, and two LACS, myself and a bloke called Yarrow. The RAF Construction battalion were still in residence finishing off the Nissen hut construction and the surrounding blast wall protection. There were also a couple of civilians on the site – Jack, the man in charge, and his mate. Their task was to install all the internal wiring and racking necessary to connect all these 8 consoles, the transmitters and receivers and this monitoring device. You can imagine that this required a tremendous amount of wiring and the task of the four airmen was to work under Jack's supervision on this wiring problem. I was most impressed with the speed and efficiency of the RAF constructors. They finished off their part of the work rapidly and well, and promptly disappeared.

Jack, however, was even more fantastic as a worker. I suppose he was on a contract basis but he really got on with the job and we were infected with his enthusiasm and worked hard ourselves. My attitude to the job had changed very much here. Perhaps because I was older, perhaps because of my responsibilities as a potential father - but anyway I knew the Mark III equipment as well as anyone and better than most and with the opportunity which Jack's work provided, I really put my back into it.

The wiring was carried around the six huts on overhead racking which Jack himself was putting up and the co-axial cables were run from machine to machine by the RAF lads and lashed together neatly and tidily along the racks. There were I believe about 60 cables along the main channel linking the huts.

This period was of course during the build up to the invasion of Europe and Swanage was full of Americans. The 2nd and 5th Ranger battalions were in town and they were to spearhead the assaults on the Utah and Omaha beaches. Tough though these lads undoubtedly were, they seemed peculiarly susceptible to English beer, even the wartime variety, and a couple of pints in one of the many locals seemed to get them seeking a fight. Their immediate target was blacks and I came face to face with Southern prejudice in its most virulent form. Blacks were expected to get off the pavement into the road to allow the whites to pass by and failure to do so led inevitably to a punch-up. We ourselves kept a low profile, helped by a shortage of money to spend in the pubs, but I never came across any instance of Americans setting about the British. In fact our relations with them were generally very good.

BEFORE I FORGET

We were working on day shift at this time and under the general supervision of a Flt Lt from Worth. Eventually the equipment appeared, was installed and connected up and Jack and his mate disappeared. The Flt Lt, whose name escapes me, recommended me for promotion to Corporal but had to depend on the approval of the new CO when he arrived. Who should it be but my old enemy Flt Lt Conway. So my chances of promotion went straight down the drain.

It was obvious that the site would not be ready in time for the invasion and so, as accurate bombing of gun sites etc. was to be vital, a mobile trailer was brought in with a separate crew and it was this trailer that took on the bulk of OBOE attacks – culminating on the night immediately prior to the invasion when no less than 35 separate attacks took place. I think OBOE can claim a lot of success in eliminating most of these gun sites at a crucial point of the invasion. The Sergeant Mechanic in charge of this site eventually received an OBE for his work.

Personnel began to pour into the site now, both male mechanics, very many of them Canadian, and female operators. I want to say at once that whereas at Trimingham I said the girls were the nicest I ever worked with, here at Tillywhim, we had the greatest bunch of men that I ever had the privilege of working with. We had begun to operate a watch system and I had charge of one of the watches which at one time rose to about 10 personnel including a couple of NCOs. My knowledge of the gear was, however, good enough to keep me in charge despite being still an LAC. On my watch I had Finn Macdonald who has remained a friend of mine to this very day and Ken Wells, and Harry Laurie and we had a fine time together both on site and off duty too.

Another notable personality on the site was New Zealander Corporal Ray Walker, of whom one of the girls once said "I always feel whenever he looks at me that he's mentally undressing me." Knowing Ray, he probably was, too.

Recreation on this station was well organised. Down in the town the Malvern Institute was taken over as a NAAFI and there was a little card room upstairs where many an evening was spent playing Solo. I rather fancied myself as a Solo player (and still do) and at any rate was much more venturesome than most players and generally used to make a small profit. I can remember introducing the group on a couple of occasions to *Misére Ouverte*[9] which although they had heard of, I don't think any had ventured to play.

Also operating in watch system meant plenty of time to go on the beach and so part of almost every day was spent with a pleasant mixed party down there. The municipal tennis courts were also available and I played quite a bit usually with a pair of twins amongst the WAAF called Pam and Paula Everett. The softball team was rapidly constituted and although I played a bit, there were by now so many Canadians on site that I could not get a place on a regular basis. We had one very keen match against one of the US Ranger battalions. Bill Fritz was captain and organiser of the team and was also the pitcher. He was a very good pitcher too and in this game up to about the 7th Innings, held the Yanks down so well that we were in the lead by several runs. Unfortunately he then tired and although we had a useful relief pitcher warming up, Bill was too obstinate to take himself off and so we blew it in the end. Probably just as well, as a defeat by a bunch of Limeys (even if all Canadians) would have destroyed the Rangers' morale just prior to the invasion.

Up at the site, a Flight Sergeant Nicholson had arrived to take charge of the Mechs. Whereas Slack and Ewing had been radio men, Nicholson was a banker – and it showed! He was excellent on organisation – every mechanics watch was presented with a worksheet as it came on duty. His knowledge of the Mark III OBOE, however, was absolutely nil and he had to tread very warily with people like myself because he was dependent on us to keep the site running. After all you can polish the floor, dust the equipment, fix the brackets tidy the site etc. till you're blue in the face but if the equipment doesn't

---

9   In *Misére Ouverte* declarer contracts to take no tricks at all, with all his cards laid open on the table

work when the bombers were over Germany – then you're OUT. However, Old Nick did teach me one Cardinal Principle useful in later life which I recommend to any reader. It happened this way – just past the entrance to the site, there was a Notice Board. And on this board, Nick placed his Organisational Chart in a very prominent position. On the site, the CO was Ft Lt Conway and he appeared top right with his adjutant and other technical officers. Top left contained the controllers from Wing Commander downwards. Centre left were the NCO operators with the operating watches below them. Centre right were the Mechs and their watches, with the Admin staff floating round the bottom. BUT, right in the middle with all lines floating in and out from him was Flight Sergeant Nicholson and it was crystal clear that once he was removed the site would absolutely collapse! So the principle is this. IT DOESN'T MATTER WHAT YOU DO, BUT WHAT YOU TELL PEOPLE YOU ARE DOING. And I firmly believe that I owe my fist step on the Management ladder at Powers-Samas[10] to application of this very principle.

One morning on site I came face to face with my one real case of fault-finding. I don't mean bottle changing or loose connection repairing but real fault diagnosis and repair. One of the consoles which was supposed to display the target marker as an extra brilliant area of the trace line, displayed instead a huge downward pulse causing the trace to dip almost to the bottom of the tube. We got the Circuit Diagrams out and I finally isolated the circuit directly involved, deducing that an extra signal must be filtering through to the grid of the strobe valve. And so it proved, a small condenser had developed a leak – not sufficient to overload the valve but just enough to cause this signal to appear.

Now I ought to introduce you to Doug Hogg. Doug was i/c of the watch immediately preceding ours and a first class technical man. I met him again many years later when he was in charge of Magnetic Tape development at Ferranti Ltd so you can see he was a real electronics wizard. The first characteristic of Doug's that I remember was his radio set. He had built himself a radio set, just completed when he arrived at

---

10 An early computer manufacturer for whom the author began working in 1955

Tillywhim. It was, I thought, a very good set with excellent reproduction and a wide range – but it didn't satisfy Doug! There was some minor defect here and another there and he tinkered away at it until he finally reduced it to a wreck of what it once was!

However, Doug's main claim to fame was that he was i/c the watch on the night of the FIRE. Apparently somewhere about 7 a.m. the consoles were put on the air and something in No 3 shorted and ignited the whole thing. In no time at all the console was blazing furiously and the heat generated was terrific. The mechanics on watch got to it very smartly but even so it took ten pyrene extinguishers and two of foam to get it out. The whole of the console was a complete write off and the heat generated was so great that the glass of the tubes was melted and shrank inwards on to the electrodes. When our watch arrived at eight, the fire was safely out but the mess everywhere was indescribable. A fair amount of badinage took place mainly concerning the inaccurate aim of the men with the foam extinguisher as there seemed to be foam everywhere.

With this incident in my mind is associated Finn Macdonald's Indian War Dance. When we finally sorted out the mess and restored some sort of order, we were required to start dismantling the console and its associated equipment. This included an electronic clock assembly alongside the operator position. Finn had of course checked that the master switch disconnecting the electrical supply to the console was off, but unfortunately he was not aware that the clock was on a separate supply. So that as he endeavoured to disconnect the clock he managed to take a firm grasp of two live wires!

Finn Macdonald on the steps of the Ops Trailer

BEFORE I FORGET

It took him probably about 20 seconds before he could throw away the wires but in that time any Iroquois would have been proud of the War Dance that poor old Finn performed!

The rising tide of personnel caused the RAF to get organised and our cushy civilian billets disappeared. We were all moved into empty houses taken over - ours was actually next door to Mrs Phippard – and we also had to take meals at the Victoria Hotel in town – known locally as the Chinese Embassy due to the frequency of the serving of rice pudding!

I had previously mentioned the American Army's inability to cope with English beer. Often as we waited on Swanage Square at 10.30 for the truck taking us up to the site we would see the drunks staggering out. One evening sitting on the coping, an American truck pulled up in front of us and an individual rose out of the back and addressed us. "I'm a Major in the American Military Police" he said, "These lads are going to be in the forefront of the action when the invasion takes place. So when they have had a few too many and a punch-up starts after closing time, I just push them down on the beach and let them finish it off there!" You can imagine, we listened to this with our jaws agape. Why he thought it necessary to justify himself to us, I do not know. I couldn't imagine it happening with English MPs.

By now the invasion was very near and the whole of Poole Harbour was crowded with ships of every shape, type and size. Fighter sweeps roared off to sea many times a day and activities generally were reaching a crescendo. Censorship was imposed on all units and our letters home had to be submitted to the CO for censorship. I didn't much care for this idea and while I fed a few innocuous ones to the censor to keep him busy – whenever I wanted to send a love letter to Mary, I posted it in the ordinary Postbox which seemed to work quite OK.

Unfortunately, I was having a difficult time personally during this period. My father had suffered a bout of pneumonia during the winter which turned to pleurisy. This in turn weakened his heart and the doctors told him that he would have to abandon his outside activities and take it easy at home. Now my father had always been a very active man and could not face this sort of inactivity so he seemed to go into a decline and at the beginning of June suffered a heart attack and was sent into St Thomas' Hospital. I managed to get compassionate leave to see him and so was actually away from the site on the day of the invasion. At least I saw him but he was obviously declining fast and on June 16th 1944 he died. I had again to apply for compassionate leave to attend the funeral.

Somewhere about the 18th June Hitler started his V-bomb attacks on London and so life became very wearisome for my mother and Mary. This culminated somewhere in July when a V-bomb landed on the corner of Mayfield Avenue in Chiswick and the resulting blast wrecked 98 Thornton Avenue where they were living. They were not hurt because they were sheltering at the foot of the stairs but were taken round to the local Aid Centre where, when friends turned up to see how they were, they were identified as two grey-haired old ladies sitting in a corner covered with dust and debris from the explosion. We were rapidly offered alternative accommodation in Flanders Road not far away but my mother was so depressed at the time that she would have abandoned all her goods and chattels were it not for the vigorous intervention of the Hopcroft family who set to work with a will not only to keep more things around but also to get Mother on her feet again. By this time I had arrived on yet another bout of compassionate leave and by pressing the pram we had bought in anticipation of David's birth into use as a trolley we managed to rescue the household belongings. It didn't do the pram much good however, especially as it was a cheap utility model!

During this move, we were sleeping round at my Aunt Maud's place in Shepherds Bush and the whole trip was full of incident. As the train arrived at Waterloo Station, an air-raid alarm was on so the station staff had entirely disappeared. I walked out and towards Waterloo Bridge when suddenly a V-1 appeared overhead making its customary spluttering noise. Suddenly the engine cut out meaning a bomb fall. I threw myself flat on the pavement and it actually fell along a street lying at right-angles to the Bridge road. Lying there on the pavement I saw the blue flash and heard the roar of the explosion but no worse than that and I was able to hurry across the bridge to the Underground.

While at Maud's, I shared a camp bed with Mary and as she was now a fair size (about six months pregnant) she filled most of the bed and I balanced precariously on one of the struts! One night was enlivened by a terrible crash. We leapt up and looked out to see where the V1 had fallen. Nowhere to be seen and only next morning did we discover that a picture had fallen off the wall. Eventually I overran my leave pass trying to get the move finished and was 48 hours late back on the unit. This resulted in a fairly nominal 3 days Jankers which I spent in scrubbing the floor of the WAAF Cookhouse. Not at all a bad task since the cooks used to provide me with a steak and chips supper afterwards!

In these early days, one mechanic had to man the site at night more as a night watchman than anything else. One night when I was on duty, I heard a buzzing noise from the PBX telephone exchange which had just been installed. Now I had never been trained to operate this type though I had seen a rather different type while working at Tribe Clarke before the war. Anyway I managed to answer this and it turned out to be a Controller calling from Walmer who was in the middle of organising a raid and had discovered a complete breakdown of telephone communication with his opposite site at Winterton. He sounded desperate as he tried to establish the link via ourselves. Eventually I managed to figure out how to raise Winterton and connect them successfully.

The Americans did a lot of their operational training in the fields surrounding our site and they had firing ranges set up nearby. Their approach to range discipline was very casual by British standards and I used to get a slightly uneasy feeling as they lobbed mortar bombs right over the top of our site. On another occasion several of our lads were watching them practice firing a Browning machine gun. After all the Yanks had had their turn, the Sergeant turned to the idle onlookers "Anyone else care to have a shot?" and so all our lads had a turn as well!

To return to the entertainment front! Every Saturday night the WAAFERY at Sentryfields had a dance (to records) and the Grosvenor Hotel also used to run regular dances. I rather fancied myself at the light fantastic at this time and enjoyed myself to the strains of Glenn Miller who was all the rage then. As a reasonable dancer I did well for partners but managed to avoid any regular attachments until rather later in my stay at Tillywhim, of which more later.

At the Grosvenor, which was a large commercial hotel, the barman was of the type known nowadays as "Gay" though in my time, the word "Pansy" was more often applied. This barman used to take a terrible ribbing at every dance with a tornado of remarks every time he said anything. Writing this made me think about homosexuality in the RAF and I can think of very few individuals who I would identify in this way. There were a couple of lads at Sir John Cass and later on perhaps a couple more on the mobile unit which we eventually took on the Continent, but those apart I can think of no others. I suppose I might not have noticed being really rather sexually naïve at this time but generally these things did become known and were treated rather cruelly by the rest of the unit.

Eventually the invasion day arrived and the Ranger Battalions were flying into the heart of the action. You will recall that on one of the beaches, Omaha, the Americans ran into very severe resistance and were badly mauled. This brings me to the sad tale of Lesley Warrell one of the nicer WAAFs on the site. She had begun to go out with one of the American Rangers. They had only been out together about twice and as he seemed a nice lad, they were still very much at the platonic stage. Anyway, it was said that of the thousand men of this battalion only four survived. One of them was this boyfriend of Lesley's and he was very badly injured indeed. So much so that he would be bound to be badly crippled for the rest of his life. Poor Lesley, stricken by conscience, felt that she ought to marry him and act as his nursemaid forever afterwards. All this on the strength of a couple of evenings out. Anyway Ray Walker, Finn and myself set ourselves the task of rescuing her from this burden and we used to argue relentlessly with her.

BEFORE I FORGET

Eventually I believe we prevailed but her conscience took an awful amount of beating down.

Sometime during my stay at Tillywhim, the RAF had another fit of turning airmen into soldiers and I was sent on an Assault Course up on the Yorkshire Wolds. This trip was for a week and though I did not look forward to it, it turned out to be one of the most hilarious weeks I ever spent in the RAF.

The course contained a number of elements. First, there was a certain amount of weapons training centred largely on Bren and Browning machine guns. This also included the opportunity to toss a grenade – a purposeless exercise I always thought, except for the excitement of wondering whether some fool's clammy hands will drop the damned thing. The CO of this unit obviously believed that the best way to teach weapons was to do the thing badly to start with, thus generating a few laughs and then to show how it was really done. This made the instructional part of the course quite amusing. Next was the Assault Course. This was the usual type consisting of high walls to climb over, ravines to swing across, tunnels to crawl through and finally a rope climb back up from the bottom of a quarry. However, the course was built on the side of the escarpment so we started off like rockets going down the hill but the rope climb back up again was agony. However, as the village pub was down at the bottom of the hill, it didn't seem to stop the lads running the course again each evening.

The third element was theoretical training in elementary tactics i.e. out-flanking manoeuvres, containing fire, cover, field of fire, smoke grenades etc. – all followed by practical exercises. This was where the fun really began.

The first exercise divided the course into 2 halves. The first lot were sent out to take up a position and the second lot (of which I was a part) sent out to attack them. The NCOs on the course were given the briefing and the maps and the erks just trailed along behind. The major problem was that nobody could really read a map though all maintained they could.

Anyway we trailed off through the countryside and almost immediately were ambushed by a party left behind by the defenders. I remember having to run like mad and dive into some cover to try and set up a machine gun post that would cover the attackers while a flanking body moved in. By the time we had it set up, they had fled anyway. So we marched on, eventually arriving at the spot we were supposed to attack only to find no enemy. They had apparently got lost. After some fruitless discussion on what to do next, we decided to continue onwards and we were trailing along a path taking us up and around the side of a hill when suddenly the leaders of the two parties came around a corner and literally bumped into each other. Our mob had no idea what to do and just dived for cover but the other side remembered all their instructions about out flanking and threw a party down the hill to do just that. Unfortunately this means that the final thrust had to take place up the hill and I can tell you that it's not very easy to maintain full enthusiasm for a charge up a 45 degree hill. So I reckon we won that on points.

The next exercise was at night and the briefing session told us that we were to defend the radar site against an attack organised by the instructors. This site was surrounded by a fence about 8 feet high and made up of solid iron bars bolted together.

My prime concern (as ever) was for personal comfort and I went out with my full uniform over my pyjamas. I seized the first opportunity to volunteer to man a single slit trench. Where I settled down to a quiet snooze. Suddenly I awoke to the sound of rifle-fire and exploding charges. Continuously putting my head above the trench there seemed to be a lot of people running about and shouting. I pointed my rifle in the general direction of the action and blasted off a couple of rounds just to show some activity and then I retreated into my former position When we were finally summoned back to HQ, it transpired that the instructors had managed to reach the perimeter undetected, remove a chunk of fencing, penetrate the site, put their X marks on all the operation blocks without anyone noticing. Eventually in desperation they threw some grenades about and generated the action. Perhaps all the course were doing the same as me.

BEFORE I FORGET

The final exercise was to be a *pièce de resistance*. The defending group, of which I was one, was sent out to take up a defensive position which was in a shallow ditch behind some useful hedge cover. We duly arrived and took up our positions. After an hour or so with nothing happening we began to appreciate that the attackers had got lost. So we abandoned our positions and gathered in a group to discuss what to do next. Suddenly a cry arose, "There they are!" and the attackers (who had also abandoned the search) were marching down the road in column of route. We dived back into our positions and let them have a volley just to see them jump. They ran for cover and then threw smoke grenades over the hedge into the field so as to deploy behind the screen. However, the wind soon blew away the smoke and left their frontal assault cruelly exposed in the field. They then tried an outflanking movement in the opposite direction but as this involved crossing the main road, it was too wide a sweep and broke up in confusion. Anyway it was now near tea time so we gave up by mutual agreement and set off to return.

Back at Tillywhim, we had a more serious and indeed tragic encounter with the war. Two Canadians on our unit were exploring the cliff top nearby where the wire had been disturbed and a rough path along the cliff had been excavated. They were misguided enough to run down this path and one of them chanced to land heavily on a concealed mine. They were both blown to pieces and Bill Fritz had the unenviable task of identifying what remained of the bodies.

By now the mobile units were in regular use and even some consoles got into action in the main block, though of course our raids were confined to France. Once the breakout occurred and the Germans forced to retreat from France our *raison d'etre* disappeared and the flood of mechanics were really only getting trained so as to man the mobile units which were being assembled for use in Europe.

As a part of this preparation, we were required to learn to drive and the local driving schools were mobilised to train everyone. So I duly had my first introduction to car driving which was useful but generally uneventful except for one instance when the instructor had to mount the pavement to avoid a rogue truck. Eventually I graduated to 30 cwt trucks and had a lesson or two but without really mastering the technique of double de-clutching.

During this period we continued to enjoy the dances at Sentryfields the WAAFERY and I became acquainted with a WAAF called Midge Thirlby. She was a delightful girl and really very good-looking. In accordance with my usual custom I let it be known that I was married and it was as well that I did because I could easily have fallen for this lovely girl.

Another brief incident from this period was an opportunity to see a boxing exhibition by Joe Louis, then the world heavy-weight champion. It was pretty banal stuff but there was just one incident I recall where Louis let go a punch like lightning and his partner nearly fell over backwards to avoid it.

My mother and Mary were by this time safely installed in Flanders Road which was really quite a nice little flat with a big Studio as its main room. Unfortunately the building stood back from the road and in consequence the bedroom was about 5 yards from the Underground track and the early morning train was guaranteed to shake you out of bed at 5 a.m. The baby was now getting close and was scheduled to arrive on August 24th. I had felt somewhat aggrieved as I appeared to have suffered all the morning sickness. Mary had kept remarkably well but had been accepted into Queen Charlotte's Hospital in Hammersmith to have the baby. This was excellent news generally because it was the top maternity hospital in the country – however it did mean that she was examined and prodded by hordes of students every time she went in for an examination.

So finally on August 24th, the very day, a telegram arrived. Was it a boy or a girl. Neither actually, it was a flying bomb. They had been bombed out again with a bomb landing on the Polytechnic building on the corner of Flanders Road, bringing down ceilings everywhere. Mary had been caught in a most embarrassing position, sitting on the loo, when the bomb struck. Anyway fortunately no one was hurt but in no time at all, they were removed again, this time to Wavendon Avenue, off Dukes Avenue in Chiswick.

However, some 10 days later, the magical telegram did arrive – a boy about 9 lbs – fair hair and dark blue eyes. Name David George already agreed upon. I had had so much compassionate leave that there was no early prospect of seeing them both. I had to content myself with descriptions by letter. Mary had had a long labour and eventually a forceps delivery but recovered quite quickly afterwards. A few days passed (mothers had 14 days in hospital at that time) and a disturbing letter arrived talking about a gas-main explosion in Chiswick. A combination of factual news and inspired guesses convinced me that this was no gas-main but the first of the V2 rockets which had descended on Staveley Road, Chiswick.

Mary with David, b. Sept 3rd 1944

Simultaneously, a bombshell descended on me – proceed to Durnford in Wiltshire, and thence to Cardington to assemble into the No. 1 9000 Unit, ready to go overseas.

NINE

Going Overseas

I decided that come what may, Mary and the baby had to be rescued from London and shipped up to Broughton in Northamptonshire to stay in safety with Mary's mother.

So I disappeared from my billet en route to Durnford, donned my civvies and caught an early train to London. When I arrived at Waterloo, no MPs were to be seen fortunately, as there was a raid on. As I came out of the Station and on to Waterloo Bridge Road a V1 chugged overhead and suddenly the engine cut out – always a sign of imminent explosion – I hit the deck smartly and as I reached the ground, I saw the blue-white flash of the explosion reflected on the buildings opposite the road I had just left. However, no damage nearby and I was soon on my way.

When I arrived at Queen Charlotte's they were very reluctant to accede to my request to release Mary and David (after 10 days in hospital). Very different to practice nowadays. However, I eventually persuaded them and we were soon on our way to Broughton. I cannot leave this episode, however, without recording my absolute delight in holding my son in my arms for the first time. Can there be anything more satisfying in the world than this?

I wasted no time in Broughton and returned smartly to Durnford hoping that my late arrival by about 3 days would not be noticed. It was, however, but the general chaos of setting up the new crew resulted in only a nominal bout of Jankers which was rapidly worked off.

BEFORE I FORGET

Our short stay at Durnford was enlivened by a few lectures on how we were to survive abroad. One was on how to recognise the various types of mine. Another on the delights of iron rations – K rations – for the fighting troops on active service – to C Rations where you could spend more time brewing up.

I cherish particularly the description of the magical cube that you place in your tin mug and pour on boiling water to make a nice cup of tea. As the sergeant said, "There's everything in this little cube to make a nice cup of tea – there's tea in it, there's milk in it and for those of you that like sugar there's sugar as well – all in this little cube. For those of you that DON'T like sugar – well there's not enough to taste anyway!"

Durnford was a camp with a Guard House and barbed wire but there was more traffic through the barbed wire than past the Guard House and some fond farewells were said in Swanage. Happily for me, Finn Macdonald, Harry Lawrie and Ken Wells, all Canadians, were all assigned to our crew from our watch at Tillywhim so we were among friends.

After a few days, the order came to move to Bedfordshire – to Cardington where the unit was to be fitted out with its four mobile trailers carrying the Radar equipment and a variety of trucks to carry all the other equipment necessary for the crew. This, of course, necessitated the urgent provision of drivers and those who had received any Driver training were first in line. My experience on trucks was very limited so I did not volunteer. Those who did were given Driving Tests at Cardington and as far as one could see providing you did not change directly from first into reverse you passed. I'm not really sure whether I missed out on this or not. Certainly I would have obtained a Driving Licence which could have been continued into Civvy Street after the war, when actually it took me till 1959 to get a licence. On the other hand I would have had to drive a 3 ton truck from Cardington eventually to Alsace and back. On the whole I think my choice was a wise one.

While at Cardington we encountered one of the very few Australians I ever met in the Air Force – a Sergeant who appeared to "know it all". He had acquired a Jeep and while demonstrating his knowledge of the vehicle, he managed somehow – I don't really see how – to let the clutch in while standing outside the vehicle. Where upon the Jeep took off – the clever dick Sergeant having to run after it across the field. That took him down a peg or two.

We were anticipating a life in tents at this time and the boys were always on the look out for something to make life easier. Seeing what looked like a large bundle of balloon fabric lying about – they "organised" it before our departure. More of this later.

After a few days and one last 48 hour leave when I took Finn with me to Broughton to see Mary and David – all the driving seats were occupied and the convoy set off. First to Old Sarum on Salisbury Plain. This may seem a peculiar route to the continent but perhaps it was intended to put the Germans off the scent.

Only a day or two there and then we were on our way to what turned out to be Tilbury, though we had an overnight stop in a camp at Aveley outside Dagenham. I remember this night well because we were billeted twelve to a Bell-tent – all sleeping feet to the centre. These tents were permanent fixtures and properly erected, which was just as well as it poured with rain all night. The atmosphere inside the tent that night apart from being stuffy was particularly gloomy as well.

Next day, the convoy moved into Tilbury Docks and was loaded on board an LST (Landing Ship, Tank) - quite a large vessel of, I would guess, several thousand tons. Most of our vehicles, including the trailers, were stored on deck because there were lots of other supplies of all kinds for other sections of the forces, including in the hold, as I discovered by wandering around, 30 Sherman Tanks. To use the Duke of Wellington's phrase, I don't know whether they frightened the enemy, but by God they frightened me!

BEFORE I FORGET

We must, I think, have sailed by night and as part of a very large convoy of ships carrying supplies. There was a hell of a lot on our ship alone so it made one appreciate how very big the problem of supplying the Allied armies really was. Anyway next morning we were storming our way across the beaches of Ostend with our distinctly amateur drivers brought face to face with driving on the right. A few miles inland and we found an appropriate stop so we could partake of breakfast. We eagerly crumbled our compressed cake of porridge oats into a mess tin, poured on the boiling water, stirred vigorously and the result – Revolting! The tea wasn't much better with the undissolved tea-leaves floating on top of the brew. Still I suppose if you were desperate!

We were soon on our way again and must have moved quite well as I don't recall any night spent on the road. Our destination was a site not far from the American Air Force base at Florennes which gave its name to our site, though the nearest village was a tiny place called Flavion.

TEN

Flavion

60 Group Headquarters which controlled all the Radar activities of the RAF in Europe had its centre in Mons. I am sure therefore that our progress to Flavion was interrupted by a stop in Mons. However, we stopped in Mons several times whilst on the Continent and I now can't distinguish one stop from another – so I propose to discuss Mons when we are en route from Flavion to Alsace.

I always believe that if there is one place in the world where it rains more persistently and more miserably than England – it is Belgium. So my prime memory of the site near Florennes where we established our site was of MUD. Thick, glutinous, heavily liquefied mud. I suppose we had been trained to erect tents somewhere because they seemed to appear quite rapidly. Finn and I, Paddy Clulow and another Canadian called Macarthy were in one tent. We broke open our bundle of balloon fabric – Disappointment! Only the outside was fabric, inside was a mess of waste rope, netting etc. Nevertheless, there was enough to put down a floor to the tent of balloon fabric and woe betide any visitors who trod on our floor in his muddy boots. Even the C.O. coming round to inspect the tents, baulked at entering faced by four airmen staring fixedly at his muddy boots. Outside we erected a sign saying ACHTUNG - MINEN with a skull and crossbones, which we had appropriated en route and we were at home to all visitors.

The mud rapidly became all-pervading at the site and we soon had to construct a turning area for the trucks made out of railway sleepers. On one occasion I recall leaping over the back of the truck and somehow missing the sleepers so that one of my legs slid down into the liquid mud almost to knee-height. Another interesting experience on this site was when one of our amateur truck drivers actually did manage to change from first to reverse and spilled all the men in the back into a heap on the floor.

Anyway within a very few days the CO had decided that the muddy site was simply uninhabitable and had explored the village of Flavion, discovering that they had a *Salle des Fêtes* – on the first floor of a building with stables underneath.

The room was about 50 feet square and we had about 60 airmen inside, so there was very little room to do anything. I often wonder how the overcrowded prisoners of Strangeways would have enjoyed the *Salle des Fêtes* at Flavion. The sanitary arrangements consisted of two buckets stationed half-way down the stairs. Inevitably when I came to use them they were brimming over! Next morning slopping out consisted of taking these buckets out and tipping them into the middle of Flavion's main street (which was on a slope) so that the effluent ran through the centre of town. Do not, however, condemn us as barbarians. This system was Flavion's main drainage method so everyone in the village did the same.

We rapidly made friends with a young urchin of the neighbourhood, of about 7-9 years of age who intrigued us by being already addicted to a clay pipe.

It was during this idyllic sojourn that I was introduced to the 2 mess-tin bath. One tin for the application of soap and the second for the rinse water!

We very soon had the opportunity to visit the nearest large town which was Charleroi. Charleroi is a heavily-industrialised town and my only memories of it were of the large Department Stores on the main square. I should have explained that a part of the kitting-out process at Cardington was to exchange our ordinary uniforms for battledress, the first being in Air Force Blue, the other in Khaki. We were instructed to wear the khaki as our normal working dress, presumably to avoid confusion with the enemy but we all hated the idea especially to be considered a "Squaddie" i.e. an Army type. So when we had the chance we always got into Blue. This caused a lot of interest in Charleroi and I remember an incident in the *Grand Magasin des Bourses* (as I believe the store was called). I had purchased some ink and somehow managed to leak some on to my uniform. The lady assistant produced some soap and water for me to try and wash it out, but this gave me a chance to see how deprived they had been during the war as the soap was obviously made out of fish heads and had very little cleaning qualities.

We then retired to a nearby café and after a beer, the group was leaving the café with myself and Paddy bringing up the rear. Two charming young ladies seated near the exit smiled at us and one said in excellent English "How would you like to kiss my pussy!" We couldn't get out of the café quick enough but only relating this incident to the party outside, two of the bolder (and older) spirits, Ted and Ray, headed back inside. That was the last we saw of them till returning on the truck. It would appear, or so they said, that these were "ladies of the town" and that they had spent most of the afternoon trying to inveigle Ted and Ray into the shops and land them with bills for purchases. Ted and Ray were too wise old kinds to be caught out like that.

Charleroi was full of Americans and although this was still only a few weeks since Liberation, they were already becoming disliked by the locals. This due mainly to their belief that any female was fair game for their sexual exploits and generally in full view on the main square. The English were at least more discreet.

During one of these trips to Charleroi I determined to do what I thought of as a good deed. My old school friend Doug Webb had married a girl who was a Belgian refugee at the time of Dunkirk her name was Sylva Boelens and her family (who had all fled) were from a mining area called Gilly on the outskirts of Charleroi. I suspect they had fled because they were active Communists. Doug was in the Army and due to his undisciplined behaviour managed to get himself transhipped to Singapore just before the collapse. So at this time he was

BEFORE I FORGET

still a prisoner of the Japanese. The only news Sylva had had of him was that he was alive – though of course with the conditions out there, that could have changed. Nevertheless, very little of this had penetrated through to Sylva's family in Gilly. So I made my way out there to visit them, and pass on what information I had. They made a great fuss of me especially as I could speak a little French but I could see what primitive conditions they lived in in that area. Not far removed from the description of mining life in Emile Zola's "Germinal". The best educated of the family was a cousin called Emile who conducted most of the conversation and who, a few years later, came over to England to visit us.

It was in Charleroi, that my meagre knowledge of French was finally exposed. We were in a café and had enjoyed a main course when someone suggested a sweet. Seeing *Pommes Frites* advertised on the wall, I ordered this all round expecting to get some kind of Apple Fritters. Instead the Belgians, no doubt thinking "these crazy English!", served plates of chips to all.

Back in Flavion, Ted and Ray were pursuing their policy of fraternising with the natives and produced the apocryphal story of how Ray, intercepting a local housewife on her way home from the bakers, succeeded in pleasuring her against a village wall with the family supply of baguettes still tucked under her arm.

A spell of KP (Kitchen Patrol) improved my performance at spud-bashing. Spuds for 60 gives plenty of opportunity for practice.

Eventually, however, towards the third week of November 1944, following further advances by the Allied armies and particularly the invasion of Southern France and the drive by the American 7th Army up the Rhône Valley which had terminated in the capture of Strasbourg on the Rhine. There was, however, still a large body of Germans on the West Bank of the Rhine in what became known as the Colmar Pocket for the obvious reason of it being centred on the town of Colmar. At the same time, north of Strasbourg, the Germans were occupying Haguenau and the district around it in some strength. Thus

Strasbourg was reached through a fairly narrow corridor perhaps 10 kilometres wide and about 40 kilometres long. In the centre of this corridor about 25 kilometres from Strasbourg stands the delightful old village of Mutzig, famous then and now for the beer produced by the Brasserie Wagner. In the words of the old Air Force song, "They said that's what we're looking for, we'll send our Air Force there".

Of course no one told us! We only knew that crews 9452 (my own) and 9451 were to join up with 9431 and 9422 to constitute a new unit to be despatched to the southern end of the front in France.

Eventually, the trailers were packed and the trucks assembled on site and we were on our way. First stop – Mons.

BEFORE I FORGET

ELEVEN

Mons

Initially, accommodation was in a large *Caserne* or Barracks used by the Belgian Army. This, while quite adequate, was a bit primitive for the 60 Group Headquarters staff who commandeered a school and moved themselves (and transit travellers like ourselves) in.

In addition to the Air Force there were extensive American Army units stationed in or near Mons and very little love was lost between these units of the Allied Forces. Near the *Caserne* was a café, called the *Café Ostende* where the enterprising owners provided music and a small floor for dancing every night. Since a reasonable supply of girls appeared at the café it was, needless to say, packed every night.

The music provided at the *Café Ostende* was very much oriented towards the Americans – swing music of the time tending towards rock and roll but also of the smoochy variety. I rather fancied myself as a dancer at this time and I headed for the *Ostende* whenever I could.

One evening, the Belgians present complained bitterly that they never got a chance to dance the Belgian way and the Band leader, getting fed up with these complaints, suddenly announced an old-fashioned Waltz. This excluded the Americans and most of the English, but I, seizing the opportunity of a less crowded floor, grabbed one of the local girls and launched myself into it. The Band leader obviously thought "I'll teach these so-and-sos to complain" and so he continued the waltz on and on. Whilst the dancers, including myself, refused to give up. Eventually the leader had to admit defeat but only after the dance had lasted for three quarters of an hour!

The Americans in Mons were no better at drinking the Belgian beer than they had been at British beer and so there were often fights around the Town, generally dealt with quickly and ruthlessly by the Military Police. Nevertheless, it was very unwise to venture out alone or even in pairs into the back streets of Mons though I never got into any fracas.

One incident, however, took place outside the *Café Ostende*. An RAF sergeant and crony of his were walking past the *Ostende* on their way back to the barracks after an evening at the cinema, when out hurtled an American clutching a chair which he proceeded to smash over the head of the Sergeant. It appears that there had been an argument inside and the Air Force man involved had made a hasty retreat. By the time the American came out, he simply hit the first thing in Air Force Blue he could see – hence the Sergeant's unlucky night.

Another similar incident took place at the school taken over by the Air Force. I should explain that the buildings of the school were arranged in a square around a central playground. They were two storeys in height and in one corner there was a passageway through the lower floor constituting the entrance and exit, leading inside to a staircase to the first floor where most airmen were billeted. This passageway was manned by Air Force Police, generally the older sedentary types whose task it was to check airmen in and out.

One evening, an airman entered looking somewhat hot and bothered, signed himself in and disappeared upstairs. A few seconds later, several American entered obviously in hot pursuit and proceeded to grab the unfortunate Policeman on duty and beat him up. The airman meanwhile had rounded up his mates and they all came rushing back down the stairs to join in the fray. In no time, the small passageway about 10 feet square was a seething mob of Americans and airmen all flailing away. Eventually the Americans were thrown into the street but not before the unfortunate SP had suffered severe damage.

Talking about fights, I encountered a most unusual fellow in Mons. He was a Sergeant in the Army Signals Corps and when we were out drinking together, he reacted very differently to the rest of us. To most of us, every drink rendered us more and more stupefied and less and less capable of doing anything, much less fight. But to this Sergeant, each drink seemed to sharpen up his reactions until he was on an absolute razors edge and simply had to go out to seek a fight somewhere. A dangerous man to get involved with and I avoided him where possible.

A much nicer place to go and drink and dance in Mons was the Royal Albert and Elizabeth Club. This was a very smart club situated on the Grand Place in Mons and at this time open to all Service personnel. We didn't discover it until later visits, by which time 60 group had begun to import WAAF's. On one occasion, a small mixed party was at the Club when we set up a little practical joke on one of these girls.

The attitude of the Belgians to the provision of toilet facilities was a little more free and easy than the English and at the Club, the entrance door let into a communal toilet. In front were several cabins to which the ladies would obviously proceed but to the right, in full view, were a number of standing urinals for the men, usually at this time fully occupied. Anyway the WAAFs were duly fed quantities of beer until one unfortunate enquired the whereabouts of the Ladies. We indicated the door and waited. She reappeared in a few seconds covered in confusion and somewhat annoyed at what she saw as a wrong directive. However, when explained, she took it in good part and soon the girls had adopted the Belgian attitude without embarrassment.

Another excursion belonging to the later visits to Mons was to an American Forces Club for a Jazz concert. This was the era of the great swing bands such an Benny Goodman, Tommy Dorsey, etc. and many of these musicians were in the Forces and were formed into Big Bands of their own. One of these bands appeared at this Forces Club and we enjoyed a great evening of really top class American Swing Band music. The joint was really jumping!

BEFORE I FORGET

TWELVE

Mutzig

At last, the convoy was on its way, four seventeen-ton Radar trailers with dishes mounted on the top of each, pulled by Matador trucks. Diesel engine generators, assorted workshops and Utility trucks, Jeeps etc. with sixty odd Radar Personnel followed by a completely separate Wireless Telegraphy unit with about thirty personnel of their own. The whole convoy proceeded at a snails pace and took, as I recall, about three days to get down to Alsace.

On the way, I recall a stop either at Reims or somewhere nearby when an enthusiastic Frenchman, delighted to see the British as against the Americans, produced a bottle of home-distilled schnapps (or probably he called it *Eau de Vie*) into which he had inserted cherries until the bottles was completely filled. The flavour of the cherries had penetrated the liquor and it made quite an acceptable drink.

I remember another stop in Colombey–les-Belles in Joan of Arc country. In fact just down the road from her birthplace at Domremy. However, what I particularly remember Colombey for was an introduction to the mirabelle – a small sweet, yellowish plum – and even more for the liquor distilled from the fruit. So you can see, we were not missing the opportunity to explore the local folklore.

On the third day, we had to face the task of crossing the Vosges Mountains particularly across the Col du Donon a fairly steep twisting pass and we arrived there after nightfall. We were, of course, well aware that Alsace was different from the rest of France, in the sense that

BEFORE I FORGET

Hitler had made it a part of Germany and the inhabitants in general spoke a Germanic dialect and might well consider themselves Germans.

The CO, no doubt well briefed by the boffins of 60 Group, ordered the convoy to proceed on side-lights only (to avoid air attack!) which did not make the task of crossing a mountain pass any easier. The snail began to slow even further. Our morale sagged further still when we were overtaken by American Army convoys travelling at about 30 mph and with headlights blazing.

We, of course, were totally unaware of our destination as we crept further towards the enemy front-line. Eventually, we halted in a village obviously Alsatian in manner. It was by now fairly late at night ad we were wondering where we were going to stop. The convoy was allowed a break here and the enterprising among us soon discovered the village was called Mutzig. It was indeed our destination, though we were not yet aware of this. Soon the order came to remount and we were on our way further forward. Presumably this was intended to be a move to the actual site where the wagons would be located but it proved a foolish move indeed since the chances of locating a country site at night with a large and heavy convoy must have been less than zero.

First we moved forward when we should have moved back. Then we headed off the main road along a country track. Once the whole convoy was fully committed to the route the country track petered out into a simple cart track. The soil in Alsace was, though not quite as muddy as Belgium, still fairly soft and before long the first seventeen-ton trailer had sunk up to its axles. The trailers themselves were hauled by powerful Matador trucks - each equipped with a cable for pulling loads. So the first Matador was sent forward and the cable extended to the trailer. Full power ahead, but the trailer would not budge and the Matador slid slowly backwards up to its axles in the mire.

It was felt that what was needed was a second Matador. But to deploy this to position, it had to penetrate the nearest field and circle round to position. As it did so, it of course sank up to its axles as well. Various other vehicles now joined in either to help or to get a better position to direct affairs. And, of course, they in turn slid into the mire in a state of total confusion.

Eventually the CO had had enough and ordered the rescue attempts to be abandoned for the night and the unit to bed down there as best they could. During the night, a light fall of snow enlivened the scene the next morning, at first light, the full extent of the chaos was revealed.

However, the mud had saved us really, as the track we were following, if pursued for another few kilometres, would have led to the German positions in front of Haguenau and we would have delivered all the latest (and most accurate) blind-bombing technology direct to the enemy.

At least next morning more sensible decisions could be taken and the drop in temperature had hardened the ground. We were able to recover all the vehicles and trailers, retrace our steps and find the correct route to the chosen site.

This site was a most interesting one. Firstly, it stood on the last foothill of the Vosges overlooking the Rhine Valley. By this I mean the Rhine Valley in its fullest sense including the areas of plain on either side of the river. From our site we could easily see the cathedral of Strasbourg, about 25 kilometres away and on a clear day, the heights of the Black Forest on the other side of the river. Secondly, the country was most fertile with grapevines and cherry trees everywhere. Thirdly the site was on top of a Maginot Line fort, now of course more or less derelict but where I imagine there might have been some slight action when clearing the Germans out, as one of the fort's buildings had a dead horse lying there.

At a later stage, some limited exploration of this fort was possible and I recall an incident when one airman, forgetting his mining lecture, picked up a German wooden box mine and opened it. The remainder of the party hit the deck in a flash but fortunately the box was empty. Nevertheless, a look at this fort did underline the effort and money the

BEFORE I FORGET

French had put into fighting the 1914-18 War in 1939-40 when concepts of war had completely changed.

On the way to the site we encountered an American Army Signals unit with all their trucks, huts and tents very carefully camouflaged and their communications network of wires neatly mounted on poles and strung through the air at heights of about ten feet. Our Diesel Generator trucks were about fifteen feet high and were promptly driven by our amateur drivers right through the network lines. The ground was still very wet and the first heavy trailer and trucks by passed the Army Unit on one side scoring a heavy muddy track as they went. Since this made the track fairly slippery and difficult to use, later trailers decided to bypass the site on the opposite side, thus completely delineating this carefully camouflaged site by muddy tracks all around and with their communications to anywhere totally cut off. One could hardly have blamed them if they had opened fire on these hostile invaders from the RAF. Anyway, they rapidly packed up their gear and cleared off. Glad no doubt to be rid of us.

RAF #1-9000 (Oboe), Mutzig

fr. center Alf Cassidy, bk. center Finn Macdonald

Eventually we, that is the Radar section of the convoy, settled in Mutzig. Mutzig was surrounded by other villages all with the suffix heim. Slightly to the North, Molsheim, which was the correctly designated name of our station. Though I didn't discover it till many years later, Molsheim was the site where Bugatti manufactured many of his early racing cars. Further back towards the Vosges was Dinsheim-sur-Bruche where we later met the family Rathgeber and where I encountered what I thought a very sad and poignant sight – the 1914-18 War Memorial with 7 dead in the French Army and 4 in the German. Surely a monument to the futility of war.

Finally a few kilometres further towards Strasbourg, Dorlisheim, where the WT unit made its base and where we subsequently played our football. There were three different billets which we commandeered to act as our living quarters. The last was a school opposite the *Café Klaeyle* at the Dinsheim edge of the village and in that I shared a tiny room with Dennis Reed. There was only room for one of the ubiquitous double-decker wooden bunks which we must have seized from the German Army and on which we slept during all our stay in Mutzig.

I cannot, however, recall which of the other two billets came first, nor indeed where one of them was. Our stay in Mutzig was divided into two halves – the first from Dec 1944 to early January 1945, when we retreated back across the Vosges (more anon), and the second from March 1945 when we returned to December 1945 when the unit finally broke up.

One billet, which I suspect was the first, was a long room with all the unit sharing, and where I remember the dispensing of the Christmas beer in 1944 and the subsequent fracas between myself and a Canadian, Ron Marshall. God knows what it was about but we hurled insults at each other across the room. I was lying on my bunk in the upper position. Eventually Ron decided to punch it out and tried to climb on to my section of the bunk. The wooden structure promptly expanded and we both fell through into the lower deck. Anyway no damage was done to either of us and we quickly forgot the source of our quarrel.

BEFORE I FORGET

The other billet was at the rear of a central café and here the accommodation was packed as tightly as at Flavion. I remember it particularly because of our attempts to set up a voluntary duty roster to clean and tidy the place were frustrated by the refusal of Taff Thomas to cooperate and do his share. I reckon that here was the source of my dislike of the Welsh. Another incident recalled from here was seeing in the yard some Moroccan soldiers kill a chicken by severing its neck with the bayonet and seeing the headless body run aimlessly round the yard for some minutes before collapsing.

During all these moves, we had been compelled to wear our Khaki uniforms but as I pointed out, we disliked this intensely and Finn and I took an early opportunity to don our Air Force Blues and enter this café for an evening drink. At the bar, the blonde landlady talked with a few of her cronies and the only other occupant was an old peasant already well under the weather with drinks. We sat down at the next table with our beers and he immediately staggered over and joined us. He spoke in Alsatian German and my school German enabled me to reply with a few encouraging words to keep him going. He had obviously mistaken us for Luftwaffe personnel because he began to give us instructions as to how we could penetrate the Allied screen and find our way back to the German lines.

A stunned silence fell on the small group at the bar as they obviously expected retribution to overtake the old peasant. However, we were not the Luftwaffe or any kind of Nazi and Finn and I regarded the whole thing as a huge joke.

Up in the hills, a fairly large number of German prisoners were held in a camp which appeared to be run by the local branch of the French Resistance. They might not have set up Concentration Camps but they certainly wasted no sympathy on the Germans.

One of the boys had managed to take a clandestine photograph of the prisoners lined up on the sides of a square where in the centre a prisoner was being flogged for trying to escape. We used to collect a few German prisoners to do the chores in the kitchens which had been established in the abandoned brewery of the Brasserie Wagner. It was always said, though I did not see it myself, that these prisoners were confined in what was a reasonable facsimile of the Black Hole of Calcutta and when the doors were unbarred in the mornings, several prisoners invariably fell out. The Germans of course were delighted to be picked for the kitchen duties with the RAF as it meant that they got some decent food which they certainly didn't get from the French. Consequently they would seize your mess tins after a meal and clean them meticulously so as to ensure being reselected the next day.

Please don't think that I am being unduly critical of the French – when subsequently they started to renew their conscript army – the new recruits received only one C-ration per day as against the correct allocation of three.

In these early days, I remember one descent from the site on the mountain top to the village, riding on the pillion of a motorbike. The descent chosen by the rider was so precipitate that I spent most of the trip climbing up his back.

An even more hair-raising descent of the mountain was on a half-track. The MT Unit had found an abandoned German half-track and managed to get it going. They decided to take the watch down on this thing and in consequence not only was the interior filled to overflowing but they were sitting on the bonnet and hanging on to the sides and the rear. I was one of those hanging on to the rear. Unfortunately the MT driver did not know how to control this vehicle and on every corner he overshot badly – took too wide a sweep – mounted the grass verges, cut down nearby hedges etc. and generally swept the odd airman or two off the vehicle. I managed to hang on myself but was virtually the only one left outside.

Christmas was now approaching and the CO had managed to organise a very large cask of beer for the troops' festivities. However, a shadow was looming over our peaceful activities. So far on the continent we had managed to avoid any connection with the war but the war was about to pursue us.

BEFORE I FORGET

The 9000 chain in Europe was organised on three centres. Venlo in Holland, Laroche in the Belgian Ardennes, and ourselves in Alsace. Any combination of two could play CAT and MOUSE to OBOE operations over most of Europe.

However, on December 18th 1944, Hitler launched his totally unexpected Ardennes offensive. Though it never quite had the success he expected from it, due largely to the individual heroism of American Army units, nevertheless a large salient was created through the American 1st Army. By Christmas, the Panzers were well on the way towards Laroche and the 9000 site there had to make a very hurried exit. Bearing in mind the remarks I have previously made about Belgian mud, which applied equally to the site at Laroche, it says a great deal for the trojan efforts of that 9000 unit that all Radar units were successfully retrieved and the only loss to the unit was a single workshop van.

So in Mutzig Christmas came and went with the only notable incident being when a Canadian, Gordie MacKay, threw up into the toilet at the *Café Klaeyle* and his false teeth disappeared into the cess pit system.

Suddenly Hitler's armies launched another attack from the Bitche area towards the Saverne Gap which formed the channel towards Strasbourg. It was in fact only a diversionary attack intended to prevent the US 3rd Army turning north to counter attack in the Ardennes, but no one at the time knew that. The CO became very jumpy and every day sent a truck up to US 7th Army HQ at Sarrebourg to check on the current front line situation. Every day the US 7th Army, with that confidence that always characterises the Americans replied, "We'll give those Krauts hell – don't worry everything is OK".

Then one morning the truck arrived in Sarrebourg and the US 7th Army had vanished! The truck came back in panic and the CO sent another scouting expedition south towards the Colmar pocket. They arrived on the outskirts of Sélestat, known to be in German hands, without seeing a single Allied Soldier. We appeared to be the last Allied unit east of the Vosges.

The CO urgently contacted 60 Group HQ in Mons for instructions (or rather a confirmation of his intent to retreat). They got their information from 2nd TAF in Brussels who got theirs from SHAEF in Reims who got theirs from 7th Army HQ. Which of course was 24 hours out of date and therefore consisted of, "We'll give those Krauts hell!" So he was instructed to stay put.

In the billets, the lads determined that Jerry should not capture the vital stores! So we drank the rest of the Christmas beer. At the end of a convivial evening 50% of the unit were for going out to fight Jerry single-handed. The rest were too drunk to care!

Unbeknownst to us, General de Gaulle was making urgent representations to Eisenhower, Churchill and anybody else he could think of, to save Strasbourg, the loss of which would be a severe blow to French morale. So eventually they agreed that the French 1st Army should take over the sector and by next morning their tanks were pouring in from the South. At this very moment, the latest information arrived at 60 Group HQ (24 hours late). "Get out at once and at all costs", came the orders from 60 Group. So our unit, already packed and ready, was immediately on the move retreating towards the Vosges and obstructing the 1st French moving in the opposite direction!

Finn, Al Rattray and myself managed to get ourselves allocated to the Workshop unit which also carried the unit blanket store. Very comfortable, the more so because as we approached the Vosges, the snow began to fall and winter set in.

The Col du Donon was deemed to be too dangerously near the German front and so we took a more southerly route towards St Dié and Epinal. Heavy falls of snow caused very slow progress punctuated by sliding off the road etc. Dennis Reed, always the conscientious type could be heard outside exhorting the pullers and the pushers to deal with these crises. We snuggled down amongst the blankets and let them get on with it. This crossing was even more difficult and following morning the unit staggered into Commercy, well into Lorraine, where we intended to regroup.

BEFORE I FORGET

We remained for a few days in Commercy and there made the acquaintance of a lady who had received a medal from Marshal Pétain, no less, for services to the Republic, as she had had ten children. I don't think she thought the medal was sufficient reward!

We were also pestered constantly by a kid of 11 or 12 who was already a tearaway. I felt really sorry for this kid, though he was such a nuisance, as his mother was a whore and his stones and abuse were countered by our cowardly jeers about his mother. What chance did the poor devil have?

We got to know something about the Pétain regime here which had substituted for the old revolutionary cry of Liberté, Egalité, Fraternité, the more prosaic sounds of Travail, Famille, Patrie.

After a few days, it was decided that we should re-deploy to Baccarat slightly to the east where we were to remain for a couple of months and to get well in with the local inhabitants. The unit was quartered on the local population and Finn, Al, Dennis and myself were allocated to the village hunter. He was an oldish man, married to a woman perhaps 20 years younger and who carried a double-barrelled shotgun under his arm all the time. Unfortunately the wife took a fancy to Al and began to try to manoeuvre him into bed. These advances were not received with favour by any of us, primarily because the lady was addicted to garlic and one simply could not look her directly in the eye. The four of us, therefore, looked distinctly shifty when speaking to her as we were always turning aside. The fact the old man was a crack shot didn't help either.

What the hunter actually hunted was primarily wild boar which seemed to abound in the Lorraine forests and we received an invitation to dine on wild boar (for the only time in my life) and very nice it was too - rather like a gamey pork. He also had captured a baby wild boar and kept it in the yard. It was about 10 inches long and already very aggressive. It would hurl itself at your ankles and if you were not a quick mover, you would get a nasty bang.

Of course, in Baccarat, we had no operational work to do so there was no impediment to getting to know the local population. In no time, the unit was well dug in with all the local inhabitants. We (that is Finn, Al, Dennis and myself) were very fortunate to get to know the Crouvezier family. Henri was a typical Frenchman, short, sporting a beret and smoking Gaulois. Germaine, his wife, again a typical Frenchwoman, broad in the beam, very hospitable. I must admit also that a major attraction for all of us in the Crouvezier household was their lodger, a young teacher called Marcelle Kirstetter. A very nice girl, quite oblivious to any approaches by the RAF and I particularly remember one encouraging remark she made to me and I quote, "The French don't use the subjunctive much". Since I never understood why anybody should use this, when at school, this cheered me up particularly.

Baccarat church was in ruins, having been hit by an American bomb, so this made the British all the more welcome as Allies. We all liked the people of Baccarat so much that we seized every opportunity of returning there from Mutzig when we finally advanced again.

Baccarat of course was and is the centre of a thriving cut glass industry and many of the townsfolk were engaged in the factory. Everyone in town had beautiful specimens of cut glass and in particular those types of glassware, where coloured glass is melded on to plain glass and the cuts made through the coloured section to the plain. Beautiful specimens everywhere and it's here I first decided that any free money that I ever obtained would be invested in glass. It's a pity I never succeeded in achieving it. Anyway I did finally return with six small liqueur glasses and two small decanters in Baccarat glass – some of which still survive.

To return to the war – the threat to the Saverne Gap and Strasbourg never materialised and it became apparent that it had only ever been a diversion. The Ardennes Salient was pinched off and the Germans retreated to the Rhine – the Colmar Pocket was closed off and the Germans were evacuated across the Rhine. Finally the RAF plucked up their courage and allowed the No 1 9000 unit to return to Mutzig.

BEFORE I FORGET

This would have been about the beginning of March 1945 and before the end of that month, the decisive crossings of the Rhine took place and it became apparent that the war was heading towards a close. I don't quite know how this came about but at the time, we seemed to receive appraisals of the situation - where the Allied troops had reached, what opposition they were encountering and indeed an appraisal of what actions they were likely to take. These bulletins were posted up on site and so were available to all.

A great deal of attention in the early days of April 1945 was concentrated on whether Hitler and his cronies would try to make a last stand in the mountainous areas around Berchtesgaden. It was thought that if this took place OBOE precision bombing would take a very active part in the attack on this so-called "Bavarian Redoubt". So a more advanced site was selected around Ulm on the Danube and an advance party assembled to explore the possibilities. This included Finn Macdonald and they were despatched in April. More anon about their adventures and the effect on our unit in Mutzig.

In the meantime, the site at Mutzig required protection and a rota of Guard duties were established. This proved wildly unpopular with the erks and prominent among the protestors was one LAC Ash, an operator. Ash was a flamboyant character with very little regard for authority but somehow he managed to become LAC in charge of one of the Guard watches. A log book was issued and the i/c guard required to enter all incidents. For a day or two Ash found nothing to enter but Guard ON and Guard OFF. Not surprising really as most of the time was spend in the Guard tent playing cards. The CO complained bitterly about the lack of incident in the Log Book and Ash, ever obliging, filled up the next watch with a detailed account of the progress of the card game concluding with a lament on the extent of his losses. This resulted in a "Fizzer" – 14 days jankers for the unrepentant Ash.

Guards were also required for the MT Unit and I recall doing a stint there, notable mainly for the sounds of creaking bedsprings as the MT unit (a randy lot) entertained their girlfriends. The guard was run on strict RAF lines, however, and at 11pm the Guard closed down and we all went to bed. Rumour also had it, that an inspection carried out by one of the officers focussed his torch on the bare behind of one of the MT personnel hard at it with his girlfriend. Anyway, the authorities soon got fed up with this and abandoned the guards, leaving the site vulnerable to any saboteur. Fortunately none appeared.

The unit was thus able to turn its attention to the more important task of rebuilding its social life. The village of Mutzig contained one hotel and this hotel had a very passable dance hall attached, with a nice stage. Some instrumentalists were discovered among the German POWs and a band was assembled to play at the weekly dance. This group were withdrawn from the POW camp on permanent secondment and placed on regular RAF rations. They were of course delighted and all the others who worked in the cook house and in the MT unit had a very much improved time of it and so were extremely co-operative.

One interesting feature of the hotel was that in the corridor approaching the dance-hall, were two conspicuous doors labelled very clearly DAMEN and HERREN. However both separate doors led into the same unisex loo of the standard type.

The dance was an excellent meeting place and the girls of the village turned up in force bringing with them their mothers to ensure that none fell victims to the rough soldiery, and I rapidly made the acquaintance of the Diebold family, dancing with their charming daughter Jacqueline and practising my French on Mama. Mrs Diebold was a very nice woman, most hospitable and we became fast friends for the remainder of my stay in Mutzig. I was given "Open House" with the Diebolds and could drop in at any time – which I did at almost all times when not on duty. Mr Diebold worked on the railway and belonged to a co-operative club which provided him with a regular cheap source of red wine. I always suspected that it fell off the back of trucks passing through, but I could be doing him an injustice.

The Diebolds owned a small plot of land on which they grew both apple and cherry trees which they converted in to Cider and Schnapps (more about this process later). I was able to add cans of fruit juice and cigarettes to the supply, so you can see we were all set for some very convivial evenings. Grapefruit juice enlivened with Schnapps and little sugar makes a very acceptable (and potent!) cocktail.

Finn Macdonald similarly made the acquaintance of the Rathgeber family who lived in Dinsheim and had a very nice daughter called Odette. She was I think, a little older than Jacqui, who was only 17, but they were both very nice girls.

I remember once being invited to dinner at the Rathgebers. They lived in a house at the back of a farmyard and the approach to it was through a glutinous mixture of mud, cowpats, squawking chickens and probably a pig or two. However, the house itself was absolutely spotless. How on earth Mrs Rathgeber managed it was beyond me. One of the dishes served was a salad with slices of home-cured ham or bacon which turned out to be so tough and raw-tasting to our palates that we both had a problem trying to be polite to our hosts and to eat it. Our taste for the salad was also somewhat dented when after the meal, Mr Rathgeber fertilised his garden by peeing directly on it. I don't know why we should have felt squeamish as no doubt it was thoroughly washed and anyway the local fields were frequently watered from a tanker filled with the village urine. The smell resulting from this exercise was pretty revolting but nothing was wasted.

A small stream ran through Mutzig village – fairly fast running and used by the village women for washing purposes. One frequently saw sheets subsequently spread out on the fields for bleaching by the sun.

My French was making rapid progress now and this resulted in my advice being sought from time to time. On one occasion, a very nice widow approached me through Jacqui. She had been receiving visits from one Sergeant Humphries – his protestations of undying love were about to succeed but she would like to know whether he was married in England. I should explain here that Jacqui was well aware that I was married, in accordance with my regular policy of revealing this fact as soon as reasonably possible.

I, of course, knew that Sid was married but loyalty to comrades had to be maintained. So I came out with some lame excuse that he was a Sergeant and I was an ordinary Soldier and we did not mix. This seemed quite an acceptable idea to the French. However, I did go on to lay it on thick that we were all soldiers, here today and gone tomorrow, and to counsel caution to the widow.

An even more embarrassing incident occurred with a very striking young blonde girl called Denise, only 16 years of age. Denise was very keen to improve her English and resolutely refused to speak French. "What is the meaning of this word 'fucking' that the English are always using", she says to me in English. I am rather pleased that this conversation is in English as we are surrounded by Mamas at the time with their ears wagging. I duck the issue! "Do you hear me using it?" I demand. "Well no," she says. "There you are," I say, "it is a naughty word – they should not use it – and if you take my advice, you will avoid these airmen who do use it." Thereby I hope blighting the chances of those villains with designs on the delectable Denise.

By this time, the value of cigarettes as currency was well established. We received an allowance of 250 cigarettes a week. 200 (10 packs of 20) American cigarettes in a carton – Marlboro, Camels, Lucky Strike etc. and 50 English cigarettes all packed into a round tin. The going rate then was 200 francs for a packet of 20 and the Exchange rate was 480 francs to the pound. This may not seem expensive by today's standards but was very expensive then. However, the village was full of troops of the French 1st Army. Some of these were *Goums* – Moroccan tribesmen with a sinister look and a large kukri up their sleeves. What they smoked, I don't know, but fortunately not often our cigarettes. There were also Algerian troops who looked much more civilized and were paid sufficiently high rates that they could afford cigarettes and this was our main source of buyers. Funnily enough, the Algerians were paid much more than the French conscripts who began to appear once the war was over.

Dennis Reed, ever a moralist, lectured me on the damage which the black-market operations were doing to the English economy. To no avail, but I noticed that when subsequently the price rose to 300 francs, his moral obligations faded away.

He and I were now sharing a room as we had moved into our third billet, a small building opposite the *Café Klaeyle* whose takings began to rise astronomically. Outside the window of our little room, a lilac bush climbed the wall and as the spring time wore on, the scent of lilac was deliciously overpowering. This billet was confined to the Radar personnel and it was pestered by a small group of 11-12 year old girls, presumably with their eyes on chocolate bars, who used to flirt outrageously with the airmen. It is, I think, a tribute to the inherent decency of the group that none of these kids ever got into trouble because they were certainly playing a very dangerous game.

The easy access to this billet must have tempted others as we caught a 14 year old lad helping himself to sweets and cigarettes. He was shouted at, in what to him was a foreign language, and must have been terrified as to what might happen once in the hands of soldiers with guns. Some discussion ensued as to what we should actually do and eventually I was deputed to tell him that we were going to throw him into the river. He wasn't too keen on this either but I suppose must have thought it better than summary execution. Anyway, he was frog marched towards the river but after about 200 yards everyone got fed up with this and let him go free. Perhaps he was taught a lesson as we never saw him again.

Sport was something we rapidly turned our attention to and in particular football. Having discovered a suitable field at Dorlisheim, we soon established some matches. The football talent on the unit divided into three groups. The first from the WT unit at Dorlisheim itself who considered themselves far superior to the other groups. We shall see how they got their comeuppance shortly. The next group was the Radar Operators who could put together quite a useful side which could easily white-wash the third group – that made up of Radar Mechanics. Quite a large proportion of these were Canadian anyway so they had to be taught the game from scratch.

One Man's Radar War

My first game was the initial game for the Mechanics against the Operators. I started on the right wing with the avowed intention of swiftly kicking away any ball which came in my direction under the guise of a "cross from the right". I had an easy first half as most of the action was concentrated around our goal and we finished the half 6-0 down. The goalkeeper had distinguished himself by not having the slightest idea of how to save or perform any function. He was to put it bluntly, hopeless. In a moment of aberration at half-time I volunteered to change places which offer he thankfully accepted and the change could hardly really be said to have improved the situation as I let in 7 more goals and we lost 13-0 but I must have saved a few and generally looked more the part – so that is how I came to join the unhappy Goalkeepers Union. I say unhappy because whereas if you make a mistake in midfield there's always a chance someone will rescue you – in goal if you make a mistake there it is in the back of the net. So I have more sympathy than most when Peter Schmeichel shows a very occasional lack of judgement!

Some other footballing memories vary from the disastrous to the mildly successful. In one pick-up game with Finn Macdonald playing centre forward for the other side, suddenly a long ball from the opposition came towards the edge of my penalty area and Finn and I are racing for it. Finn had an unusual high-stepping run rather like a horse and I could see these boots approaching the ball and me at speed. What was required was to snatch the ball from his feet and roll sideways out of the way. I rolled sideways all right but completely missed the snatch leaving him with an open goal!

In another game Ray Burgess, the referee, awarded three penalties to the opposition in the space of 10 minutes. The first was hit neatly into the corner of the net with me nowhere near. The second I got my hand to but it ricocheted on to the post and went in but the third, obligingly delivered a bit nearer I made a spectacular save – catching the ball neatly as I fell to the left.

I was never noted for my dead-ball kicking but on one of the rare occasions when I played on the wing, I managed to get a corner placed into the centre of the goal mouth where one of our forwards headed it in!

I never got to play against the WT unit who considered themselves so good that we poor Mechanics never got a game. So arrogant were this bunch – a team selected from only 35 possible choices – that they actually had the nerve to challenge Strasbourg, a French First Division side to a game. And this is where they finally got their comeuppance, Strasbourg beat them 9-0!

But we must return to the war – you remember that there was a war going on at this time even though it was drawing to an end.

With our advance party established in Ulm, the unit was suddenly warned to standby to move at 24 hours notice. The urgent necessity was of course, to organise a Farewell Dance. This was rapidly achieved and the village turned up in force to bid us farewell. By now well established in the village and with no chance of the Germans returning, there were many tearful farewells and a good time was had by all.

Next morning, an urgent message received, delay departure by 24 hours! Time for another Farewell Dance. Equally enjoyable – and the following morning a further 24 hours delay. Believe it or not, we had 10 successive Farewell Dances before they finally gave up the whole idea and left us still in Mutzig. I suppose the village must have been a bit sceptical about it all but the end of the 10 days but most of them continued loyally to attend.

The returning Advance Party had arrived in Ulm a little too late to indulge in any full scale looting but they had managed to "organise" certain things. Finn had discovered a linen store in the German School they had taken over and had brought me back a pair of sheets. Sheets! What bliss, after four years of sleeping between the blankets .

One of the other things he had managed to find was film, printing paper and the materials for processing film. I can't remember whether he also "found" a camera but I know he was able to take pictures of lots of things and people and this led to an episode which caused me to consider Finn a friend for life which he has certainly turned out to be.

In the *Café Klaeyle* there was a maid of all work - a lady in her late thirties who had married a German Soldier during the occupation and was now heavily pregnant by him. The father had of course to retreat with the German Army and abandon his wife. When the baby was born, Finn took pictures of the baby and the mother, processed them and presented her with the prints so that she could send them through the Red Cross to the father in Germany. This, while the war was still in progress. To me this represents humanity at its very best, transcending all the foolish violence of hatred and war and it is a foundation of my very high regard for Finn as a friend and human being of the highest class.

About this time we must have received one of the first of many invitations to return to Baccarat. This time it was to attend the First Communion of one of the junior members of the family. This was, of course, a part of the turnout of all the youngsters of Baccarat in the First Communion parade and despite the obvious difficulties of wartime, all the girls appeared in their miniature versions of a Wedding Dress and the boys in their now long trousered suits with elaborate sashes and buttonholes. How very nice it all looked, especially in the happy and euphoric mood caused by Liberation, with France free once again.

We, of course, could not attend the religious ceremony as Protestants but we could and did attend the feasting afterwards. Baccarat is, of course, a country town and the produce of the countryside was no doubt saved for this special occasion but I must say that I have never participated in such a sustained bout of eating and drinking before or since. Lunch began at about midday and lasted till around four in the afternoon at which time we rose from the groaning table for a saunter round town just to give the digestive juices a chance to work. By six, we were again at the table for dinner and it must have been nearly 10 before we finally gave up and considered putting the children to bed. Of course, the whole thing was taken in a leisurely way and the interruptions for speeches and toasts were many and varied but it gave us a fascinating insight into the lives of the good people of Baccarat, France.

Every day now brought further news of the imminent collapse of Germany. Hitler's suicide and replacement by Doenitz. Daily advances deeper into Germany. The meeting of American and Russians on the Elbe, and finally the surrender of the German forces on Lüneberg Heath. The German war was over! It was May 7th 1945 and a time for celebration and happiness. What better way in Mutzig than a Victory Dance. And with the speed of light, this was organised. Also a Victory Parade. This was to be a joint affair between ourselves and the Algerian units in Mutzig. We hastily tried to remember our drill and determined that our smart turn-out would stand comparison with the French 1st Army.

Eventually we assembled and trying desperately to swing our arms high and keep in step, we marched through the village to rendezvous with the Algerians. When we arrived, we found that the Algerians were all carrying Chinese lanterns and shuffling along with little semblance of order, so our barrack square formation looked a bit out of place.

After individual celebrations with the respective families, Finn and I took the girls, Odette Rathgeber and Jacqueline Diebold to the dance. Only to find on arrival that the hotel dance floor was absolutely solid and the crush trying to get in was halfway down the corridor. So we gave up and buying a couple of bottles of white wine, we took ourselves off up the hills outside Mutzig to a little shrine with an altar and seats where we sat ourselves down to watch the fireworks exploding over Mutzig accompanied by the Algerians firing off all their surplus ammunition, and of course to drink the white wine. I suppose, in a shrine, we should have prayed, but we didn't but I'm sure that as we enjoyed our little innocent celebration with such delightful and friendly companions, we each gave thanks in our own way for the end of this terrible war.

Next day, we discovered, had been designated Victory in Europe Day. VE Day, May 8th 1945 and there was just time to jump on the truck and head for Baccarat and the official celebrations with all our French friends.

The dance at Baccarat, for there was always a dance, was in the open air and arranged to take place on a park area covered with cinders. Finn and I had our army boots on and survived the wear and tear well, but Al Rattray, who had put on his civilian shoes, danced right through the soles in one night. It was that kind of dance anyway and for the only time in my life, I danced till dawn and we finally staggered back to the Crouvezier's in daylight at 6.30 a.m. But how marvellous it was, the relief and joy that it was finally over and the nightmare of Nazism had gone for ever.

Now began the period of visits. I suppose that being in a pseudo-American sector (behind the French 1st) petrol was readily available, but the unit's trucks were used to organise visits to interesting places.

In the very early days, there were problems as the officers commandeered the trucks and disappeared off to Germany across the temporary bridge linking Strasbourg with Kehl. Perhaps they were sightseeing too, but the prevailing opinion on the unit was that these were looting expeditions.

Anyway Finn and I hitched a lift to Strasbourg on a French Army 15 cwt truck. I particularly remember the trip in, because the driver was a young French girl who was one of the best drivers I ever encountered. She drove at a furious pace, threw the truck all over the road but somehow you felt she was always in full control.

Strasbourg we enjoyed very much, though the Cathedral windows and in particular the famous clocks were still bricked up and not available. Strasbourg is a bilingual town and we were impressed by the way the Strasbourgers switched from French to German and back again in ordinary conversation. There were a lot of Americans in the town and they were doing what they did best i.e. chasing the women. On the

BEFORE I FORGET

Place Kleber, main square of Strasbourg, they appeared to be using a 15 cwt. truck as a mobile brothel!

Other visits we made that summer in Alsace were to the Monastery de St Odile (actually a nunnery) where we were somewhat surprised to see the nuns unloading crates of beer from a truck, obviously already operating a tourist service. Another Alsatian visit was to the Castle of Haut Königsberg which is a medieval castle commanding excellent views over the Rhine valley. I also participated in two excursions into Germany. One to Baden-Baden of which I remember nothing, mainly I think because we took so long getting there, that we had no time to look round. And the second to Karlsrühe, a town quite substantially damaged – again I remember little of the place. On the way out of town we picked up a couple of girl hitch-hikers. Remember we were all sporting our regulation blue uniforms and not khaki. So the girls thought we were Luftwaffe and once on board they were astonished (and terrified) to discover that they were in the hands of what they obviously believed were the fanatical killers of Bomber Command. Needless to say nothing whatever happened to them, except that they had to listen to our fractured German.

As well as the visits, leave passes were now available and I got my chance to have three days in Brussels. I forget the exact date but it coincided with the General Election in the UK and the results were announced in Brussels. Arrangements had been made for all Forces Personnel to vote and it was generally felt that the Forces vote was the main reason for the astonishing result – a total rejection of Churchill and the Conservative Party and a landslide to Labour. I don't think that Churchill himself was rejected but the Conservative Party was and we felt that we deserved a better and fairer world, fit as they said, for heroes to live in.

I can tell you that there was dancing in the streets of Brussels that night. Joyous festivities as we felt that a new era was about to dawn. At one of the Forces Clubs, I made the acquaintance of Reine de Wilde, a delightful 21 year old Bruxelloise who lived in Ganshoren, a suburb of Brussels with her two sisters who were very much older than she was.

A few years later, I was lucky enough to be able to return to Brussels with my wife, Mary, and to visit the de Wilde family again. And at that time to realise a recommendation that Reine made in 1945 to visit the modern cathedral at Koekelberg which was a very impressive building.

In the meantime, I managed to visit St. Gudule, the Grand Place and of course the Maneken Pis. We also managed to get to Laeken to see the oriental palaces.

Finally, the leave I had been waiting and longing for - a 7 day pass to England to see my beloved wife Mary and the baby I had had to desert at 10 days old and who was now 9 months old. How marvellous that was to play with David and to see how much he had grown and how much it made me long to get out and to resume ordinary civilian life again. At this time, however, (June 1945) there were still the Japanese and we were still hoping desperately to avoid being transferred to the Far East. There still seemed to be a major task ahead to overcome the fanatical resistance of the Japanese.

One amusing sideline on the UK trip concerned blankets. We were instructed to take one blanket with us – to protect us on the Channel crossing. This would be handed in on leaving the ship at Newhaven and another collected back on the return journey to France. On arrival at Newhaven very few indeed of the squaddies and erks returning to the UK had bothered to bring blankets and the cries of the collection NCO at the foot of the gangplank were totally brushed aside as the boys swarmed onshore. However, on the return journey, everyone meticulously collected a blanket because these could be sold very readily on the already booming black market. How many blankets the British authorities fed into Europe that way, one could never discover but I should think it roughly equalled the Marshall Plan.

By now, the full horrors of Nazi Germany had been well publicised with pictures of Belsen, Dachau and Auschwitz though even then the worst extermination camps were not yet known. So we were very interested to have a chance to visit this camp though of course all the prisoners had been dispersed long before.

BEFORE I FORGET

Lets get the name sorted out first. The camp was called Struthof, the nearest village Natzweiler and the nearest town Schirmeck. It was a relatively small camp – only (!) 30,000 people died there and it was notorious really for two reasons. One, that it was a centre for some frightful medical experiments and two, that it was the place where the four British WAAF's who had been dropped into France to join the Resistance met their deaths – the most well known being Violette Szabo, others being Andrée Borrel, Vera Leigh and Diana Rowden[11].

The details of the Concentration Camps were so horrific and indeed almost unbelievable that I made up my mind that I would record what I actually saw, and to distinguish this from the tales of what had allegedly happened – though I have no reason to doubt that they may well be true.

Main Gate of Struthof Concentration Camp 1945

The camp was still in use, being full of Alsatian collaborators placed there by the French. The whole camp was very clean and tidy but obviously run with iron discipline. The paths were of gravel – all swept clean and into neat patterns which were attended by prisoners stationed every 10 yards with brushes who replaced the pattern immediately you had passed. The prisoners were compelled to doff their caps and bow as

---

11 It appears that the author is wrong about Violette Szabo, who was in fact executed at Ravensbrück in February 1945. The fourth woman executed at Natzwiller on 6th July 1944 alongside Borrel, Leigh and Rowden was Sonya Olschanezky.

anyone passed by and the camp had a large clock face (with no works to it) and the hands were moved on every minute by a prisoner armed with an alarm clock.

What did I actually see? The camp was surrounded with barbed wire and inside that, an electrified fence. It was built on a slight slope with the living accommodation at the upper end and the furnace block at the lower end. There were two huge open pits filled with what were undoubtedly human bones and skeletons. Whether there were 30,000 or less, I could not tell, but there were very many. About halfway down the camp, among the living quarters there was a gibbet.

The furnaces themselves were at the very bottom of the site and were entered from the lower side, i.e. out of sight of the main camp. There were two furnaces, of a type which I have frequently seen on the TV at various places. The entrance was reached by descending several steps from either side. It was said that victims were shot in the back of the neck as they descended these steps. There were certainly many bullet holes in the walls alongside these steps. The furnaces were not large and I would think not capable of holding more than a couple of bodies each, so that disposal of bodies must have been a long-winded process.

Inside the block, we were shown a pile of human hair. At least it looked like human hair but when and under what circumstances it was removed I cannot say. We next saw a room labelled *Desinfektionsraum* where disinfecting and fumigation took place. It was like a cold room for meat with huge meat hooks hanging from bars below the ceiling.

In another room there were two huge vats, large enough to contain several men. It was said that this was a torture practised by filling one with boiling water and the other with ice cold water and throwing the victims from one to the other. It could have been possible but whether it did I could not say. Finally we were shown an Operating Table. This had a tiled top, very solidly built with drainage channels cut in arrowed shapes leading down from the edges to a central main channel. Obviously it was an operating table but under what circumstances it was used, I could not tell.

BEFORE I FORGET

I have recounted what I actually saw with my own eyes and from what evidence has been gathered from prisoners at Struthof and elsewhere, I have no reason to doubt the tales of what went on. From what I saw, it certainly could have happened. A chilling experience!

Finally, on the way out from the camp, we passed a cart being manhandled up the hill by a team of prisoners in lieu of horses. I'm afraid we took the opportunity to jeer at the Master Race reduced to such circumstances.

To return to more congenial visits. I have to recount two more trips to Baccarat. The first on July 14th 1944 – Bastille Day – the first after Liberation. What a celebration. There was a procession round the streets in which we were participants. The streets were strangely silent – this was because everybody but everybody was in the procession. The village band incessantly played the Marseillaise and the local marching song Alsace et la Lorraine – the only words of which I can now recall are the last line – *Et, malgré vous, nous resterons Francais!*

By this time, the Hotel de Ville had been reopened and so the dancing was inside. The walls were decorated with murals depicting the Boar Hunts – you remember I mentioned our acquaintance with the village boar hunter. Also, the French Army had begun to exercise its conscription and some of the local lads had been called up. Midway through the dance, these young men paraded round the hall with a large tricolor held horizontally into which the good citizens of Baccarat hurled gifts of cash to be shared among the conscripts. They undoubtedly needed this as they were currently being paid 5 francs a day (about 3d)

The second visit was for the only football match that I recall our crew playing against the locals. This was organised to take place at Raon L'Étape another village not far from Baccarat. They not only possessed a football team but also a football stadium, albeit a small one. Somehow, the first choice goalkeeper was not available and so I was drafted for the job. Once again, it was a festive occasion and the stadium was packed with people. At a guess I would say about 1,500 people. Unfortunately for us, the Raon team was quite useful and I had a very busy time. We lost 3-0 but I did manage one or two quite useful saves including saving a penalty. This is not quite as heroic as it sounds. The referee was Ray Burgess, one of our crew, and he, seeking no doubt to be ultra impartial awarded the penalty in what were very doubtful circumstances. The Raon team captain, not wishing to be outdone at the *Entente Cordiale*, and recognising the fallacy of this decision, took the penalty and kicked it straight at me at a fairly gentle pace so even I could hardly miss it.

On one or other of these visits, Mr Crouvezier had arranged a tour of the glass factory which was most interesting, particularly to see the craftsmen cutting the most delicate of patterns and indeed sculptures in the glass by hand using tiny rotating wheels against which they pressed the glass to carve out the figures. Beautiful work indeed. We also saw the processes for overlaying the coloured glass onto the clear glass so that the cuts can be made through the coloured glass to the clear, so typical of Baccarat glass.

We also saw there, the complete glassware collections made for Marshal Pétain and for Hermann Goering which had been completed but never delivered. They featured respectively the Axe symbol of Vichy France and the Swastika prominently cut into each separate piece.

As spring gave way to summer, the thoughts of the Canadians turned to playing softball and games were very soon being arranged. Some of the lads constructed a backstop of wire netting which they erected on the field. It lasted precisely 24 hours when someone obviously thought it better employed as a chicken coop.

Anyway, we had many enjoyable games of softball and I as usual hung around the edges of these games – not really good enough to match the Canadians but always glad to get a game to make up the team. Al Rattray did a lot of pitching and Finn used to delight in teasing him over his pitching. Finn was actually ambidextrous and could bat either right or left-handed. He would change from one to the other while at bat against Al which used to quite throw Al's delivery and to enrage him to boot.

Softball, Mutzig 1945

From left, Alf Cassidy, Ken Wells, Ray Anderson, Mel Stewart, Gord Mackay

Otherwise the Canadians were very preoccupied with getting back home which was being organised for them, and somewhere around August they finally departed. Strangely, I don't remember much about their actual departure though we missed their congenial company very much indeed. What good companions they all were and I cherish very much my continued friendship with Finn which has endured till today. I remained in touch also with Al Rattray for many years after the war and only lost contact when his personal affairs got too complicated.

My own preoccupation during this time was to avoid being sent out to the Far East where the war with Japan still continued and looked as if it would go on for a long time. The Air Force at this time launched an Educational Initiative which allowed airmen waiting for demobilisation to study for an examination equivalent to the Matriculation exams prevalent in schools at that time. This was called something like the Forces Special Education Certificate and it enabled lads who had missed out on Secondary education to catch up during their waiting time. Anyway, they needed instruction for this, so I put my name forward. An additional advantage was that they offered promotion to Acting Sergeant and on my grading this resulted in 12/6 per day pay which pretty well doubled my existing pay.

60 Group HQ had by now moved itself from Mons to Bonn and so in September when the No1 9000 unit was finally broken up, we were despatched to Bonn to the Johanniter Krankenhaus – a hospital taken over as billets. We could not have remained there for long as Taff Thomas and I were soon advised that our applications to serve as Educational Instructors were accepted and we were to be posted to a GEE station just outside Reims.

BEFORE I FORGET

THIRTEEN

Witry-les-Reims

The unit to which we were posted was stationed at a village called Witry-les-Reims about 7 kilometres outside Reims. It was one of the first GEE stations to be established in France and the crew had remained there ever since so that they were well dug in with the local population.

GEE is a General Navigational System not specific to any aircraft but one which can be utilised by any aircraft flying in the reasonable vicinity which was equipped with the appropriate set. I was not there as a Radar Mechanic and so was not involved with the system and cannot therefore speak with any real knowledge. However, the broad principle was this: There was a Master Station (Witry) and Slave stations at Aix-en-Othe and two or three others whose locations I do not recall). The Master sends out a pulse which is repeated by the Slaves, and the receiving set in the aircraft by timing the distance between pulses received from Master and Slave can plot with quite reasonable accuracy the position on a map.

Witry was a fairly nondescript village more or less strung out along the Reims-Rethel road. At one end of the village was a small château which had been taken over by the RAF. In its grounds they had erected a large hut which was the main living accommodation. It contained about 30 beds and had two entrances only – one halfway along the side nearest to the château and the other midway along one of the ends. Through this one exited towards the loos which were a serried rank of Elsans.

BEFORE I FORGET

Meals were cooked and served inside the château. The unit's officers lived further down the village and they made very few contacts with the main site. The CO was a Squadron Leader who made so little impact on me that I cannot even recall his name.

Eventually, I was to be allocated a room in the château for use as a classroom but this was some way into the future. Halfway through the village was the *Café Paulette* – round which most of our social life revolved. This was not the real name of the café but it appeared to be owned and run by a quite young and attractive lady called Paulette. Many of the airmen on that unit had designs on Paulette, but her eyes were clearly on the money she was making in the café – and she must have been making a small fortune! Nevertheless, let it be said that Paulette was a very nice girl and if you were in her good books she would never take advantage of you by overcharging.

The other village notable was the laundress – a lady who undertook the laundry for such of the unit as cared to employ her services. Outside her house she had erected a notice obviously garnered from a dictionary which read: Washerwoman, Washing, Wash and in consequence the poor old dear was know thereafter as Mrs Washerwoman, Washing, Wash.

At the back of Paulette's café was a hall that was occasionally used for dances but these more often took place at a converted cinema further down the village and by the time I arrived on this unit the practice of having a Saturday night dance was well established.

What was also well established on this unit was a gigantic booze racket which provided every single man on the unit with an extensive and varied supply of the most exotic booze. It operated in collusion (and really organised by) the civilian NAAFI unit located in Reims. The function of this unit was to buy (at wholesale prices) all kinds of French wines and liqueurs to supply all the units of the British Army on the Rhine (BAOR). The unit was able therefore (illegally) to supply all the cafés in and around Reims with supplies free of all government taxes. To do this, it required transport and this was provided by the GEE unit at Witry. The prime movers in this were the MT unit but I cannot imagine it being done without the connivance of the unit's officers.

Anyway I recall acquiring myself among others, bottles of Remy Martin VSOP and Green Chartreuse for 6/- (6 shillings to you). Unfortunately for me the whole racket blew up after my being only a week on the unit and as we understood it the NAAFI personnel were arrested and we heard eventually that the ring leader got 5 years. Nevertheless, it was good while it lasted.

A side effect of this more or less free supply of booze was not to enhance my reputation. In all my life (so far) – I have only been seriously drunk on 4 occasions. Two of them occurred during the 1st month on this site. Every Saturday night there was a party and the drinks came out of this extraordinary Pandora's Box. You grabbed a half tumbler glass and sat there holding it, gassing away to your mates and someone would keep appearing and filling it up with some mysterious liquid in glorious technicolor – brown, green, yellow, colourless and so on. Taff Thomas and I were not used to this but I only remember the first occasion when I finally gave up while still capable of moving and staggered to the door of the bar only to find outside that winter had arrived and the ground was covered with a hard frost. Anyway I took one long gulp of the cold winter air and passed out. In fact for the first four weeks, Taff and I took it in turns on Saturday nights to pass out and to put the other to bed. However, after four weeks we either got used to it or we learned a bit of discretion.

Of course another result of this exercise was to provide the M.T. unit with enormous amounts of money – most of which they threw about with reckless abandon. I never got to know the MT blokes at all and so can't remember any of their names but one incident I do recall was at a village dance when one drunken MT driver, to display his contempt for the French currency, of which he had so much, began to publicly tear up French banknotes of 100 francs and scatter them like confetti. The French were incensed by this (not surprisingly) and we had the greatest difficulty in bustling him outside before he got himself lynched.

BEFORE I FORGET

At this time, rations were being drawn from the American stores at SHAEF in Reims and therefore there was always plenty of PX stuff available - towels and cigarette lighters costing only a few francs. Suddenly, it was alleged – though I could never find any real justification for it – that the airmen had complained about the US rations and asked to be transferred to British rations, saying, would you believe, that they didn't get enough bread. Anyway, somehow it was arranged that food rations would be drawn from British Army stores in Paris - though fortunately the cigarette ration still came from the US. I say this, of course, because cigarettes were money to me as a non-smoker.

The result of this twice weekly trip to Paris turned out to be another bonanza for the MT unit. So much so that I wonder if they were not the source of the complaints about the food. For some reason, I had to accompany the truck on one occasion and I learnt how the whole thing worked. A little more than halfway to Paris was a village called Claye-Souilly where a comfort stop was made at a village café run by a delightful old French couple who remembered the Tommies from the 14-18 War and could be persuaded after a cognac or two to sing the old British Army songs to which everyone added their own contribution and a good time was had by all. However, it transpired that the old proprietor had also a good business sense and was a key player in the latest MT racket. It operated thus – the truck left Witry and headed for the US depot in Reims. There it picked up a load of US cigarettes and perhaps a drum or two of petrol ON TICK. On stopping at Claye-Souilly, the petrol (and some of the cigarettes) would be fed into the French Black Market for cash. The truck would them proceed to Paris where it would take on food (with extra rations being exchanged for cigarettes). Then to the liquor store where the remaining cigarettes would be exchanged for Scotch whisky and gin. The truck then returned stopping at Claye-Souilly where the extra food rations disappeared into the French black market for more cash. On arriving in Reims, Scotch whisky and gin paid for the advances of cigarettes. And this trip used to take place twice a week.

This unit was very strong on sport and had already established a quite useful football team. They already had a very good goalkeeper in Bob Voce but I could sometimes get a game if he was on duty and even occasionally as a half-back. Shortly after I arrived there also appeared a young man called Derek Stansfield who had had a trial for Blackburn Rovers. He was a very good centre-forward (or striker as we would now call him) and his addition to the team made them a very useful outfit. Generally we played either local villages or factory teams in Reims but occasionally would venture further afield, like the occasion when we took on the Paris Police and beat them 6-0. We often played in the Parc Pommery in Reims and I recall playing both Pommery and the Prat Frères (Noilly Prat) teams there. There was one occasion just as I arrived but before I had established myself when they played Reims Junior side in the main Reims stadium as a curtain raiser before the first division game. They lost 1-0. I myself played in a rerun of this game later but not in the stadium – in one of the Reims parks. I was playing right half and the Reims team contained two first team players who were having a try out after injury. One of these was the outside right Batteux who later on actually became a manager of the French national side for a short time. I think we won the game 3-2 and I actually got a mention in the local rag – I think they must have mistaken me for someone else!

Perhaps the most interesting games, however, were those against local villages. These were never Pontfaverger-Moronvilliers v the RAF GEE unit at Witry. They were France v Angleterre to the village and they would decorate the field with flags and handover bouquets before the start and generally lay on festivities afterwards. Our toughest time in these matches (generally on a Sunday) was the first 15 minutes when we were all sweating off the booze of the night before. So our policy was always to kick it anywhere during that time and once we had got our second wind, we were generally strong enough to win fairly handsomely.

One particular needle match I remember was with the local village Witry-les-Reims. On this occasion I was not playing but just a spectator. There was a lot of feeling among the local lads because their chances with the girls were generally not improved by the RAF in the village. They were a good side too but the reason I remember it well was that it was my only experience of wartime combat. It happened this way. They had gained a corner and I and another Frenchman (also called Georges and a most unusual blond) stood behind the goal. Georges said to the French centre forward, "Never mind the ball knock the goalkeeper over". I of course understood this in French and vociferously warned Bob Voce of this likely fate. Georges was incensed at this and shouted fiercely at me "Ferme la gueule" – Shut your trap. "What's that you say", I cried in English also fiercely and for my pains received a sudden punch on the jaw from Georges. At that I charged him and he fell backwards with me on top of him. Before I could exact revenge various other spectators grabbed me and pulled me away. However, Ted Evans the cook, jumped in and took my place and gave poor Georges a punch on the jaw in exchange. Then they pulled him off and finally proceeded with the game.

The other sport particularly popular in Witry was Darts. We played Darts interminably and in rather a different way to that at Mutzig. In Mutzig most games were between the Canadians and the British and were games of Cricket (on the Dartboard of course). Here in Witry, most were of the 301 start and finish on double type, though we often played 101 only. Generally the games were between teams representing the North, the Midlands (or really Birmingham) and the South (or really London). Dick Salmon and I were the London team and we were easily the most successful team. In fact I think I played better Darts here than at any other time in my life.

Generally speaking, the dirty work around the camp was done by German POWs, who were drawn from a camp located just outside Reims. This camp was controlled by Americans and the result was a very different attitude among the prisoners. In Mutzig, they were extremely cooperative because their chances of a decent meal depended on it but here they were reasonably fed anyway so they couldn't really care less. The Americans ran the camp in a very economical way. First, they extracted from the prisoners all those not of German origin. Then they stuck guns in their hands and made these guards. I recently saw a feature on TV which purported to show how badly the Americans treated the German POWs. From my knowledge of this camp, I can easily refute that claim.

There were some odd circumstances surrounding these POWs. I can remember on one occasion as a Sergeant, being charged with responsibility for repainting the hut ceiling. I first set the German POWs to work but after a time it became apparent that they were doing such a rotten job that I had to replace them with RAF personnel. I often think of that incident when the Germans are put forward as paragons of hard work.

One of the tasks given to the POWs was to empty the Elsan portable loos into the communal cesspit and then to disinfect the containers with Chloride of Lime. They always used to throw in far too much Chloride of Lime with the result that the first users to pee in the appropriate containers found that they were assailed by clouds of Chlorine Gas or something equally repulsive. This was know amongst the erks as "Hitler's Revenge".

On one visit to the Camp for a routine pick up of-prisoners the drivers were accosted thus, "Say, you guys are from the RAF. Does this belong to you?" and they were offered a truck containing a fully operational diesel generator painted in RAF colours. I thought of that classroom in Mons where 60 group chalked up on the board details of all diesel generators allocated to all the Radar sites in the European theatre and wondered how they had accounted for this one going astray.

I also have a picture in mind at Christmas 1945 of a POW from the MT section, staggering along the main street of Witry, stoned out of his mind and with a bottle of whisky in his hand. I think the War was over as far as he was concerned.

One of the interesting characters at Witry was Ken Wrigley. He was a Mech and quite an intellectual type with a good knowledge of French and German. One of his favourite pastimes after a few jars down in the Forces Club in Reims was to lean out of the back of Liberty truck on its way back to Witry shouting subjunctive phrases at the unsuspecting passers-by. No doubt contributing to the French belief that the English are crazy anyway.

One amusing and somewhat salutary evening was spent with Ken at the Forces Club with two young French girls who were there as guests. I had some knowledge of German having studied it at school though Ken's was much better. Anyway we asked these girls in English whether they spoke English – "No" they replied, "Do you speak German?" " Yes a little – wir haben kein Französisch" – and so having denied a knowledge of French, we carried on a conversation in halting German at the same time listening to what the girls said to each other in French. It was not always flattering.

In the hut at the back of the Château where we all lived and slept, we had an old radio set, almost invariably tuned to the American Forces Network request programmes. Another memory of Ken Wrigley is when on one evening returning to the billet three sheets to the wind and shouting "I want to listen to Moscow", he endeavoured to find Moscow by frantically twiddling the dials while two of us tried desperately to hold the radio set down and prevent it from crashing to the floor. Incidentally the AFN request programme presenters had at that time to cope with overwhelming requests for the Andrews Sisters singing "Rum and Coca-Cola" which was wildly popular with all the troops.

You might perhaps be excused for thinking ,"Well, did anybody ever do any work at this station?" Of course the GEE station was up and running continuously and my promotion to acting Sergeant was because of my appointment as a Forces Educational Instructor. My pay had risen to 12/6d a day and I was very anxious to keep what to me was a very good salary. Remember my civilian pay on joining up was 47/6d per week so I'm now on almost double that. My objective was to persuade the erks on the unit to study for the Forces Education Certificate. This was considered to be the equivalent of the General Schools Certificate of those days i.e. the O Levels or GCSE of today. In fact the standard was below that level so it did really represent an

excellent opportunity for educational dropouts to improve their prospects while waiting for demobilisation. By strenuous exertions I finally managed to recruit half a dozen hopefuls to the classroom. In the course of doing this I had to visit the outlying Slave stations of the GEE chain the only one of which I can remember as being at Aix-en-Othe. The course we were to follow was the usual English/Maths/
Foreign Language (French, of course) type and I rather imagine that the French lessons were the main attraction. Teaching Maths and French I found quite easy but teaching English I found to be hellishly difficult.

The other major problem I had was to ensure attendance. Most of the time this could only be achieved by more of less physically hauling the reluctant students from their beds. I suffered from frequent absenteeism, some justified by duties or leave but other just malingering. So my regular attendance varied between 3 and 4. I received very little in the way of materials from HQ and had to provide most text books from my own study materials. However, suddenly out of the blue, a booklet of over 50 close-typed foolscap sheets appeared scheduling the materials needed for an Educational establishment. Obviously it was designed for a unit the size of Cranwell. I suppose, if I had been the entrepreneurial type I would have ordered the lot and sold them off to the French black market but I hadn't got the nerve. The result of this haphazard type of scholastic enterprise was that I lived in fear and trembling of a visit by the authorities and the consequent disappearance of my three stripes and the 12/6 a day. Finally I was advised that the HQ Educational Officer was to visit and I thought the game was up. However, to my surprise, when he did appear I discovered that my little enterprise was the ONLY one flourishing throughout the GEE chain from Denmark to South Germany and in consequence I was the apple of his eye. He was, on reflection, probably expecting his own appointment to go up in smoke.

We actually had another Educational Instructor on the unit. This was a Sergeant Macmillan who was the Storeman. He was actually a Master Builder and was recruited to teach Building Construction but his chances of being able to do anything on a unit of some 50 blokes in the wilds of France was absolutely nil. He actually did earn his Sergeant's pay, however, by rebuilding the bar with the aid of POWs and making a very cosy little club out of it. More about the activities inside the bar later.

The hut in which most of us slept warrants a little more attention. It was a properly constructed hut and not just a Nissen and so was watertight and with the aid of the usual wood-burning stove as comfortable as might be expected with about 30 beds sharing the space. Something which is very easy to forget is that life in the Services very often consisted of doing nothing, or just lying around waiting for the next meal, or for something to happen. So that at any time there might be ten or so individuals just lying on their bunks. Very often the ritual cry would arise from some despairing individual "Dear Mother, it's a bastard". To which would come the chorused reply "Dear Son, so are you!" Or a variation "Dear Mother, it's a bugger. Sell the pig, buy me out." And the chorused reply "Dear Son, pig dead – soldier on!"

You may recall that this hut had two doors. One in the middle of one long side and the other in the middle of one end. Very frequently, people in transit to one of the Slave Stations would stay overnight in the hut. The exit at the end was the one which led to the outside loos and I recall one transitee rising from his bed in urgent need of the loo after an evening drinking and taking a turn to the right instead of the left and trying desperately to find the door in the blank end wall while the irate sleepers aroused by the noise of his trying to beat a hole in the wall, offered shouted advice, generally obscene, as to what he should do.

I remember myself being caught in the same urgent situation after a jolly evening on the town. I rolled out of bed, slipped my feet into my army boots and grabbed my great coat over my pyjamas and headed for the door. However, the weather had broken during the night and when the door opened, it revealed a wild night of pouring rain and wind whistling around. I realised that to travel the 20 yards or so to the loo would result in my being soaked to the skin, including my pyjamas. So after a moment's hesitation, I whipped it out and peed through the door. Unfortunately, the wind was in the wrong direction and threw a fine spray straight back inside and all over the unfortunate individual sleeping in the bed next to the door. Roused from his slumbers, he roundly cursed me for letting the rain in through the door. What he would have said if he'd known the spray was a mixture of rain and urine I hate to think.

Another incident I recall very clearly concerning the hut has lain on my conscience ever since. I suppose its not really serious but I have always felt that I behaved rather meanly and have regretted it ever since. It's a bizarre event and I cannot imagine how a mother could actually do this but it's true. One afternoon, as I exited the hut en route for the château, a little boy appeared. He was four years of age, as I discovered when talking to him. His mother, would you believe, had sent him, clutching a 50 franc note into this RAF unit full of the usual licentious soldiery to buy a tablet of soap. Fortunately he was spotted by me – so I dealt perfectly honestly with him by taking his 50 francs and giving him a nice tablet of Palmolive to take back to his mamma. Where I feel guilty is that I had a box full of bars of chocolate that I could have given him but I just didn't think of it. Poor kid, he was sent, at the age of 4, to do a job that his mother didn't gave the nerve to do herself – he deserved that chocolate that I didn't give him and for many years that's lain on my conscience.

To return to the social life of Witry centred around the weekly dance. I suppose the dance was run by the proprietor of the cinema and he usually charged 30 francs entrance fee. I remember on one occasion he subcontracted to the local Communist Party and they promptly put the price up to 40 francs. We had a lengthy argument on the doorstep with me pointing out that this represented a bourgeois exploitation of the masses. However, we paid up eventually. Generally the atmosphere between the British and the French was reasonably friendly though they certainly did not like the competition for the girls. But when the Americans turned up as they did from time to time, there was usually trouble. At this time, they were already beginning to outlive their welcome as liberators by their general arrogance and offensive behaviour.

BEFORE I FORGET

There was one particular incident where a group of white Americans appeared at the dance, pretty drunk as usual, and proceeded to try to compel the French girls to dance with them. These were protected by some of the French men and a heated argument broke out culminating in one of the Frenchmen pulling a knife. The Americans then did a hasty retreat to outside the dance hall where they regrouped and having found on old metal café table, ripped the legs off it to arm themselves to return to the hall to exact their revenge on the French. In the meantime, the English including me, were waltzing round the outskirts of this fracas trying to look as though nothing was happening. However, with the return of the Americans, we decided that discretion was the better part of valour and sidled our way past the belligerents and out of the hall. Outside, one of our number Clem Clementson, a dyed-in-the wool Geordie who had apparently taken the side of the French, was hurling threats at the Americans in his thick Geordie accent. Probably they couldn't understand what he was saying and he wasn't going to be a great help to the French as he was lying horizontal at the time! So we dragged him to his feet and outside to the street just in time as the American Military Police hurtled up with their batons at the ready and charged into the hall to sort everything out. As their usual method was to club everything in sight, we had escaped just in time.

On another occasion just before Christmas 1945, three black Americans appeared clutching three bottles of Moët et Chandon 1943 vintage champagne. The mercenary English leapt on this opportunity and managed to persuade them to part with these bottles of excellent champagne in exchange for a very inferior bottle of alleged Armagnac. It actually tasted like Wood Alcohol. So on Christmas morning, Ted Evans, the chief negotiator served us champagne in our tin mugs for breakfast.

As the spring of 1946 arrived, it suddenly became possible to get up to Paris at the weekend. Sometimes as a Sergeant I had certain duties to perform but otherwise I could contemplate catching the 8 p.m. train from Reims station arriving in Paris about 10.30 p.m. and after a weekend in Paris you could return on Sunday evening to be back on duty on Monday morning. In those days, Paris was a magical city – the English were still the most favoured nation and I loved these weekend trips.

On one rail trip up to Paris I got a first class chance to compare rates of pay. In the compartment with us were an American master-sergeant and a new French army recruit (a private). My pay was then 12/6d a day, the French private got 6 francs (3d) per day and the American £48 per month.

We generally stayed in some modest hotels near the Gare de L'Est. A lot of the life centred around the Forces Club known as the Skittlealley Club. I can't remember a lot about the food there but I remember the beer was 3d per pint. I was most impressed with the manageress of the Club when I overheard her dealing with the French suppliers of goods to the Club. She sounded exactly what I imagined a Frenchwoman would sound like in those circumstances. Yet, to talk to her you would be absolutely convinced that you were speaking to an upper-class cultivated Englishwoman. I never discovered whether she was English or French but I would absolutely have believed either. She was the most perfect example of bilingualism that I ever encountered.

It was also at the Skittlealley Club that I first met Nelly Desroches. The Club used to invite French girls to attend the dances to liven up the evenings for the Servicemen in attendance. Nelly was a student at the Sorbonne at the time, 20 years old and studying medicine. She had quite an attractive face, perhaps more interesting than beautiful but otherwise you could only describe her as fat. She really was burdened with a surplus weight that I suppose you could call puppy fat. Nevertheless, she was the most vivacious personality and a fascinating conversationalist. I enjoyed her company immensely and made a beeline for her whenever I could. These girls were always met by their parent when they left the Club (a very necessary precaution) and so I also met her mother – she had no father. In my usual way I was quite open about my marital status and so I was able to retain her friendship for many years after the war. If I can diverge from the wartime for a few moments – I met her again twice after the war, initially with Mary and then subsequently after Mary died with my two children. Nelly took quite a long time to obtain her medical degree but eventually she qualified and she married Jacques Azerad. They both became neurosurgeons and I believe Jacques at least to have been (and maybe still is) one of the foremost neurosurgeons in France.

My first visit to see Nelly after the war was in 1953. Mary and I were staying in a rather grotty café in St Ouen but we were invited to dinner by Nelly who had just recently married Jacques. Nelly by this time was 27 and had lost all that puppy fat and was now a very attractive woman indeed. She had long jet black hair and a magnificent figure and her features, always attractive, had become beautiful with maturity. They met us at around 7.30 and asked us what we would like to see before dinner. We eventually settled for a visit to the Château of St Germain and they drove us out there. We were too late to tour the Château but enjoyed the exterior gardens and the view along the river. Time began to pass and it was now after 9 and I had begun to wonder whether I had mistaken the invitation to dinner. But no – finally we arrived at the house of Mrs Desroches and dinner began at 10 p.m. and went on till 1 a.m. next morning. It was a sumptuous repast, with Mrs Desroches upholding very well the reputation of French cuisine. I remember it particularly for my own faux pas. In the middle of the meal, I felt the pressure on the bladder so in the usual circumlocutory English way – I asked if I could "Wash my hands". They must have thought me crazy but obligingly produced a hand-basin, towel and soap – whereupon I had humiliatingly to admit that what I really wanted was a "pee".

My next visit must have been in about 1960 – the Azerads had established themselves at 54 Rue Blanche in Montmartre. This street is fairly old and grotty–looking on the exterior but in the interior the Azerads has constructed a really modern, well appointed flat as befitted two successful brain surgeons. Nelly had returned to the silhouette she had at the Skittlealley club and had lost her magnificent figure and become once again "fat" but her personality was as scintillating as ever. The flat was furnished with a whole series of very modernistic paintings – all pretty excruciating to my taste – but to my surprise the painter was living on the premises. The Azerads had decided to sponsor a painter and so they picked him up, moved him in and let him get on with his painting. I never learnt his name though.

To return to the Skittlealley Club (why it had that name, I do not know – there was no skittlealley there!). One evening I bumped into a sergeant operator who had been briefly at Mutzig. He had gone up to Denmark on a GEE station when the Mutzig crew broke up and had spent 6 months there, putting on about 3 stones in weight due to the very high living standards being enjoyed in Denmark at this time. We also fell in with a couple of Army officers who were intent on sampling the Parisian nightlife. So we got ourselves into a cheery mood at the Club (at 3d a pint) and then went off to the Bal Tabarin, at that time one of the most famous nightclubs in Paris. We got seated at a table – acquired one bottle of champagne at the usual extortionate prices – carefully making it last throughout the show.

On leaving the show, we were accosted by a tout and after some length discussion on what our intentions were we finally agreed to visit what would be my one and only ever visit to a brothel. This was in the Rue Navarin – I was immediately astonished by the high standard of the accommodation – sumptuous carpets, discreet lighting and generally luxurious surroundings. Our carefully agreed intention was that we would see a "show" but that we would stand back to back and refuse any further invitations. We were seated on a comfortable sofa and five ladies were produced for our inspection and selection of three to perform. All were completely naked and it must be admitted had quite attractive appearances. With a great deal of embarrassment we picked on 3 of them and they proceeded to give us a rapid selection of 35 different ways of performing the act, using a dildo to simulate the male function. They finished with the production of what seemed to be some kind of electric drill with a soft rubber ending to the bit, with which they proceeded to stimulate each other. This appeared to have a great effect on them though I suppose it could all have been simulated to intrigue the potential customers. Anyway on our rising to leave, the naked beauties approached us with arms around our necks and honeyed words to persuade us to go upstairs with them but with true British grit, we stuck together and made our escape. So I was able to maintain my lifetime stance of never having used the services of a prostitute. Though that I suppose was the narrowest squeak I ever had.

A more respectable excursion on one Paris visit was a visit to the Paris Six Day[12], then running at the Vel d'Hiv (Velodrome d'Hiver). I was a keen enthusiast for Six Day racing and had attended all those held in London before the war, so many of the riders were familiar to me. What was different was the surroundings. The track was larger (250 metres) and my ticket took me to a standing location in the centre of the track. Around the ends of the track, on the inside, were the cabins of the riders where they rested, ate and received massage etc. but immediately on the trackside alongside the straights were tables serving dinner to the more affluent fans. So that I, in my cheaper standing location, watched the race across the heads of the diners. I remember being very impressed with the smart attire of the ladies at the tables and thinking – this is the Paris of sophistication, *haute couture* etc.

On one occasion, looking out of my hotel window at about 1 a.m. I saw a line of about twenty students linked arm in arm strolling down the road (less traffic in those days) singing. Paris in those days was newly liberated, less expensive, gay and cheerfully optimistic. I fell in love with the city then and when, a few months later, I passed through for the last time on my way to demobilisation, I stood on the Place de la Concorde looking up the Champs Elysées towards the Arc de Triomphe by night (that magnificent view!) with tears in my eyes, wondering if I would ever see it again.

Back at Witry, the reconstruction of the bar supervised by the other Vocational Instructor, Sergeant Macmillan, was now complete and a very congenial centre was produced with an excellent bar area and comfortable chairs and tables to sit at. A good Belgian beer was in excellent supply at 25 francs a litre and as the current price of a 200 pack of cigarettes was 500 francs, the beer flowed freely. My situation was even better as the boys in the MT unit were extremely partial to a sing-song and I was the possessor of a very large repertoire of the old

---

12 An indoor track cycling event.

music hall songs "learnt at my mother's knee" – I could always be relied upon to keep the singing going when liberally supplied with free beer. Suffice it to say, that during this period my consumption of booze reached very high levels though I never again finished totally drunk as I had been during the first month of our stay in Witry. I dutifully reported this long round of steady drinking to Mary at home, so much so that she wrote many times with some concern that I was turning into a potential alcoholic. She need not have worried – as one glance at the prices demanded back in the UK after my return to that country sobered me up and overnight I became almost a teetotaller.

All sergeants on the unit had to take a regular turn at running the bar and in being responsible for the takings. There were of course no restrictions on closing time so many sessions ran on into the small hours. My method of deciding closing time was to run on until I began to feel that one more litre would remove my capacity to count the takings. At that point I called time, cashed up and handed in the proceeds to the admin section who were not always too pleased at being aroused in the middle of the night to receive the takings. On one occasion, however, I arrived to find them having their own celebration back at the billet. I staggered in, deposited the takings and having claimed a raging thirst, was offered a tumbler of water. On the point of swigging it down, I had just enough left of my senses to realise it was neat gin and to politely decline what would have rendered me paralytic.

Strictly speaking, the bar was for Service personnel only and as there were no WAAFs on the station, it was almost invariably an entirely male clientèle. However, on one occasion when I was in charge I found myself landed with a problem. I happened thus. Down in Reims, there was a regular licensed brothel called the Oriental, quite frequently patronised by certain members of our unit but never, I hasten to add, by me! Indeed, I never actually found out where it was. At this time, the reconstituted French National Assembly in Paris included a dynamic lady deputy whose name escapes me, who had taken upon herself, the missionary task of closing the licensed brothels all over France. The belief existing at that time was that brothels were going to exist anyway and that you would control the situation better if they were actually licensed. All prostitutes had to carry a card showing the dates of their medical inspections. Anyway, this deputy succeeded in her aim and passed a bill closing all these licensed premises. The girls at the Oriental were thereupon slung into the street. Two of them, no doubt remembering their clients at Witry, turned up this evening with me on duty behind the bar. Closing time arrives and the airmen are persuaded to return to their beds – I busy myself with cashing up and counting the takings – and when I finally raise my head, the only occupants of the bar are these two girls. They maintain that they have nowhere to sleep and indicate that they think it up to me to find accommodation for them. Can you imagine the furore of introducing two whores into a barrack-room of 30 men? Indeed my permitting them to remain anywhere on the site is going to lead to my reduction to the ranks forthwith. However, they are threatening to scream the place down if I throw them out. Eventually I agree to find them a couple of mattresses to kip down in the bar providing they agree to depart first thing in the morning. Next morning, I appear around 6 a.m. to find the ladies very reluctant to rise. However by this time I am desperate and eventually after all sorts of shouting matches and threats I finally eject them from the premises just in time to save myself and my 12/6 a day.

So time passed while we all waited anxiously for our demobilisation. Every soldier and airman had been allocated a number based on age and length of service and demobilisation was applied to the numbers in ascending order. Mine was 39 and gradually the numbers rose and rose and finally in early September 1946, the magic number 39 was reached. It turned out that I was the only 39 on the unit. No truck would therefore be available to transport me to 60 group HQ, now in Bonn, and so I would have to make my own way there armed with Railway Warrants. A desperate rush ensued to realise my last remaining saleable assets, retaining a few cigarettes to enliven what I hoped would be a short stay in Bonn. In particular, I was keen to do my bit to improve the French clothing situation as enterprising seamstresses could turn a British Army blanket into a passable coat. My last night at Witry was therefore spent wearing all my kit including my greatcoat as I had flogged every last one of my blankets!

One Man's Radar War

To get to Bonn was going to involve a lengthy rail trip as follows. Reims to Paris, where I contrive to stay overnight to have my last look around as mentioned above. Paris to Brussels and then Brussels to Bonn. I have to remain in Bonn for about a week while papers are processed. So I cash a pack of 20 outside the Forces Club in Bonn for 80 marks. Inside the club, the beer is ½ mark a pint so I have plenty left over to acquire 7 more packs of 20 in the NAAFI plus a few bars of chocolate and to take myself to Bad Godesberg on the Rhine where I cross on the ferry and take myself up the Drachenfels with a marvellous view of the Rhine. In the café at the top, I order a beer for ½ mark and am faced with the problem of a tip for the poor old waiter. 5 pfennigs hardly seems suitable or even possible since nobody bothered with pfennigs in those days. I decide to break open a pack and give him a couple of fags which amounted to an 8 mark tip for ½ mark bill.

The situation on fraternisation with the Germans had changed by this time. Originally it was off limits, but very shortly it seemed to be possible again. Somehow, and I can't quite recall how, I finished up in a party with some German girls in a flat in Bonn and I recall the hostess being very bitter about the Americans who had apparently smashed up her piano and used it for firewood. One could hardly blame her! Another very convivial evening was spent in the Sergeants Mess at Bad Godesberg. About the only time in the Air Force that I had been able to press my Sergeant's stripes into service and to get into a proper mess. Here the food was better, nicely served by German waitresses and the spirits flowed freely (at favourable prices).

Finally my instructions arrived to depart. Bonn to Hamburg, Hamburg to Cuxhaven. A boat from Cuxhaven to Hull. The train journey from Bonn to Hamburg is extremely long, best part of a full day as far as I can recall but the interesting thing to me was that it took me through some of the German cities that we had plastered with OBOE. In particular Essen and Hanover. The destruction was indescribable. In Essen streets had been cleared but on either side were just heaps and heaps of rubble. Virtually no buildings existed in any recognisable form. I have subsequently read that production was restored by moving underground but I always found this hard to believe bearing in mind those pictures I saw of destruction in Essen and Hanover. I remember very little else of that trip. The boat from Cuxhaven to Hull must have taken at least a couple of days but the sea was calm and it passed without incident. Arriving at Hull, we were then despatched to Gatwick where the kitting out with demob suits took place. I managed to acquire a fairly ghastly blue number which nevertheless had to do its turn in impoverished Civvy street. Also I picked up a trilby hat which hung about for years but I really could never face wearing.

From Gatwick back to Cardington for a final night's stay. Full circle back to the place where I had started the 5 ¼ year stint. I went in at 20 years of age and came out at 25. The best years of my life, they say, and wasted on this futile exercise. Was it wasted – I wonder? At least we could say that we had destroyed the regime that ran places like Struthof and, as we were to find out gradually, much worse places like Auschwitz and Treblinka. And I had survived – when many millions had not!

On my last night at Cardington the RAF issued me with a pair of sheets. SHEETS! For the only single night in 5 ¼ years of service. Were they trying to get me to volunteer to stay on? If so, they hadn't a chance.

No distance at all from Cardington to Bedford. Bedford to Kettering and Kettering to Broughton. What joy! To embrace my dear Mary and our little son David, now 2 years old and to know that we would be able to start our real life together. Times would be hard. We would have many problems to earn a living and make a career and home without the automatic support of the RAF but what joy to be together at last and to put all the artificiality that I have described in these pages behind us and to look forward to our future together.

POSTSCRIPT

Life didn't turn out quite the way George expected. Returning to civilian life he worked hard to qualify as a Chartered Accountant. This entailed studying and working simultaneously for several years on a very low income. And five years after my brother was born I arrived in the middle of all this – so there was now a wife and two children to support. But he worked hard and qualified in the early 1950s. He wasn't really cut-out for life as a Chartered Accountant though, and by 1955 he'd found a job in the emerging computer industry. It was in this field that he would build a life-long career.

But in 1958 Mary, his wife and my mother, died of breast cancer. I was then nine years old and my brother David fourteen. So Dad became both mother and father to us two boys. It hindered his career, for sure, but he nevertheless rose to a well-paid job and gave my brother and me a good start in life. He married again. Twice – the first a disaster, the second time to Joan, who remained a constant companion for twenty-five years until he nursed her through dementia to her death. They lived for several years in Australia and then Spain – I think my father had learned much in the war about making the most of what you have at any one time. Joan came with a ready-made family, two girls and two boys, and as they grew older and started families of their own, my Dad became a surrogate grandfather to their children – a role which gave him enormous pleasure.

After Joan's death he entered into another relationship, with Sally. In eleven years with her they travelled widely, often returning to France, a country, and a people, he fell in love with during the war. Many of those friendships forged in wartime lasted a lifetime.

In his early 80s he began to suffer mini-strokes and became progressively incapacitated. Never, though, did he lose that sense of fun, and could always come up with a sharp comment or a new joke, even when confined to an armchair. And never, ever, did he lose his eye for a pretty girl. The last woman to really love my father was Lucy his Slovakian carer, some sixty years his junior. Lucy could see through the wrinkles to the young man you have read about in these pages. And she, to him, must have been just like one of those young WAAFs who turned up at Trimingham in 1942. If only he could have taken her to a dance.

George Phelps died in March 2008. Jack Rook, best man at his wedding in 1942 and the first of those lifelong friends, came along to the funeral to say his farewell. And so my father's journey was complete.

One Man's Radar War

BEFORE I FORGET

George Phelps

wrote one other memoir, about his life and work in the fledgling British computer industry from 1955 to 1976. It is a fascinating insight into the people involved in the early development of a technology that has come to dominate our lives in the years since his retirement. It amused him to be able to tell people that... "when I left the computer industry Microsoft Corporation was less than a year old and had less than a dozen employees". We hope to publish this memoir shortly.

Stephen Phelps

is a television producer, radio dramatist, and author. His book on The Tizard Mission, a little-known but vital event in the development of WWII Allied technologies, from hydraulic gun turrets to the jet engine and microwave radar, can be found at:

The Tizard Mission: The Top-Secret Operation That Changed the Course of World War II
by Stephen Phelps
Link: http://amzn.com/1594161631

Reviews of **The Tizard Mission**

> *One of this book's many attractions is its emphasis on the importance of inter-relationships among social, political, and technical worlds in bringing ideas to reality.*
>
> The Wall Street Journal

> *As Stephen Phelps reveals in this much needed book, the United Kingdom's decision to share its secrets with the United States was a key turning point in the Second World War.*
>
> John Liffen, Science Museum, London

> *An erudite, literate, and thoroughly absorbing piece of WWII history.*
>
> American Library Association's Booklist

Printed in Great Britain
by Amazon

DEPRESSION
Anxiety, & Other Mental Illnesses
Caused by Medical Diseases:
It's not all in your Head.

By David. H. Skaer, Ph.D.

Copyright ©2017
All Rights Reserved
Feedback Welcomed
www.DavidSkaer.com

Contents

1: What If You're the One? 1

2: How to Tell If You Have a Biology Problem 15

3: What Does Chemical Imbalance Mean? 21

4: Hypothyroidism: A Sneaky, Common Cause of "Mental Illness" 31

5: Vitamin B-12 Deficiency 45

6: Understanding Hypoglycemia and Mental Problems 69

7: Hyperthyroidism 85

8: Cushing's 89

9: Polycystic Ovary Syndrome (PCOS) 99

10: Iron Deficiency Anemia (IDA) 103

11: Viruses, Bacteria, and a Parasite 109

12: Pheochromocytoma 117

13: Hyperprolactinemia (also prolactinoma) 121

14: Porphyria: High Carbs May Be Good for You! 127

15: And There's More! 135

16: The Mental Health Dilemma 145

References and Further Reading by Chapter 157

Meet the author 201

1

What If You're the One?

Would you go to a psychologist for a broken leg? I doubt it. Would you go to a psychiatrist and get an antidepressant for that broken leg? I think not—either of those approaches for a broken leg wouldn't help much.

But for depression and other mental illnesses, many sufferers do just that. What if you had a medical disease, such as hypothyroidism, vitamin B-12 deficiency, or other medical (biological, physiological, physical) problems mentioned in this book? Would getting talk therapy or anti-depressants be the answer? Not on your life. You need to treat the real issue—the medical problem. In our society, too many health-care workers believe if you have a mental problem, it requires "mental" treatment such as therapy or medication. The result? They overlook the medical issue and people suffer needlessly. What's more, many patients have a medical illness and don't even know it! This problem of not looking for the medical issue has been highlighted by many researchers (e.g., Castro & Billick, 2013).

Are all mental illnesses caused by a physical disease? No, but it happens much more often than both health-care providers and the general public realize. "If you're the one" who has an undiagnosed medical disease causing your mental illness, then this book is for you.

Allow me a little diversion. Shark attacks are more common in Florida than any other state, including my home state, Wisconsin. I now live in Florida and fry my hide before cooling off in the Gulf water at St. Pete Beach. I realize sharks are in the same water searching for food (maybe me), but I doubt a shark will attack me, since hundreds of swimmers are tempting fate in the same way. However, if I'm the one a shark bites, the rarity argument wouldn't console me. I would "be the one."

So, why do I mention such unusual phenomena? Because many people don't know medical diseases trigger and masquerade as mental illnesses. It's rare that a doctor or therapist looks for physical causes of a mental illness. Such a problem of misdiagnosis is serious. You don't want to be "the one" who was misdiagnosed and given an anti-depressant or talk therapy when you have a medical illness causing the mental problem. I don't want to be the one the shark bit and I don't want you to be the one whose real problem (the medical issue) was missed. The rare part is that few practitioners are looking for the real problem.

Medical illnesses commonly cause mental problems—believe it. Too often medical personnel think only of the mental, so you or a loved one could be "the one," missing the right treatment. The usual treatment of mental illnesses (e.g., depression, anxiety, and schizophrenia) includes medication and psychotherapy. I'm not against either, but if you're the one with a medical illness causing your problem, medications such as anti-depressants won't help much. Counseling, except for providing comfort, won't help either. This book will help you discover if you or a loved one might be the one who is missing the right treatment.

Back in 1976, I was "the one." A shark didn't bite me but the flu bug did. I had a 100°F fever on Thursday night, which jumped to 104°F on Friday night. Saturday was a rotten, horrible, headachey day—a fever "hangover." Now, lots of folks get the flu, but that wasn't what made me special enough to call myself "the one." Monday, however, brought new meaning to the term *depression*—I was one in whom the flu caused depression. Unusual, yes, but when you're the one, percentages mean nothing. In my psychology training, I wasn't taught that the flu caused depression. In fact, I've found that few had ever heard of it—have you?

My doctor said stress must have caused it since my blood test was normal. I was in the middle of a stress-free vacation for five weeks, so his diagnosis made little sense. One of my psychology friends said I was having a pity party and just needed to entertain positive thoughts to overcome the depression. When you're as depressed as I was, however, a pity party is normal, and there's no light at the end of the tunnel—at least you can't see it. I learned to avoid talking about my depression in the 1970s as it wasn't acceptable back then to have a mental problem. I was depressed, the cause was physical, but I beat myself up thinking crummy thoughts. Everything seemed bleak.

Wednesday of that week, I visited the psychology department at my university (U of Miami). I told the department secretary I was feeling down after having the flu. She said, "Be careful, Dave. My husband had the flu in October and became so depressed that he threatened suicide." I told her I didn't know the flu caused depression, but she insisted it did.

What does she know? I thought, *I have a Ph.D.* Her husband's testimony, however, intrigued me. Could the flu have caused my depression?

The following week, after pulling out of my depression, I visited family in a nearby city and heard a second layperson's testimony of flu-induced depression. My sister's husband was returning from fishing in the Everglades with an old buddy of his. I asked his 72-year-old friend if he'd received the swine flu vaccination yet. He said, "No. That shot can give you the flu. I'm not going through that again." I asked when he'd had the swine flu. He replied, "The flu pandemic of 1918."

I later learned that the swine flu had killed 500,000 to 800,000 people in the USA and 40 million to 100 million worldwide (Barry, 2004). The stuff I didn't learn while getting a Ph.D. was that the flu can cause depression and a pandemic I'd never knew about rocked the world.

The man continued, "If I get that flu, I'm going home, taking my double-barrel shotgun, and blowing my head off."

"That must have been a bad flu," I said.

"The flu is horrible," he said, "but that's not the worst part. After the flu is over, when you think you're on your way to recovery, the depression hits you. As a result many people committed suicide back then."

This amazed me! Here was a cause of depression I hadn't heard of in my 160+ credits in psychology. I visited the University of Miami's medical library and researched "influenza and depression." No Google back then. There were many articles on flu-induced mental illness soon after 1918, including depression, schizophrenia, anxiety, and manic-depressive disorder. I found similar articles dating back to the 1890s following a less severe flu outbreak. My education had kept me ignorant of something horrible—and something every therapist should know: there are physiological (medical) causes of depression.

Could counseling have helped me with my depression? No, because the flu (something biological) had caused it. The counselor could have encouraged me by saying I'd get over it, but it wouldn't have been the answer for me. If my body had not recovered, I could have suffered for months, or longer.

In 1976, the flu shot caused many people to become depressed. One of my clients, a female nurse, agreed to get the vaccine, due to hospital staff pressure, despite having negative feelings about it. Within a few days of getting the shot, she went into deep depression. Her poor husband cried as he explained she was an excellent wife and mother, yet she wanted to die. She denied being a good mother, wife, and nurse—severe depression can make you think crazy thoughts.

Most people didn't get depressed from the vaccine, but she fit the category as one whom the flu affected mentally. Thousands of citizens sued the Federal Government because they believed the flu shot had paralyzed them; I'd never heard of anyone suing because depression hit them. Why? Paralysis is more apparent because it's physical. Depression is mental, however, and few people, including professionals, know something physical, such as a flu vaccine, can cause a mental reaction. It was sad for those sufferers.

This principle applies to your mental health because physicians and therapists often overlook the physical causes of a mental problem. If you're the one whose depression resulted from a medical illness, professionals could miss the physical cause. My doctor thought stress caused my depression. Many doctors might have recommended an anti-depressant or a therapist—neither would have helped.

What if you're the one who's depressed because of a medical illness, but no one looks for it? If that's the case, you're in deep trouble. The good news for me was that my severe depression only lasted six days. Had it affected me for six months, I'm not sure what might have happened. My thoughts at the time were similar to the illogical, depressive thinking the nurse had. I thought I was a horrible husband, father, professor, and anything else upon which I could judge myself.

Here's another interesting case—hypoglycemia (low blood sugar). Mark, a student, came to see me every so often complaining of depression. I didn't suspect hypoglycemia because he didn't eat desserts when he'd go out for dinner with my family. I didn't think he ate enough sugar to cause a problem.

One Thursday, he came to my office in tears, as he was in deep depression. I tried to convince him that it was biological, since he had a wonderful life, from my perspective. He thought he had a spiritual problem that was causing the depression, yet he read his Bible an hour a day and prayed for an hour a day. I told him it was not a spiritual problem—it was physical—and that we had to be detectives and solve the mystery.

It didn't take long. Two days later, Mark said his roommate had bought cookies on Wednesday night, since they would be studying into the wee hours of the morning. I asked him how many he had eaten. His answer was "two-thirds of a large pack!"

I told him he might have had a hypoglycemic reaction from eating so many cookies on an empty stomach. Hypoglycemia bothers some people, although not all—it did Mark. He then shared other times that sweets had possibly caused depression. Someone made him a Devil's food cake for his birthday, and he'd eaten two pieces every night for a week. He said it was the worst week of his life. After he had shared two or three similar experiences, I convinced him he'd have to change a few things to see if that was the cause.

We changed his diet by increasing his protein, since he wasn't getting enough, and cutting out all sweets. Within a few days, he was a new person with no depression. He woke up refreshed and had energy he hadn't experienced in 15 years. His doctor told him hypoglycemia couldn't cause his depression, but Mark knew better. The proof was in the pudding (which he shouldn't eat, either).

After Mark's amazing recovery, he asked how many other people got depressed from biological causes (he knew of my flu problem). I told him I didn't know, and he said, "Let's find out." So, off we went to the University of Miami medical library every Saturday for four weeks. I searched "depression" matched with "endocrine," "vitamins," "minerals," and "flu" on the computer. We brought home 40-50 articles every week! The number of articles regarding medical problems causing depression astounded me. I didn't learn anything about such causes in my schooling.

Mark said I should synthesize the information and give a seminar to enlighten others who might suffer from a biologically caused depression. I did and continued to give them for years. It's been an incredible trip—sometimes rocky when health providers thought I was crazy, but helping my counselees and seminar attendees made it worthwhile.

How much depression is due to a biological problem is a matter of debate. I know, however, that I've helped many people over my lifetime of counseling by discovering the physical causes of their depression. Some researchers believe major illnesses cause 10-60% of depression (e.g., Marian, et al., 2010) but those are just educated guesses. I believe it's way more than 10% but less than 60%. There's no way of really knowing.

Finding the biological causes of mental illness will save money and reduce lost work days, which affect the sufferers and their employers. Also, wasting time and money on psychotherapy or anti-depressants is a poor use of resources. Most tragic is the individual's untold suffering. Though the stigma of depression is not like it was, people still avoid seeking help when they think something is wrong with them mentally. Once we understand that many mental problems are due to physical problems, we can treat them by correcting the physical ailment and help reduce the stigma of mental illness. People may be more open to getting help if they realize it might be a medical problem causing the issue. The good news about most of the medical problems in this book is there are adequate treatments.

Too many doctors, including psychiatrists and therapists, overlook the real, physical cause of mental illness. Take a couple of hours to read "Brain on Fire," by Susannah Cahalan (2012). Doctors diagnosed her with extreme mental symptoms indicating bipolar disorder, depression, schizophrenia, etc. After terrible suffering, a specialist got it right; he found brain inflammation due to an autoimmune problem. As you can imagine, it changed her life. She was one of the ones with a biological problem masquerading as psychological problems.

Consider the case of a man with a vitamin B-12 deficiency—something easily corrected. The original physicians, however, treated him with anti-psychotics and anti-depressants, to no avail. After all, he had a mental problem, right? But the problem wasn't really mental—it was physical. Years later, other doctors discovered his B-12 deficiency, treated it, and brought the man out of his depression. He was the one! He went through unnecessary suffering due to misdiagnosis and inappropriate treatment, until the new doctors figured it out (Bar-Shai, Gott, & Marmor, 2011). See Castro & Billick (2013) for more like this.

In another case, a 26-year-old professional woman had problems with anger, anxiety, and obsessive-compulsive disorder (OCD). She also wanted to shower for hours, which may have been part of her OCD. These problems plagued her off and on for 12 years until she was diagnosed with porphyria (see the chapter on porphyria). In their article, the doctors encouraged practitioners to seek organic (physical) causes of mental symptoms instead of assuming the cause is psychological. Imagine suffering needlessly for 12 years; fortunately, someone investigated more thoroughly and found the biological cause (Auchincloss & Pridmore, 2001).

Over my years of counseling, I encouraged many patients to have their doctors test them for illnesses that may have been missed. The doctors often said, "It couldn't be that." It was embarrassing for the doctors, since they had referred these patients to me, but I sent them back with a possible physical diagnosis. I didn't always discover a physical illness as the cause of someone's depression, schizophrenia, or anger problem, but I helped many who would have otherwise continued suffering. What a change it made in their lives. They were the ones.

One of my counselees, who suffered from depression, was the one. She shared her family problems about her husband and teenagers which made me infer that her depression had a psychological cause. I did my best to counsel her for three weeks, but my advice did nothing. I admitted defeat and asked her if she'd had any physical problems in the last few months. Yes: she'd had her tubes tied. Aha!

I told her that such an operation could sometimes result in depression, so she talked to her OBGYN. He said, "You don't get depression from having your tubes tied." Not only that, but he called me a quack! I dried my tears and tried to save face by giving her a journal article that explained how tubal ligation could mess with hormones. I recommended that she ask her doctor for a test to see if she might be in need of estrogen, progesterone, or both. Once again, he said I was wrong, because she still had her ovaries; he refused to check her levels. This time, he told her to find a marriage counselor who knew his stuff. More tears.

The good news is that the journal article and my insistence made her wonder if her hormones were in fact the problem. I suggested that she see an endocrinologist for the hormone test. He put her on estrogen, which fixed her low estrogen levels, and within two weeks, she no longer needed my counseling. In fact, she never needed my help, except to point her to the physiological issue. She was one of the ones with a significant hormone imbalance from getting her tubes tied. Had she gone to a "real" psychologist and not a "quack" like me, she may have suffered for weeks, months, or years. The treatment changed her life.

I encountered another interesting case when I was a therapist in a psychiatric hospital. A 74-year-old patient came in for a few weeks and acted most strangely. Sometimes, he was as lucid as anyone, but he could switch to a psychotic state within a minute. He was the talk of our psychiatric hospital. The doctor diagnosed him with "dementia with psychosis" and tried to place him in a locked Alzheimer's unit, since he was a wanderer. Fortunately, we couldn't find an available unit.

In a counseling session, he told me he had taken B-12 shots for years, but hadn't had one in a long time. I checked his medical chart and discovered that his B-12 level was far below normal, so at my prodding, the doctor ordered a shot. The next day, the patient was lucid and remained so. We released him a few days later, and the doctor admitted he didn't know B-12 deficiency could cause such a severe mental problem. That patient was "one of the ones." We intended to send him to a home, but we sent him home, instead.

There are similar reports in which a psychological explanation other than the actual, physical one, postponed a person from getting the correct medical treatment. The book, *Masquerading Symptoms* (2014), by Barbara Schildkrout, M.D., has many such cases. She wrote her book for healthcare workers (counselors, psychotherapists, and doctors), so it is a tad technical, but it's an eye-opener regarding physical problems causing psychological symptoms. I highly recommend it.

There's a good chance you will find counselors and doctors who disagree with what you'll learn from my book or your own research on biological causes. Be empathetic with therapists and physicians, though, because many don't know how often the physical affects the mental. Don't let that deter you; search for answers until you get the right help. Scour the internet and you'll find information that was unavailable a few years ago. This book can give you a great jumping-off point to solve the riddle of your mental issues or those of someone you love.

I encourage you to become a detective and find the truth. Remember, if you're the one, it's worth the research and persistence, because it is sometimes difficult to get answers. Biological illnesses aren't always the cause of mental problems, but if you're the one, you need to know the causes and treatments. I'll point out many diseases that can cause mental problems, including some rare ones. As you might suspect, those that are least common are the most overlooked by healthcare professionals—even many of the common ones go unidentified.

I will give you the basis to identify causes and help you be a master detective. You may be able to assist your doctor to understand the physical cause—after all; you have more time to check the internet than your doctor does. A great article came out in December of 2016 entitled: "Knowing what we don't know…." (Baron & Braddock). Doctors and therapists can't know everything. I pray that this book will help you discover that you or your loved one could be the one. Best wishes in your hunt.

2
How to Tell If You Have a Biology Problem

Finding the biological problem causing what we call "mental problems" is not always easy; however, it is possible and most rewarding. Bursting out of the chains of depression or anxiety frees you to be human again and to live life to the fullest—something you can't do when mental illness holds you back.

How can someone help you, or how can you help your significant other? A depressed person can always give reasons for their depression, but those may not be the real reasons. For example, during my depression, I thought I was a horrible spouse, parent, and professor. I was terrible at making and handling money, and I had a few other choice thoughts about myself. My self-esteem was about as low as it could go.

All of those thoughts pointed to a psychological explanation of my depression, and I didn't think for one moment that I had a biological problem. I'd never heard of such a cause. When the depression lifted on the seventh day, I felt fantastic—but I hadn't changed. Why didn't those problems bother me anymore? The truth is: I wasn't as horrible as I thought. I wasn't depressed because of my "wrong" thinking; rather, depression caused my negative thinking and poor self-esteem. The healthcare profession, including counselors/therapists, has taught us to think a psychological problem has a psychological cause. It can, of course, but we overlook the biological explanation far too often. What should you do?

Here's where a significant other (spouse, parent, child, friend) can help. My wife did not understand why I was so depressed. Had we gone to counseling, I would have told the therapist all of my bad points. My wife would have said, "He's a good husband, a caring father, and his students love him. He shouldn't be depressed." On the other hand, if I had lost both my parents in a car accident and lost my job just before I'd become depressed, my wife would have had a different story. She'd have told the therapist that I had reasons for depression. No one would have denied that; however, nothing horrible had happened, except the flu.

When your significant other doesn't understand your depression, look for a physical cause. A serious problem here is that the depressive will have low self-esteem. The significant other may tell the doc, "She's depressed because she has low self-esteem," or, "she can't say one good thing about herself." DON'T FALL FOR SUCH STATEMENTS! Low self-esteem is more likely the result of the depression, not the cause! Look for something physical. When I counseled depressives, I tried to get input from significant others because the patient would give reasons that were all psychological. The significant other couldn't explain the depression and that's an important sign of something physical.

If the patient with anxiety or depression goes to therapy, the therapist MUST ask the right questions to be sure the patient doesn't have a medical cause for the depression or anxiety. The patient will give "reasons," like I did, but the therapist must see through those. Unfortunately, too many medical doctors, including psychiatrists, will just prescribe anti-depressants, and psychology-type therapists and counselors will try to work on the person's thinking, behavior, and self-esteem. If the problem is biological, those techniques have little chance of helping and the depressive has to wallow in their depression.

Can you ask your doctor, therapist, or another healthcare worker about biological causes? Of course, but many are not aware of these physiological causes. Many of my patients have been laughed or scoffed at when they asked questions about physical causes of depression. You can't expect doctors to know everything, so try to be understanding. There are, however, many articles about medical illnesses causing depression and other mental problems (e.g., Perez-Stable, et al., 1990; Schulberg, McClelland, & Burns, 1987.). Back in the 70s, Hall warned how often a medical issue could cause psychological issues (Hall, et al., 1978). What happens is doctors and therapists too often overlook medical possibilities and, surprisingly, mental illnesses often precede the medical issues (Cosci, Fava, and Sonino, 2014).

Another way you can help yourself and others is by researching physical causes of mental problems, just like I've done for this book. The issue is that so many of the explanations of causes and treatments lean toward psychiatric medications and therapy and not to the biological causes. Thus, you can get misled. Do your research to learn more about illnesses. Where can you get information about biology and "mental illness?"

See Dr. Google. Okay, it's just Google, but "he" knows so much that I call him "Dr. Google." Remember that many websites just want to sell you their products, so if you investigate B-12 deficiency, you could get deluged with ads pushing their B-12 products. Despite this, they may offer useful information. It's relatively safe to read universities' publications, although research universities don't always stress the biological problems. Of course, if you Google "vitamin B-12" and "depression," you'll get good information from most major university websites. Be careful, though; just because it's on the internet doesn't mean it's true.

How do I do an internet search to find biological information?

1. **Google (or your favorite search engine):** Use two descriptors. That is, put in "depression" or whatever mental problem tickles your fancy, and add another descriptor, such as "symptoms," "signs," "treatment," etc. The "treatment" descriptor will most likely give you information about medications and therapies, but seldom biological causes. You can put in any of the biological causes, along with "depression." For example, "hypothyroidism" and "depression," or "hypothyroidism" and "symptoms." We covered many such diseases in this book.

2. Remember: biological problems often share similar signs or symptoms. For example, vitamin B-12 deficiency, hypothyroidism, and hypoglycemia share some of the same symptoms of fatigue and depression. You must be a detective—don't go getting paranoid or jump to conclusions. Just because you're tired doesn't mean you should diagnose yourself with a vitamin B-12 deficiency. To pinpoint the culprit, we have to be thorough and careful. When you get a list of the symptoms, take them to your doctor to help with the diagnosis.

3. **Wikipedia:** A wonderful source of information. College instructors seldom allow their students to use Wikipedia, but I tell my students to use it for background information and then go to books and journals. The information you can

get from Wikipedia, including references, can be fabulous. Be careful, since contributors can provide false information. Wikipedia editors do, however, try to weed out that material and ask for citations.

4. **PubMed:** If you want to learn from the medical researchers, you might like using PubMed. These are all the medical-related articles published in the whole wide world. You'll see research summaries, which can teach you plenty, and sometimes you can get the article for free.

I've had many patients find doctors who are open-minded about vitamin B-12, hypoglycemia, and other illnesses mentioned in this book and didn't mind when the patient mentioned the internet. My own physicians have been open-minded and even like to hear about the research I've found. Some want copies of the journal articles.

Be a great detective and don't quit. You're trying to solve a mystery about a biologically-caused mental illness. The previous chapters should inspire you do your homework including asking your doctor for help with your list symptoms. You could be involved in an important mystery worth solving. Best wishes and let me know your successes whether your own or those of someone you helped.

3

What Does Chemical Imbalance Mean?

You've heard the phrase "chemical imbalance," and although I appreciate the term, I include more than most practitioners do: namely, medical illnesses, which are also chemical imbalances. For example, if you have too little thyroid hormones, that's a chemical imbalance as is a vitamin B-12 deficiency. The good news is the phrase has encouraged many to seek help for their mental problems who otherwise might not have. Why? Because "chemical imbalance" sounds much nicer than "mental illness." Here's my take on it.

WHAT ARE SYNONYMS FOR BIOLOGICAL CAUSES?

Discovering the biological cause or contributor to a mental problem is important, so let's get our terms straight. Common synonyms for the word "biological" are "medical," "physical," "physiological," and "organic." These are in contrast to "psychological" or "mental." Psychologists, psychiatrists, and counselors favor the mental or psychological terms since their training stressed the mental, not the biological causes. The public is familiar with "mental illness" since that's what we've learned from papers, books, movies, TV, friends, coworkers, and the internet. A logical outcome of thinking regarding mental illness is there must be a mental (psychological) treatment. In so doing, health care workers often miss identifying medical illnesses.

Counselors use talk therapy to help relieve mental illness; psychiatrists and other doctors use medications. Both therapy and medications are standard approaches to treating mental illnesses, such as depression and anxiety. Seldom does either group consider these problems are due to medical illnesses; rather, they believe they are mental illnesses. Of course, there are mental effects from medical illnesses, but it's all too easy to think in terms of mental treatment. I'm all for therapy and psychiatry, but the emphasis in my book is on medical diseases contributing to mental problems, which mental health experts may overlook. My primary goal is to treat the medical illness if that's the cause; let's first work on that and avoid days, months, and years of unnecessary treatment and suffering.

WHAT DO WE MEAN BY A CHEMICAL IMBALANCE?

In its simplest form, a chemical imbalance is when the chemicals in your body are out of balance—you have too much or too little of a chemical. Simple, eh? The chemicals that psychiatrists and other mental health workers usually refer to are neurotransmitters (serotonin, norepinephrine, dopamine, etc.). Hence, doctors prescribe medicines to restore the balance of body chemicals. They most often prescribe anti-depressants, anti-anxiety medications, and medications for bipolar disorder and schizophrenia.

All things in our bodies (including our bodies) are chemicals as are the foods we eat. So, my definition is much broader than those who think just medications. Believe it or not, research shows that psychotherapy and counseling can change our chemical imbalances to correct depression and anxiety. You can change your chemistry by thinking of something fun or something negative although such changes are short-lived. Thus, both medication and therapy can correct the chemical imbalance—if that is the problem. However, if the problem is a medical illness, then psychiatric meds and psychotherapy won't help much, if at all.

There are criticisms of the typical, narrow chemical imbalance view; here are the most common ones. When I say narrow view, I mean treatment simply with medications to correct the imbalance of neurotransmitters. My view includes many medical illnesses, so these arguments don't apply to my broader perspective.

1. The drugs aren't perfect by any means; they don't help everyone. For example, many researchers suggest anti-depressants aren't much or any better than placebos (Kirsch, et al., 2008). Other researchers indicate that the treatment is more effective for severely depressed patients (Ioannids, et al., 2008). I dealt with severely depressed patients in the psychiatric hospital and found the anti-depressants excellent, although they didn't help everyone. I also believe psychotherapy helps minor to moderate depression and that antidepressants may not be as effective with them. This argument that medications don't work as well as we might want is correct, but we shouldn't throw the baby out with the bathwater. Meds help and will continue to help many.

However, my argument that medical diseases cause mental problems also fits the chemical imbalance theory. Along with the authors I cite in this book, my view is broader than the chemical imbalance theory that assumes medications are the only answer. Remember: many health care workers only have the limited view that drugs are the answer and encourage their use and miss the medical diagnoses.

2. There are some who argue against the chemical imbalance hypothesis by asking, "If aspirin gets rid of your headache, does that mean you lacked aspirin?" Of course, we don't believe the lack of aspirin causes our headache. Similarly, an anti-bacterial medicine might work for a disease, but it doesn't mean we were low on penicillin. While it's a cute argument—usually made by purists who are against medication for many problems—saying we don't need psychiatric meds; it's not the perfect argument against drugs. Most medications change the chemistry of our bodies, so researchers try to produce drugs that alter the chemicals (neurotransmitters) that affect various mental problems. The hypothesis is a person with a mental problem has a lack or excess of some neurotransmitter. Why medications work for mental problems is a matter of conjecture, but many medications work. The argument against taking medication is not a sound one. My broader view of chemical imbalance includes far more than "taking a pill" since I suggest a thorough workup to rule out possible medical issues.

3. Finally, others argue there is no physical proof (blood test, brain scan, genetics) that tells us why a person is depressed, anxious, or suffering from schizophrenia. That's true, at this point. They argue that the medical field can tell if your sore throat is due to a strep or staph infection and if you have a genetic propensity toward Huntington's disease.

Although science may not help us identify a particular diagnosis based on blood tests or an MRI, it doesn't mean it won't someday. Despite this, we can identify illnesses that cause mental problems. Syphilis—a medical disease—causes many mental problems including depression and delusions among other mental symptoms (general paresis). That finding was one of the first to connect a medical illness to mental problems. Although we can't always find something in a blood test, MRI, or whatever, there are ways to diagnose the various medical diseases that cause mental problems. We must shift from always thinking mental cause to physical cause.

What is the good news about the chemical imbalance theory?

The narrow chemical imbalance view is that balancing the neurotransmitters with medication helped people feel comfortable seeking treatment instead of denying that they had a mental illness. This view makes the problem sound biological and reduces the blame or fear that "I'm mental" or "crazy." Oprah and other talk show hosts enlightened people along these lines as did a former Florida governor, Lawton Chiles, who shared he took Prozac. The results of such public information encouraged many to get help for depression, etc. and receive anti-depressants or other helpful medicines. The chemical imbalance news removed some of the mental illness stigmas.

How does my view differ from the chemical imbalance idea?

Anti-depressants aren't perfect for every case, but they've helped millions. I'm not against the chemical imbalance view, but, as you'll see in this book, I cover various medical issues, such as hypothyroidism. It is a chemical imbalance due to an underproduction of a thyroid hormone or two, but an anti-depressant won't help that kind of depression. We could say every illness I cover is a chemical imbalance, but if it's a medical illness, anti-depressants will not help. Doctors should first check for a medical problem before prescribing psychiatric medications (e.g., Castro & Billick, 2013). I also encourage counselors to be knowledgeable about medical diseases as the culprit of mental problems. Will counseling help much if the problem is physical?

I've had many patients say their doctors prescribed an anti-depressant due to symptoms, such as fatigue, lack of motivation, sleep problems, or not enjoying normal activities. Those signs fit depression, but they also are symptoms of hypothyroidism, B12 deficiency, and many other biological diseases. The right treatment should solve the medical problem and the mental issue.

Do researchers, doctors, and therapists know the relationship between medical illnesses and mental illnesses?

The answer is yes—some do; however, many miss countless medical illnesses I cover in this book. Doctors are familiar with comorbid diseases, that is, mental problems that occur with medical conditions. I discuss these in the last chapter. Examples of these are heart attacks, strokes, arthritis, Alzheimer's disease, multiple sclerosis, and diabetes, among others. Doctors will often treat and correct the illness and remedy the depression. They may also give an anti-depressant and recommend counseling (Coupland, Hill, Morriss, et al., 2016).

Take heart problems as an example. Researchers thought the depression after a heart attack was because the person now understood their mortality. Apparently, suffering from a heart attack or a stroke makes one more aware of the ephemeral nature of life. It's understandable how depression might follow in such a situation. Further research showed, however, that a heart attack changes our chemistry (e.g., Liu, et al., 2013). Working with depression after a heart attack is important—and may help avoid future heart attacks (Coupland, et al., 2016).

I'm not against medication or counseling for mental problems—in fact, I am for both. I was a therapist for 20+ years and recommended psychiatric meds in my long career. We must, however, rule out the diseases that may cause or contribute to so-called mental problems. I agree with the chemical imbalance hypothesis as far as it goes, but we must consider biological (medical) issues that might cause depression, anxiety, or psychosis.

Therefore, understand that any illness results in a chemical imbalance. Just using medication does not cover the whole imbalance spectrum nor will psychiatric drugs be the answer for many psychological (mental) problems. The mental health community must look for biological illnesses that may cause those mental problems. I will relate many of these in this book. Counseling, psychiatric medications, treatment of organic diseases, and healthy lifestyles will offer us a multi-faceted, holistic attack on mental problems. With this, we will have far more success which means better lives for those who have "mental illness."

4
Hypothyroidism: A Sneaky, Common Cause of "Mental Illness"

When I researched biological causes of depression, hypothyroidism was the most common culprit. It was also the most common problem I found while counseling. Many other medical illnesses result in similar symptoms, making it difficult to tell if it's hypothyroidism or another disease causing the depression. Have faith, though—we'll do the detective work together.

Hypothyroidism means low thyroid activity. The thyroid is your metabolism gland, and— if it's in hypo mode, then your metabolism slows and fatigue will set in along with other symptoms. If the thyroid is overactive, then you would be hyperthyroid. Hyperthyroidism gives you plenty of energy; you'll eat like crazy and still lose weight as your metabolism burns those calories. It sounds great, but you don't want to be hyperthyroid just to lose weight, because it can also cause anxiety and depression. We'll talk about that in a separate chapter.

Hypothyroidism, like many of the illnesses mentioned in this book, is also sexist: it affects up to nine times as many women as men (Wu, 2000). About 2-10% of women have hypothyroidism and are more likely to get it after the age of 30. I've seen cases in women as young as 14, but that is rare.

If the thyroid problem gets out of kilter, it can cause panic attacks, psychotic depression, bipolar (manic-depressive) disorder, and rarely, schizophrenic-like symptoms (e.g., hallucinations) (Gupta, et al., 2017.) Depression, even if mild, disrupts a person's life. You may be prescribed an anti-depressant if the doctor overlooks the biology of your illness. Don't let that happen.

Understanding the Symptoms of Hypothyroidism

These aren't the only symptoms, but they are the most common. You can Google to learn more or read excellent books I'll recommend at the end of this chapter. These symptoms are not in any order. You might have two of them and your friend may have two different ones. You may have six; some symptoms are more common than others.

4: Hypothyroidism: A Sneaky, Common Cause of "Mental Illness"

The following information is so common that I'm not going to cite medical journals.

a. Feeling cold when others don't. Males often prefer a room cooler than women prefer, so women must compare themselves to other women. If you notice you're cold when other women aren't, take notice. This is a common symptom.

b. Depression. No surprises, since that's what we're discussing. Depression could be mild, since your system has slowed, or it could be severe. The danger is in thinking you're depressed for psychological reasons. We can all find something to be upset or stressed about, but be careful with assuming such a cause. I've had many patients who thought their depression was from stress, but discovered the medical condition, got it fixed, and their depression lifted.

c. Hair loss. This is gender-specific, too. It's a typical hypo problem for women. Men lose hair for more reasons than most women do, but hypothyroidism can affect men's hair loss, too.

d. Loss of interest in things that used to be interesting. Your body knows you have a thyroid problem and slows you down, so you'll avoid many typical behaviors. Not interested in going to a movie? Why? "I couldn't stay awake," or, "I don't care to watch that film" Those are typical responses when you lose interest in life. Your sexual life can suffer, too. You may not find reading as enjoyable or even playing cards with the kids or friends. Many depressives feel guilty when their energy level drops and affects the family. Loss of interest is a common sign of depression, so a doctor or therapist overlook the real problem--hypothyroidism.

e. PMS. When a woman is hypothyroid, she will often have period problems. The thyroid affects every part of your body, and the problems with PMS are common with hypothyroidism. Let your doctor know if you're having troubles— female problems are too often overlooked and sometimes labeled "normal" when they are actually a sign of a biological issue.

f. Weight gain is common. Research varies on how much weight people gain, but I've had clients who added 10 pounds and others who picked up 60 and more in a matter of a few months. What is sneaky is that you're not eating more, but your sluggish metabolism means you don't need as much food and you store it as fat. Lack of activity due to fatigue decreases the calories burned and increases weight gain as well.

g. Constipation can be a problem, because once again, your body has slowed down and food digestion slows down, too. Constipation is common for many people, which makes it difficult to say that it is an indicator of hypothyroidism. However, it's one symptom to keep in mind. Tell the doctor about it—the more symptoms you share, the better decision can be made.

h. Fatigue is one of the first signs of hypothyroidism. Unfortunately, it can result from many other issues found in other chapters. Nonetheless, if you are more fatigued than you think you should be, don't blame it on your old age. If you're living on four hours of sleep each night for a week, fatigue is understandable. If you can't, however, explain your fatigue, get suspicious. It's a very common side effect of hypothyroidism.

i. Lack of concentration. The reason hypothyroidism affects concentration is that your slowed metabolism doesn't allow your typical quick thinking. It's like trying to focus when you're tired. Unfortunately, it's common to other problems, but keep it in mind as part of the syndrome.

j. Hoarse voice. It may take months or even years before this symptom appears. I can't imitate it on the printed page as I can while giving a seminar, but it's somewhat like the voice of someone who has smoked for 50-60 years or who has a bad cold. Since hypothyroidism develops slowly so you, your workmates, and family members may not notice the gradual change in your voice. If you only see relatives once a year, however, they might notice. Also, if you've given the doctor a few signs, he may ask about your voice thinking it's raspy.

k. Higher cholesterol is another symptom that may or may not tell you much, since high cholesterol is common. If your cholesterol levels have risen over the past year or two, it may be a sign that your thyroid is slowing. Fortunately, if you get checked for hypothyroidism, you'll get a complete blood panel showing cholesterol levels. Once you get control of your thyroid, the cholesterol will drop back to pre-hypothyroid levels.

l. Infertility. Your body is incredible: if your thyroid isn't working up to snuff, the body will try to protect you and a baby by preventing conception. One night, my wife and I attended a faculty/student get-together. A student came up, grabbed my hand, and said, "Thank you, Doc, for getting me pregnant." I looked at her and said, "That doesn't sound right." She laughed, apologized, and explained, "I took your biopsychology class in which you went over hypothyroidism. My husband and I were trying for a baby with no luck in three years. I had hypothyroid signs, got checked, got diagnosed, and got on thyroid meds. A year later, we had a baby."

Here are two cases that are interesting. Both are instructive to show how easy (and common) it is to overlook hypothyroidism.

Case #1. I was driving from Wisconsin to Miami, trying to make the trip non-stop. I wouldn't spend money on a motel (I'm frugal), but I had to eat to avoid hypoglycemia.

4: Hypothyroidism: A Sneaky, Common Cause of "Mental Illness"

So, I stopped at a southern Indiana restaurant at 6:00 AM after being up for 24 hours. It was so hot that summer that you couldn't run your car's AC without being in danger of your vehicle overheating. Thus, after 24 hours, my windblown hair was in disarray, I had a scruffy beard, was greasy, and tired. I prayed an old waitress would serve me, because she would be used to seeing her husband in the morning and my appearance wouldn't shock her. Of course, my waitress was an 18-year-old—so much for my praying! Despite my presentation, however, she took my order. Within a few minutes, a woman entered showing signs of hypothyroidism. Check out the above signs with those symptoms.

1. She was **overweight** (perhaps by 75 pounds).

2. I could see her scalp right through her permed hair—significant **hair loss**.

3. She was wearing a blouse PLUS a leather jacket. I figured she must be **cold,** despite the temperature and high humidity.

4. My waitress talked to her and the woman had a **hoarse voice**.

I could not believe a person had that many signs of hypothyroidism and had not received help. Perhaps she hadn't been to a doctor. I felt responsible for getting her on thyroid meds, but the bad news was that I didn't look presentable enough to talk medicine with her. The good news was that she apparently knew my waitress, since they were making small talk.

My waitress returned with my eggs and toast, and I asked her if she knew the woman. "Yes, she's my mother." I explained that I did medical research and I thought her mother might be hypothyroid. "Have you ever heard of that?" I asked. She shook her head, possibly wondering if 'hypothyroid' was a dirty word.

I continued and said I would write symptoms on a napkin and asked if she'd give it to her mom. "It could change her life," I added. She said she would. I left a 200% tip, hoping that would impress her enough to give the information to her mom. I'll never know if she did, but this woman had four signs of hypothyroidism that were apparent from 20 feet away.

Case #2. I had a neighbor, Susan, who asked if I would hypnotize her friend to help her lose 20 stubborn pounds that refused to budge. I agreed to meet them Thursday evening at my house, but I told Susan it would be best if she'd come with her friend, since I she didn't know me. She agreed, and they both came.

Susan came dressed in Miami, summer style: short shorts, a sleeveless top, and sandals. Her friend came with jeans, a blouse, and a jacket. I asked her if she was cold all the time. She gave a big "yes" and added that people at work (at an outside plant nursery) kidded her about always wearing jackets. As I questioned her, I found out that she'd had a hysterectomy because she had

4: Hypothyroidism: A Sneaky, Common Cause of "Mental Illness"

so many female problems. I asked her if she was losing hair. She leaned over and showed me a bald spot on the crown of her head as large as a silver dollar.

I told her that I didn't think hypnosis was the proper treatment until she got a thyroid check. She went to her doctor and asked for a T-4 and TSH test. He had not heard of those tests (this was in 1984), so I sent her to my doctor, who put her on thyroid medication. He told me she had more symptoms of hypothyroidism than any patient he'd seen. She lost the weight, was warmer, and her hair grew back. Her doctor should have caught hypothyroidism years ago—she may not have even needed the hysterectomy.

Once you get the label of depression, the doctor's next step is often prescribing an anti-depressant, rather than finding the cause. If you're depressed, you'll want freedom from your depression, but that doesn't mean you need an anti-depressant. That's another reason to do your homework and take the symptom list to the doctor. They are busy folks and can use your detective skills. If you have good reasons to get tested, your doctor will be more than happy to help.

So, be prepared and take a list of your symptoms from the list I gave you and from other information you glean from books and the internet. If your doctor asks you where you learned this, don't say from the internet, since many health care workers don't like that source. Say you were reading a book (this book) by a doctor and copied your symptoms.

Hypothyroidism is Insidious

You may not suspect hypothyroidism, but if you keep an eye on the symptoms, you might identify a problem a year or two before it becomes a serious issue, e.g., depression. Many of my patients should have gotten help long before they saw me, but they didn't notice the slow progression of hypothyroidism.

Like many diseases, hypothyroidism comes on slowly—it's gradual and sneaky with an unfortunate result. That's why the word "insidious" applies. Here's an example of insidiousness from my life. I'm not hypothyroid, but years ago I gained weight (15 pounds—a lot for a little guy) and, with aging, lost hair. A friend who hadn't seen me in five years came to visit. The first thing he said was, "Dave, you've gained a lot of weight and lost a lot of hair!" What a friend. My wife said, "Has he?" She didn't notice, because she was with me every day and didn't see the slow weight gain and hair loss. That's what's nasty about hypothyroidism: with the slow progression, you get used to the symptoms and wait too long before getting help. So, learn the symptoms and see if you might have hypothyroidism and languish—maybe for years—before getting help and avoid unnecessary anti-depressants.

Getting Tested

If you suspect hypothyroidism, get a thyroid test. Most doctors recommend the TSH test (TSH = thyroid stimulating hormone). Your amazing

4: Hypothyroidism: A Sneaky, Common Cause of "Mental Illness"

hypothalamus (the size of a pea and hidden in your brain) tests your blood for all kinds of things, including thyroid hormones. When you get hypothyroid, your hypothalamus sends a message to your pituitary (called the master gland) telling it that the body is low on thyroid hormone and to stimulate the thyroid with TSH. The pituitary does it thing and sends TSH into the bloodstream, which excites the thyroid to produce more thyroid hormones.

The doctor tests your TSH levels, because if TSH is high, it means something is wrong; often the thyroid gland is at fault. There are many tests the doctor can give you to figure out the cause, but the treatment is usually the same: thyroid hormones. You can check out your favorite search engine for what tests are available. One problem with the TSH test is that the accepted, normal values have changed. Years ago, TSH scores were okay if within the range of 1-5. Endocrinologists changed what they believe the best range is, however, and suggest 0.3 to 3.0 (Shomon, 2005). Many labs still report the standard as 1-5. The accepted levels are controversial, and your doctor can give you other tests to be sure of a hypothyroid diagnosis, including considering your symptoms. Testing for hypothyroidism is a bit tricky and may require more than the TSH. If you have many symptoms, you can't rely on the TSH test alone (Welsh, 2016; Kharrazian 2010).

Treatment with thyroid supplements will probably be a lifetime medication. I've known folks, however, who were on thyroid meds for a few months and then taken off and did well. What will happen is your TSH scores will drop if your thyroid's working better, and you won't need the meds. Be careful with assuming you're cured, though, because your thyroid might get sluggish again. Get your TSH checked every so often and keep your symptom list nearby.

MEDICATION ISSUES

You should know that there are different medications for hypothyroidism and many are synthetic (e.g., Synthroid). These work well for most patients, but pig thyroid (e.g., Armour) may work better for some. It doesn't sound appetizing, but I've known folks who managed better on the natural rather than the synthetic supplements. Some doctors don't deal with natural thyroid preparations while others do. Research "Armour thyroid" and see if it's something you may want to try. Many swear by it but many doctors don't prescribe it. Also, check out Shomon's book (2005) or Rubin's (2006)—or both—in the references for more on this topic.

The second problem with medication is the amount you should be taking. As you might suspect, a person who has a reasonably good, but not great thyroid will need less supplementation than someone whose thyroid is extremely sluggish. Get regular testing during the first couple of years; many doctors recommend testing every three months until you are stable and then, every six months. I've spoken to thyroid groups and others only got tested every two years. I don't recommend that, because your body changes, so you need to get checked to make sure you're at the correct level.

What other illnesses occur with hypothyroidism?

Hypothyroidism is an autoimmune disease, which means your immune system attacked your thyroid. Vitamin B-12 deficiency and diabetes (Chaker, et al., 2016) can both be autoimmune diseases. Thus, when I had patients who were hypothyroid, I would get them checked for vitamin B-12 deficiency. Likewise, if they had vitamin B-12 deficiency, I'd get them tested for hypothyroidism, and if diabetic, I'd get them checked for both hypothyroidism and B-12. When my body blessed me with rheumatoid arthritis 16 years ago, my doctor checked my thyroid. Why? He knew that arthritis is an autoimmune disease. Thank goodness, my thyroid was fine.

Hypothyroidism is well-known, but often overlooked. Doctors referred their patients to me for depression, and I sent them back to get their thyroid glands tested. Back in the 1970s and 1980s, many doctors weren't aware of the thyroid's impact on depression. Again, we have the problem of "if it's mental, there's a mental treatment for it." Don't let mental symptoms keep you from looking to biology since hypothyroidism is a common cause of depression. Women tend to have more depression than men, but since women also suffer from more biologically-induced depression, that's not surprising.

Remember: you will have to be a detective to help your doctor. Here are tips to help your detective work. Search Google, Bing, or PubMed. Here are terms to throw into your search engine. I recommend using two words at a time, as that narrows your search. For example:

Hypothyroidism and symptoms/signs

Hypothyroidism and medications

Hypothyroidism and depression

Hypothyroidism and mental illness

Enjoy your search and your new health or the new health of someone's life you touch. Be sure to check Shomon's book (see references).

5

Vitamin B-12 Deficiency

Vitamin B-12 deficiency causes many problems, both physical and mental. The good news is that it's easy to treat and recovery can be amazingly swift. The symptoms of vitamin B-12 deficiency often show up long before most tests will show a problem. Unfortunately, few get checked for B-12 deficiency, so you could have a problem without you or your doctor knowing. Thus, it's important to recognize the symptoms.

I refer my patients to doctors familiar with vitamin B-12 deficiency. One day, a doctor called me and asked how long I had been in town. I told him two years. He said, "Dave, you've sent me twelve patients in those two years. That's more than I've seen in the ten years I've been here. Why are you catching it so often and I'm not?" My answer was, "Because I'm looking for it."

When folks have "mental problems," they come to a therapist expecting psychological counseling. Yes, I offer counseling, but I look for physical problems when I can't figure out a psychological cause. That's why I catch so many patients with B-12 deficiency, hypothyroid, hypoglycemia, and other illnesses.

Mental Symptoms

1. **Disorientation/Confusion:** These related symptom occur with many problems, but keep them in mind. Perhaps an individual forgets too much, too often? It may be a first sign of B-12 deficiency.

2. **Concentration Problems:** This can lead to confusion and memory loss (Reynolds, 2006).

3. **Memory Problems:** If the concentration is lacking, memory could be deficient, too.

4. **Dementia**: It's sad that clinicians classify many people with dementia when patients just have low B-12 levels (Morris, Selhub, & Jacques, 2012; Ortuno & Cervera-Enguix, 2003), but it's wonderful when we discover and correct the problem.

5. **Crankiness, Negativism, and Anger:** I know some folks get cranky when they reach their elderly years; others become more relaxed. We need to make note of personality changes. Uncle Snort has always been negative, so being negative at age 68 doesn't mean as much as it

would with Uncle William, who was nice until age 70 and then got nasty.

6. **Paranoia:** People are after me, life's against me, nothing is good. The fear can range from mild to severe.

7. **Depression:** Sometimes older people have other medical problems, so health care professionals think their depression is because sadness accompanies illnesses. Hence, they are diagnosed with depression and put on meds for it without finding out if the B-12 deficiency or other illnesses are behind it. Various studies show that low vitamin B-12 level sometimes causes depression which is easily treated often with swift results (Gariballa & Forster; 2007; Robinson, et al., 2010). One patient was on anti-psychotic and anti-depressant medications to no avail; the doctors corrected his B-12 levels, and he soon recovered (Bar-Shai, Gott, & Marmor, 2011).

8. **Hallucinations, Delusions, Mania:** This can get a person diagnosed with schizophrenia (Kale, Naphade, Sapkale, et al., 2010; Engelborghs, Vloeberghs, Maertens, et al., 2004). Unfortunately, too many doctors miss a B-12 deficiency relationship and therapists seldom know about it (Brown & Roffman, 2014; Berry, Sagar, & Tripathi, 2003). The individual labeled with schizophrenia or mania will get anti-psychotic medications, instead of B-12 (Spiegel & West, 2008). Short-term

anti-psychotic meds may be necessary while they treat the B-12 problem, but not afterward.

9. **Alzheimer's:** Vitamin B-12 deficiency can mimic Alzheimer's behavior and thinking. There are plenty of cases of this mimicry in the scientific literature (Schildkrout, 2014). Always have someone check a person's nutrition status if they are exhibiting symptoms of Alzheimer's or senility. This doesn't mean B-12 deficiency is a cause of Alzheimer's, but it is an imitator. The two can also occur together (Prodan, Cowan, Stoner, & Ross, 2009).

PATIENTS WITH A VITAMIN B-12 DEFICIENCY DIAGNOSED WITH MENTAL ILLNESS

1. **Senility with Psychosis:**

Mr. K, a 74-year-old, was wandering a busy city and stopping cars. The police picked him up and placed him in our hospital. His thinking varied from normal to bizarre within an hour or two. Sometimes, he would switch within minutes. For example, when I first talked to him, he was fine and answered questions well. In an instant, he became bizarre and told me how he shot his grandmother so no one else could. He added, "It made the other person (who he said was a famous actor visiting him) furious, because the actor wanted to kill grandma." At 74, the psychiatrist would not label him with schizophrenia, but we did label him as senile with psychosis (out of touch with reality).

One day, I checked the B-12 report we had on him and found that it was low, so I suggested the doctor give him a shot. The next day, Mr. K was clear as a bell, which amazed us all. We were about to place him in an Alzheimer's unit, but thank goodness we gave him the shot. I asked him if he'd ever had a B-12 shot; he said he'd had them his whole life. Of course, he didn't tell us that upon admission, and we had no medical records for him. Rather than being sent to a "home," he went home to his wife.

2. **Schizophrenia:**

This illness often presents with hallucinations (seeing and hearing things are the most common), delusions (false beliefs), and communication problems. It's a debilitating illness that makes work and relationships tough, if not impossible. Medications control it, but none is perfect.

--A twenty-one-year-old male, Jose, came in for counseling. He was fatigued and hearing voices. One voice was that of God, who told him to get out of his car and run around it three times—on a three-lane freeway in Miami. I asked him if he still thought it was God. He said, "Not now, but when you're alone, hear a clear voice telling you what to do, you don't take chances." Doctors diagnosed him with schizophrenia and depression—the latter from his inability to work due to fatigue. He had no "get up and go."

He was wearing shorts on the summer day that he came to see me, exposing a reddish sore somewhat larger than a silver dollar on his calf. It sported a small hole in the middle that made me think he'd gotten a nail puncture wound. He said, "No, it's been there for six months. The doctors don't know why it hasn't healed." Although doctors had ruled out diabetes, they went no further. This pointed to something metabolically wrong. When a person is B-12 deficient, wound-healing can be slow or non-existent.

    Therefore, I sent him to my doctor to get a complete blood panel work-up. Jose brought the results in a few days later, and it looked like he had anemia. I told him he might be B-12 deficient, and sent him back to the doctor for a B-12 shot. My doctor called me later that day and asked, "You were using it as a placebo, right?" He did not understand that a B-12 deficiency could lead to such a "mental problem." Furthermore, he didn't believe a 21-year-old would be deficient, as it's much more common in those over 60.

    Jose got a job the next week, which he wouldn't have been able to before, due to being so tired and unable to stay at a job. One of his friends told me he was doing well—no more hallucinations and he was no longer tired. Interestingly, his mother was so happy that she came in, thanked me, and said she always thought he had a physical problem, not a psychological one.

    --A 35-year-old male, Bob, suffered from schizophrenia and had deteriorated so much that we had him on massive doses of anti-psychotics. He was getting more and more paranoid to the point that he didn't want to give me anything but fleeting eye contact. We had not tested him for

B-12 deficiency, but I asked a nurse about giving him a shot. She said, "Why not? Nothing we're doing is helping," and gave him a B-12 shot on Wednesday.

I was hoping for a miracle next day, like the earlier two cases, but nothing had changed on Thursday, Friday, Saturday, or Sunday. When I came to work on Monday, however, Bob greeted me and said, "Hi, Doc." I returned the greeting and asked him how he was doing. He said he was doing great and I asked him why. "Because they gave me a B-12 shot," he answered. I asked him if he'd ever had shots before and he said he'd had them since he was 16. Who would suspect schizophrenia symptoms from B-12 deficiency?

Please note: Schizophrenia is a label for many behavioral and thinking problems. There are many causes (Torrey, 2013). If we find someone has schizophrenic symptoms that B-12 deficiency is causing, remove the mental label from that person's history. Other illnesses can cause schizophrenic symptoms, too (e.g., see Cushing's syndrome).

1. **Depression:** I've had many patients whose B-12 deficiency caused their depression which can range from mild to severe. If it's mild, fatigue and depression will be moderate, but could still make life less than exciting.

2. **Memory, Confusion, Concentration, Headaches, and Mild Depression:** Sue, age 28, was in my abnormal psychology class in which

we go over B-12 symptoms. She had several them. She described her thinking as fuzzy and had trouble following spoken instructions for an exam. The military gave her an honorable discharge, due to her "mental condition." She could go to the VA for medical help, and the doctor suspected a B-12 deficiency. He gave her a shot, and she improved for a while. That, however, was over six months earlier.

I suggested that she go to a doctor before she went on an overseas mission as a contractor for the government. She had excellent insurance with her company, so the doctor gave her an MRI, CAT scan, and a B-12 test. The MRI and CAT scan were perfect, and the only problem was a B-12 deficiency. She had a brain problem, but it was physical, not mental. She now gets shots more regularly—not every six months.

Physical Symptoms

As with many illnesses, physical symptoms are more tell-tale than mental symptoms. Once you have a mental problem, everyone thinks of mental treatment. Don't fall for that and check the physical as I did in my counseling. Remember: you don't need all these symptoms

1. **Fatigue:** One of the first signs of B-12 deficiency. Of course, many physical issues can cause fatigue, so it isn't the best symptom to suspect a B-12 deficiency.

2. **Loss of Appetite:** Not everyone will lose their appetite. With young children, B-12 supplements often help. I've known patients, usually older, who don't care to eat and consequently lose weight. "Food just doesn't taste right," they would say. Of course, there are many reasons food may not taste good—zinc deficiency is another. I am B-12 deficient, but my appetite is fine.

3. **Headaches:** There many types of headaches, and those caused by B-12 deficiency are one of the least known. They are not severe, such as cluster, migraine, or coffee withdrawal headaches. Just keep this in mind when you're trying to analyze yourself or others for a B-12 deficiency. Don't accept the stress explanation for your headaches.

4. **Sore Tongue or Mouth:** This is the symptom that got me wondering about my B-12 levels. I kept thinking I had bitten my tongue or ate something I was allergic to. After helping folks with a B-12 deficiency for 20 years, however, I realized I might have the same problem. A nurse gave me a shot, and within two days, the sore tongue disappeared, I wasn't snoring, anymore, and I had much more energy. I didn't realize how fatigued I had been until I got that shot.

5. **Numbness or Tingling in Hands and Feet:** Many things can cause this. I lost most of my light touch sensitivity in my feet—especially

the right foot. My feeling hasn't returned, but others are more fortunate than I.

6. **Pain in the Hands and Feet Due to Neuropathy:** I don't have this, yet, but it's common for folks low in B-12. Neuropathy is more common in diabetics; since diabetes and B-12 deficiency can occur together, diabetics should get their B-12 levels checked (Kibirige & Mwebaze, 2013). Sometimes, B-12 supplementations can correct the neuropathy.

7. **Burning Feet:** Related to #6, but this is burning and not just regular pain. It's due to the neurons not functioning well and dying. Again, B-12 treatment may correct it, if caught soon enough.

8. **Balance Problems:** This symptom is sometimes the first to be noticed. People at retirement age know that falls are dangerous, so we know about balance problems. If, however, you're having balance problems, be sure to check your B-12 levels.

9. **Mimicker of Multiple Sclerosis (MS):** In its early stages, doctors have a difficult time diagnosing MS. I have read about a few cases of a person being diagnosed with MS only to find out that it was a B-12 deficiency. MS is a disease of younger folks (20-45), and healthcare professionals often consider B-12 a problem of the elderly. Thus, a 37-year-old who is B-12 deficient may get misdiagnosed with MS. Considering a B-12 deficiency might be helpful (Mansueto, et al., 2012; Kocer, et al.,

2009). Know of the possibility of the deficiency mimicking MS, even though the confusion is a rare occurrence.

Cases of B-12 Physical Problems

Larry was diabetic and his doctor, an endocrinologist, should have checked him for a B-12 deficiency. His mother was B-12 deficient, as were her mother and sister. The doctor knew that, plus the following: Larry had a sore tongue to the point that he couldn't brush his teeth, fatigue limited his physical activity, and his wife said he had an anger problem, which made him unlike his usual calm self. (That's a mental symptom, but folks often have both physical and psychological symptoms.)

I explained B-12 deficiency to him, so he trotted off to his doctor to get a test. The doctor refused, however, since Larry was only 42 years old. I sent him back to tell the doctor that his counselor (me) wouldn't see him again until he got tested. What good could I do for him if he's B-12 deficient? The doctor balked, but agreed to the test. Larry got a call two days later telling him to get in for a shot that day, since his B-12 level was 72 (far below normal). Larry got his energy back, and his wife said he was his sweet old self again.

Gretchen was a 72-year-old woman who attended my talk for the golden-agers at her church. I spoke on some sneaky causes of problems in old age, including vitamin B-12 deficiency. She marched up afterward and said, "I think I have a B-12 deficiency." I answered, "You seem too perky to have a B-12 deficiency."

She retorted with more energy, "I am NOT perky, young feller. I'm tired all the time. I don't like to eat and only do so because I know I'll die if I don't. My tongue is sore and my feet burn. No matter where I go, the feet go with me." I suggested that she go to her doctor and get tested.

Her daughter called me the next day saying that her mother was always looking for a magic bullet and now mother thought she had a B-12 problem. "My mom's a hypochondriac." That wasn't true—she was trying to find an answer that hadn't been forthcoming. I apologized, but told her a few of the B-12 symptoms. The daughter said, "She has six of them." So, off to the doctors they went. They gave her a blood profile test, but wouldn't check her B-12.

They sent me the results of the blood test, which showed that she could well have a B-12 deficiency. I told them to go back with a list of symptoms and point out the blood test indicators for the problem. The doctors checked the B-12 against their better judgment, and the next day, Gretchen got a phone call telling her to come in right away for a B-12 shot. Her level was 72—a dangerous level. Fortunately, none of the mental symptoms (like hallucinations) had affected her, yet, but they could have down the road, had she not gotten treatment.

An acquaintance of mine, Mary, was in her 70s and was having a problem with falling every so often. She knew nothing about B-12 deficiency, but her doctor did. He found that she was deficient and corrected it. No more falling! She lived alone, and a fall could have had severe consequences.

I worked with a gay couple who were both HIV-positive. They got B-12 shots after hearing my talk about it with interesting results. The next day, the Bob told me he'd lost feeling two years ago on his left thigh, but the shot had brought back the feeling. He now realized his nerves had been dying from a lack of B-12.

His partner, Jim, had a car wreck about five weeks before hearing my B-12 talk. Interestingly, he had no pain in his ankle. When I came in that morning, he pretended he was angry with me, but smiled and said, "I'm angry because I've had no ankle pain from the car wreck—until I got the B-12 shot. Now I'm on pain meds to get me through the day." We laughed about it, but he was happy he'd received help, despite the pain. His neurons were unresponsive until he got the shot.

What's interesting is that both were HIV positive for years (nine and six years) and no doctor had ever told them about the possible need for B-12, which HIV folks should watch (Schildkrout, 2014). Jim was also hypothyroid, so his doctor had two reasons to check B-12 levels, but he didn't.

B-12 deficiency is more widespread than many in the medical profession think. Years ago, doctors thought it was a disease of those over the age of 65 or 70. That's mostly right, but you can tell by my case studies that the young can have the deficiency, too. In the last 20 years, researchers have been testing younger folks (in their 40s and 50s) and finding that they, too, have some B-12 problems. Don't think, because you're younger than 60, that you can't be deficient. Get checked if you have symptoms.

It's tough to estimate what percentage of folks may suffer from it, but the estimates range from 6% to 20% with higher numbers in those over 60. Using more stringent "normal" values of B-12 levels might show higher percentages (Allen, 2009). If an older person has any illnesses (e.g., diabetes), the probability of low B-12 increases.

How Might People Become Low in Vitamin B-12?

1. **Inability to Absorb B-12:** An autoimmune problem can damage part of the stomach lining that produces intrinsic factor. We have to have it in our stomachs to absorb the B-12, whether it is in food or pills (Lanska, 2009).

    Unfortunately, one day I read a doctor's medical article which said you don't need shots and can take vitamins at higher levels than normal. So, I did so for three months, at the end of which, my wife said I was not my happy self, was too tired to do much, and was grumpy. I got back on my shots and good ol'

Dave was back within five hours. The result of swallowing pills for me was losing most of my light touch sensation in my feet. Interestingly, another doctor wrote about how he had taken pills because of the same journal article and kept getting worse to the point of almost giving up his practice. One day, he tried the shots, and now he's back to practicing medicine. He wrote a letter to the editor warning against relying on pills alone.

Why don't the pills always work? If you don't have intrinsic factor, you won't absorb vitamin B-12 from any source. Your stomach lining should make intrinsic factor, but your immune system may be the culprit—another autoimmune problem. I presume that's why I became deficient. Of course, you might have somewhat low levels of intrinsic factor; if so, taking higher doses in pill form may well help you. Be careful, though, and don't end up as that doctor and I did.

2. **Vegetarianism/Veganism:** Because only animal products provide absorbable B-12, vegetarians and especially vegans can become deficient (Sahoo, Avasthi, & Singh, 2011). Deficiency rates are much higher for vegetarians and even higher for vegans than other people (Pawlak, et al., 2013). Most vegetarians probably don't lack intrinsic factor any more than most folks, however, so taking vitamins will keep them from getting deficient.

3. **Low Stomach Acid:** People who have too little stomach acid can get low in B-12, since they need enough stomach acid to allow absorption. Many elderly have enough intrinsic factor but low levels of acid, which makes absorption difficult or impossible (Morris, Selhub, & Jacques, 2012). Individuals who take too many acid-lowering medications sometimes get low on B-12. Medications to combat stomach acid levels and GERD can bring on a deficiency.

   Diabetics (typically Type II) who take metformin to help with their diabetes may become B-12 deficient—perhaps 10-30% (Campbell, 2006). People other than diabetics take metformin for other problems, so they, too, should be aware of the possibility of a B-12 deficiency. That doesn't mean a person should stop taking metformin—just get help with the B-12.

4. **Gastric Bypass:** Anyone who has had a gastric bypass operation is a candidate for the deficiency. If you or someone you know had such an operation, talk to a doctor about B-12. I've met 80-100 people who have had the operation and, out of that many, only four were not taking vitamin B-12. Physicians who perform bypass operations realize the need for B-12 supplementation.

5. **Crohn's Disease or Irritable Bowel Syndrome:** Sufferers from these diseases are candidates for B-12 deficiency because food goes through them so fast that they don't

have time to absorb B-12. Getting the correct supplementation (see below) can help rectify the deficiency, but it does not remedy the bowel problem. Some folks with IBS have had part of the small intestine removed, and they should ask their doctor about B-12 supplementation. Sometimes part of the small intestine that was removed is the part that absorbs B-12.

6. **Pregnancy:** This can also bring on a deficiency; fortunately, doctors check for everything when a woman is pregnant.

7. **Shocks to the System:** Sometimes a shock to the system (e.g., high fever or flu) might affect the liver so much that it doesn't absorb B-12. This is unusual, but it can happen, since your liver stores B-12.

How Do I Know If I Have Vitamin B-12 Deficiency?

Some doctors will give you a B-12 shot to see if it helps. Some doctors rely solely on tests. I recommend that you get checked for vitamin B-12. A blood test can usually tell you, but there may be a problem with testing (Solomon, 2007).

Some labs list "normal" levels of B-12 from 200-900. If you test out at 275, the lab report doesn't say you're low, even though it should! Research shows that you should score from 400-500 (Pacholok & Stuart, 2011). The 72-year-old woman, Gretchen, with a score of 72, had an interesting report. The lab said they didn't have levels for older people, even though it said a 45-year-old patient should score at least 350. They added that, at 72, the levels should be much higher. I can't believe they didn't have norms for the elderly, since they have a higher chance of becoming deficient. They should have norms for all age levels, rather than a one range fits all (e.g., 200-900).

Mr. K, the 74-year-old man I mentioned earlier had a B-12 level of 212. The doctor didn't pick up on it, since the lab report said the B-12 was normal. I fault the lab for not reflecting the latest information on what should be normal. We gave him a shot that changed his life in one day.

Many tests help identify the B-12 deficiency, but the important thing to remember is labs seldom provide the right levels. I tell my patients to shoot for a level of 500. Get Pacholok's book (2011) for the best information.

Finally, there are three indicators in a blood test that hint at a B-12 deficiency (or a folic acid deficiency.) If your MCV, MCH, and MCHC levels are close to or above the standard upper level, get checked for a B-12 deficiency. Gretchen, the 72-year-old woman I mentioned earlier, scored high on all three, which made me believe she had an issue and helped the doctors decide to test her. If you get a complete blood panel, look at those three, since they may have skipped a B-12 check.

How Can You Increase Your B-12 to Livable Levels?

1. **B-12 Injection:** The quickest way to recover. Most doctors will give you a 1000-microgram shot, which is a lot. Stay at the physician's office and make sure you have no problems after an hour. There are rare cases of vitamin B-12 lowering potassium levels, which can make a person dizzy.

   The B-12 shot is by prescription; the doctor, however, can write you a script and you can get needles and give yourself the shot or have a nurse or spouse do so. Get instructions on how to give the shot. Most practitioners recommend getting the shot once a month, although sometimes, doctors will give shots every week until the B-12 levels rise.

   The monthly schedule doesn't work for everyone. I needed a shot every three weeks, or my symptoms returned in week four. A colleague of mine needed an injection once a week, or the symptoms returned. Others can get by with a shot every six months. Keep track of the symptoms; if you get symptoms by a particular week, get the injection the week before that. Don't wait until you get the symptoms, since the deficiency can damage your nerves.

2. **Sublingual Tablets (Lozenges):** Put them under your tongue or between your gum and your cheek, like when you chew tobacco. The

reason this works is because they absorb right into your blood stream, so you don't need intrinsic factor. I take a lozenge about every day to keep my levels up instead of taking the shot. They range from 500-micrograms to 5,000. If you take one a day, either dose should do the trick. Some doctors don't think the lozenges work, but my doctor tested me and I scored 1143 (way over the 900 upper level). Buy the methylcobalamin form, since it is more absorbable than cyanocobalamin. The cyan-type is cheaper than the methyl, however, if you're on a tight budget.

3. **Liquid B-12:** Swish it around in your mouth for 30 seconds to a minute. It works like the lozenges, but is more expensive.

4. **Oral Spray:** Similar to the liquid, but is even a more expensive route.

5. **Nasal Gel:** This comes in a little tube which you squeeze the B-12 gel into your nostrils and then pinch/massage your nose to get the gel exposed to all the blood vessels. A negative of the nasal gel is that it is a bit expensive.

6. **Food:** If you have no intrinsic factor, you won't absorb B-12 from your stomach. Don't be fooled—eating foods rich in B-12 (meats, eggs, dairy, and supplemented bread and cereals) won't do you much good. If you have some intrinsic factor, you might absorb B-12, but be careful and make sure it's working.

7. **Pills:** Again, if you don't have intrinsic factor, swallowing vitamins won't do you much good for a B-12 problem. Note that I'm talking about swallowing vitamins and not the sublingual form. I consumed 3000-mcgs a day (we only need 2- to 8-mcg per day) and I still lost feeling in my feet, plus had other symptoms mentioned above. Research indicates that taking massive doses can work as well as shots (Castelli, et al., 2012). Nonetheless, not everyone can absorb B12 in this manner, so be careful. Don't make the same mistake I did.

WHAT ARE OTHER ILLNESSES ASSOCIATED WITH A B-12 DEFICIENCY?

It's good to know other illnesses associated with B-12 deficiency, because if you have any of them, you should check your B-12 status. If you have a B-12 deficiency, you should check for the other related problems. The term for diseases occurring together is comorbid.

Hypothyroidism is common; some research says about 25% of hypothyroid patients will be B-12 deficient because both can be autoimmune disorders. I have two autoimmune diseases, arthritis and B-12 deficiency. When I first got diagnosed with rheumatoid arthritis, my doctor checked my thyroid function. It turns out that my immune system has left my thyroid alone, yet, but I get it checked every so often.

Diabetes is also a buddy of B-12 deficiency, especially Type I. There is discussion, however, that Type II might also be an autoimmune disorder. I've had patients who had hypothyroidism, diabetes, and vitamin B-12 deficiency. Any of those illnesses can produce many psychological symptoms. Iron deficiency anemia may also appear along with vitamin B-12 deficiency. I don't, however, think one causes the other.

The Importance of Understanding B-12 Deficiency

I hope I've convinced you of the importance. In summary, vitamin B-12 deficiency can devastate a person and family. When you realize that it can cause depression, anxiety, senility, and other mental and physical problems, you should be on top of it. Please get Pacholok and Stuart's (2011) book listed in the references. You can also search your favorite research engines, but be careful, as some of the material is incorrect and misleading.

Best wishes in identifying or ruling out B-12 problems. Remember: find a doctor knowledgeable in B-12 or consult with a neurologist or hematologist. Persist—it is part of your detective work.

Tips to Becoming a Vitamin B-12 Detective

Get on the internet, use your favorite search engine, and look! Put in:

Depression and Vitamin B-12

Alzheimer's and Vitamin B-12,

Schizophrenia and Vitamin B-12

You can also put in:

Vitamin B-12 and treatment.

Vitamin B-12 and lab results.

6

Understanding Hypoglycemia and Mental Problems

The main psychological (mental) problems I've seen from hypoglycemia are depression along with fatigue and anger. Unfortunately, medical professionals and counselors tend to overlook hypoglycemia (Salzer, 1966), so you may have a difficult time getting help. Therefore, you need to use your detective skills to discover if you're hypoglycemic. Sometimes it's easy; sometimes it's difficult.

Most doctors don't agree with my view about hypoglycemia, and I can't blame them because years ago, the popular press said hypoglycemia explained almost any problem. That was an overgeneralization, and doctors got sick of hearing their patients asking for a hypoglycemia test and diagnosis. Two researchers entitled an article in the New England Journal of Medicine, 'Non-hypoglycemia is an epidemic condition' (Yager & Young, 1974). I understand the authors' position since so many folks back in the 70s thought hypoglycemia caused almost every problem they had. Do any doctors think hypoglycemia affects us average people (non-diabetics) and causes mental problems? A few do, but most don't.

I have trouble with hypoglycemia myself, but I don't always catch it; I am good at avoiding problems which I'll cover later. Researchers don't agree on how to diagnose hypoglycemia (Pourmotabed & Kitabchi, 2001); they often report it as a rare occurrence, except in people with diabetes who take too much insulin (Messer, Morris, & Gross, 1990). Some doctors understand hypoglycemia and will help you, but unfortunately, they are the exceptions.

From my counseling experience, women have a more difficult time giving up sweets than men. The gender gap is similar in many mammals; female animals prefer sweets more than males. Also, women have about twice the depression rate as men. It's not mental differences, but biological. Women are more affected by hypoglycemia regarding depression and males are more likely to have anger issues from it.

1. Hypoglycemia simply means low blood sugar (glucose). However, researchers have various definitions of hypoglycemia, which can be confusing and misleading. For example, many

define it as glucose levels below 50, since 70-99 is "normal." Others define it as a percentage drop in glucose within a certain time, rather than a particular level. Still, others emphasize the reactions of patients after a sugar load. I prefer the latter since blood tests aren't helpful for a patient who has depression or anger from eating sweets. Thus, it's not always easy to define or figure out if you have hypoglycemia. Furthermore, doctors aren't looking for it, and most people aren't familiar with it causing depression. In fact, most of the medical articles supporting hypoglycemia as a cause of mental symptoms were published many years ago (e.g., Hunt, 1985). If doctors don't believe in it, they will not be looking for it, but the good news is that you can figure it out on your own and take corrective action.

2. There's controversy about what causes hypoglycemic episodes, but I'll explain it based on what I've learned from medical journals and counseling.

   a. Medical doctors believe the most common way to get hypoglycemia is by taking too much insulin (Pourmotabbed & Kitabchi, 2001). That would mean that diabetics are the ones—perhaps the only ones—who suffer from hypoglycemia. Of course, diabetics know hypoglycemia is a problem. I've interviewed family members of diabetics, and they assure me that depression and anger rear their ugly heads during hypoglycemic attacks. A tumor on the pancreas might overproduce insulin and cause hypoglycemia, as well, but that problem is rare, and most doctors would catch it.

b. Many people get hypoglycemic after they eat too many high carbohydrates—especially sweets. I believe this, but few doctors do (but see Salzer, 1966). So, if Susan eats ice cream at 3:00 PM on Tuesday afternoon, her sugar level spikes and then the insulin level spikes. If Susan produces too much insulin in response to the sugar, she might become fatigued or depressed when the insulin lowers her sugar level because the insulin reduced her sugar level too much. Many women report getting tired half an hour to an hour after eating sweets.

It's difficult to prove that this caused her fatigue or depression, and what's confusing is that Susan may get depressed on Tuesday, even though she ate the same amount of ice cream on Saturday without a problem. Such a finding often misleads us, and a person might say, "Well, it didn't bother me today, so it must not have been the ice cream that caused the depression on Tuesday." We must be careful with that logic, however, because our bodies vary from time to time and may handle sugar better on one day better than another. Most of us don't want to give up sugar, so we'll defend it like it's our best friend. Be careful, though, and keep better track of your mood swings and sugar intake. You don't have to give up sugar, but watch when and how much you eat.

c. You may get hypoglycemic by going too long without food. Unfortunately, medical professionals aren't big on this view, either. As you might expect, I disagree with this point, and research backs my opinion (e.g., Peroutka, 2002). I have this problem and if you don't believe me, ask my wife. I don't get depressed, but I do get angry. See my companion book, *Temper, Temper: An Effective Strategy to Conquer Your Anger and Hostility (2017)*.

If I eat breakfast but skip lunch, by 2:30, my blood sugar can drop so low that I get mad. It doesn't happen every time I skip lunch—sometimes my body handles the drop in sugar level better than other occasions. Some days, my body corrects itself, while other days it lags. So, you can see that figuring out if you're hypoglycemic can be tricky. A similar example is varying my sleep. I am used to seven hours of sleep each night. Sometimes I might get five hours one night and drag the next day. Another day, however, I'll be okay with four hours. Our bodies don't function like clockwork—they vary from time to time. How my body handles sugar varies from time to time as it did for many of my counselees. Consequently, it takes detective work to solve the riddle.

Many people wake up hypoglycemic. They feel "blah" in the morning, depressed, or have an anger problem. Let's face it: if you eat at 6:00

PM and don't wake until 7:00 AM, you've gone 13 hours without food (Peroutka, 2002). Your body tries to normalize your blood sugar, and for most people, it works. Others don't fare so well and have problems. One way your body tries to keep your sugar levels normal is by releasing sugar stored in your liver.

Years ago, I couldn't find any scientific evidence that going without food for an extended time could cause problems. That was confusing since I had seen it over and over in my practice. In the 1990s, however, research showed long hours between supper and breakfast could mess up one's sugar levels and cause issues.

Snickers' ads explain the anger problem. "You're not you when you're hungry." If a candy bar company knows it, why don't the researchers? Excellent research is difficult and expensive, and pharmaceutical companies could not sell medications for the problem, so they won't do the research. Moreover, most researchers and those in medicine rarely believe in hypoglycemia, labeling hypoglycemics as a non-disease group (Hofeldt, 1989). If they can't prove hypoglycemia, they often suggest that the patient may have had psychiatric problems to begin with (Johnson, et al. 1980). If health care workers don't believe in these last two causes of hypoglycemia, then they won't be looking for it, and they won't help you. They might even tell you you're crazy. Don't fret—it's your life, and I'm going to help you.

Here are a few so-called "mental" problems that hypoglycemia can cause. If it causes your depression, you don't need anti-depressants, because the mental problem is secondary to the hypoglycemia.

a. **Depression:** I have helped many counselees overcome depression by handling their hypoglycemia. In fact, most of them did not think hypoglycemia could cause such a horrible problem and many didn't even know about hypoglycemia or its effect on mental health. Patients would come expecting me to counsel them for their depression, so I had quite a time convincing them that the problem was hypoglycemia (Salzar, 1966).

Remember Mark and his hypoglycemia from the first chapter? Discovering how sugar affected him changed his life. Mark was one example out of many people who got relief from depression and fatigue by changing how they ate. Most people can eat about anything and still feel good; however, there are days when that might not work, and there are folks who have to be more careful.

Hypoglycemics can still eat sweets, but they should eat them right after a meal. Ice cream late at night (or most cereals) can be disastrous, and eating sweets on an empty stomach is asking for trouble. If you're hypoglycemic or wonder if you might be, eat your sweets with a meal.

b. **Anger:** As I mentioned before, hypoglycemia can make me angry. I get nasty—not violent—and I blame my temper on something someone said or did. At the time, I don't believe I'm hypoglycemic. Only after thinking it through later do I realize that the incident did not explain my temper. Have you ever experienced this? "Hangry" is the cute term for it.

I rarely get angry at dangerous drivers or slow drivers, unless I'm hypoglycemic, and that's when I get irate. Fortunately, I may just beep my horn—no finger-pointing or gun waving. When I get angry at drivers, I know I'm hypoglycemic.

Many men came to see me because they had anger problems. Their tempers were so bad that their wives were ready to divorce them, and some were in trouble at work for anger outbursts. Approximately two-thirds were hypoglycemic. At first, they thought I was crazy. Hadn't they sought a psychologist for a mental problem?

Fortunately, it was easy to discover hypoglycemia in those that had that issue. These men became angry at certain times, such as when they got home late, had skipped a meal, or had eaten junk food in the afternoon (high carbohydrates). One of them drank a gallon and a half of sweet tea every day to hydrate himself while he worked outside in the Florida sun. These guys didn't hate their wives; they simply had this uncontrollable anger like I have when hypoglycemic. Remember the Snickers' ad: "You're not you when you're hungry." Check out my book on the biological contributors to anger for more on this problem (*Temper, Temper....*).

c. **Headaches:** Most people don't suspect morning headaches are due to hypoglycemia, and of course, not all morning headaches are. When your body can't keep your sugar levels normal between the evening meal and breakfast, however, you are liable to have morning headaches (Peroutka, 2001). Most of the non-migraine, morning headache clients I worked with had habits of eating sweets, such as ice cream, cereal, or a slice of toast at night—all high carbohydrates. That raises blood sugar, followed by a severe drop in many hypoglycemics when insulin pours in. The result is morning headaches of varying degrees. The blood sugar level will be back to normal by morning, but the headache remains. I've had many clients tell me they can't skip a meal or a headache will join them. Hypoglycemics have daytime headaches, too, if they don't eat right.

Occasionally, I share hypoglycemia information in my college classes. Consequently, students will share the effects sugar has on them. One said she'd suffered from morning headaches for years and went to therapy. The therapist told her that repressed anger was the culprit. Wrong! She quit eating ice cream at night and had no more headaches, but she didn't tell me of her success until six months after going off the sweets to make sure it wasn't a placebo effect. What happened to her supposed anger? When she was in therapy, she'd believed the psychologist's hypothesis. She admitted that she had a little temper, but that was not what was causing the headaches. See how easy it is to be duped by psychological theorizing?

d. **Fatigue:** This is a typical result of hypoglycemia (Johnson, et al., 1980; Salzer, 1966). Not all fatigue is caused this way. If I get three hours of sleep, I'm tired the next day and have trouble staying awake while driving or reading. I have, however, had days when I was tired and realized I'd worked right through my lunch time. I'd grab a bite and was back to normal in no time. The hypoglycemia slowed down my metabolism resulting in fatigue.

From my experience and research, these are the main "psychological" or "mental" consequences of hypoglycemia. Unfortunately, some people's sugar level drops so low that they pass out and sometimes a coma results. Anyone who experiences such symptoms will need to see a doctor to discover the cause. Other people sweat, have anxiety attacks, or get the shakes. I've occasionally experienced shakes; it's a sign that my blood sugar is low.

3. Figuring out if you suffer from hypoglycemia is not always an easy task. Even doctors can have difficulty diagnosing many problems and, consequently, aren't sure how to treat it (Hunt, 1985). For example, I went into the hospital on a Tuesday and stayed until Sunday! They kept me that long because the doctors couldn't

figure out what was causing my jaundice. Two excellent doctors explained everything and answered my naïve questions. They said that my case was a mystery, even though I was in incredible shape—they checked my heart, lungs, blood pressure, oxygen levels, and other internal organs (they went inside to check the liver and pancreas). They finally guessed that it was a problem with my liver, so they put in a stent to see if that would help. Apparently, they guessed correctly, because I'm back to my perky self and all no more jaundice.

So doctors sometimes have a difficult time figuring out what's wrong and what is the correct treatment. How does this relate to you figuring out if you're hypoglycemic? Everything. It may not be easy to pinpoint. Here are a few suggestions.

KEEP TRACK OF REACTIONS TO WHAT YOU EAT & WHEN YOU EAT

1. If you eat cake at 3:30 PM and get shaky, that's a response to the high level of sugar—a sign you might have a sugar problem. Most people do not have that reaction. Folks often feel anxious when that happens, but it is short-lived. The problem is that your sugar level may soon drop too low and produce some of the symptoms above.

2. If, after eating sweets, you get tired, angry, or depressed in an hour, that's a sign of hypoglycemia. Your sugar level has dropped and changed the chemistry of your nerves.

Depression

It will get back to normal soon because the body corrects itself, but the emotion may hang around for a while. For Mark, his depression could last 2-4 days.

3. If you get angry, tired, or depressed from going without food for too long, that's also a sign of hypoglycemia. Anger and fatigue are my most common symptoms.

4. If you eat a salad for lunch with no protein and get tired, depressed, or angry around four of five o'clock, that's a sign of hypoglycemia. The salad didn't have enough protein or fat to keep your sugar levels normal. If you had a salad with three chicken strips (protein) and had no problem, then that's good news—that's being a detective.

5. If you don't eat breakfast and you get tired around 11 o'clock—and maybe nasty—that's another sign. I had two co-workers who would tell me to eat something because they said I was getting snippy. I wasn't nasty to them, but they could tell by my phone mannerisms that the good ol' Dave had left the building. Eating yogurt and a little peanut butter brought me back to normal. I realized that I was in one of those hypoglycemic metabolic weeks and then brought a snack every day so I could keep the sugar levels normal.

6. If you eat sweets at night (cereals, puddings, toast, a glass or two of juice, alcohol or other high carb foods), pay attention. If you wake up grumpy, depressed, or with a headache, it's a

sign that you might be hypoglycemic. See my cranberry episode below.

7. Doctors give the Oral Glucose Tolerance Test (OGTT) to pregnant women or patients suspected of being diabetic. You drink a sweet liquid, and the staff checks your sugar levels every 30 minutes to an hour. A test may require six hours; others are three hours. Most doctors do not believe it's a valid test for hypoglycemia, although I've had patients take it and get a diagnosis of hypoglycemia. It may or may not show the problem, because you may handle the OGGT sugar load that day. If you get the OGTT and the doctor tells you that the results are normal, don't take it too seriously. Pay attention to the symptoms listed above. On the other hand, if the test shows you're hypoglycemic, you probably are.

Our bodily processes vary. I have gone months without a hypoglycemia problem and can skip lunch or eat ice cream at night with no reaction. Then, without warning, I have to eat regular snacks during the day to avoid becoming hypoglycemic. Be a detective. My wife also volunteers as a detective for me. "Better eat something, Dave," she says. My wife is much happier when I'm nice, and so am I. If you're the one who suffers from hypoglycemia, controlling it will improve your life and the lives of those around you.

AVOIDING HYPOGLYCEMIA

There are steps you can take to keep hypoglycemia away. Here are three things most researchers recommend (Salzer, 1966; Pourmotabbed & Kitabchi, 2001; Leichter, 1979):

a. Follow a diabetic diet, even if you're not diabetic. Eat every three hours. Frequent meals keep your blood sugar levels normal since they are smaller than the three meals most people eat. Don't go without food for too long. When I get into a hypoglycemic stage, I eat breakfast, a snack at 10, lunch at 1:00, a snack at 4:00, and dinner at 6:00 or 7:00. Such a regimen keeps my sugar levels from ever getting too low. The snacks are NOT sweets, but protein and some fats, such as peanut butter, yogurt, cottage cheese, cheese slices, or slices of meat.

b. Cut your high carbohydrate intake—especially on an empty stomach. You need carbs, but you can get them from vegetables. Fruits are good, too, but they are often high in sugar. Fruit juices are worse for hypoglycemia than the whole fruit, so I have to avoid juice on an empty stomach. One night, I drank three quarts of cranberry juice because my back hurt, and I had read that cranberry juice is good for kidney problems. I didn't have a kidney problem—my back was out of whack. Back then, I didn't know cranberry juice contained so much sugar. In the morning, I was so angry that I couldn't believe it and neither could my wife. I didn't come around until late afternoon, even though I had eaten a good breakfast and lunch. The food had brought my sugar levels back to normal, but not my mood. Had I gotten my sugar levels checked at 10:00 AM, while I was still as ornery as a mule, the doctor would have said, "Nope, it's not hypoglycemia—your levels are normal." Separate sugar levels from the mood, because depression or anger can last far beyond the low sugar levels, as the neurotransmitters and other bodily chemicals haven't adjusted, yet (Pourmotabbed & Kitabchi, 2001). It's not just the sugar level problem, but what your sugar level did to other body chemicals, too.

c. Increase your protein and fats intake. Talk to a nutritionist for help. I get about 50-70 grams of protein a day. Mark, the student who had depressive hypoglycemia, was only getting about 25 grams per day when I analyzed his diet. He upped it to 80 by eating protein at supper (half a chicken), eggs for breakfast, and supplementing with a protein drink. Remember: not everyone can take high levels of protein or fats. Consequently, talk to a healthcare provider who knows you. Nutritionists will help you with a healthy diet plan. Both protein and fats take longer to digest and keep your sugar levels within the proper range. Moderation is the key.

I cannot emphasize enough the need to become a detective. Hardly anyone else will care about you as much as you do. See how these techniques help you discover when and why you become hypoglycemic. See how changing your diet may change your life.

Remember: many other illnesses can cause symptoms of depression, anger, fatigue, and anxiety, so you must be a detective to discern the problem that is affecting you. The other chapters will help you. If you find something that helps you, let me know via my website.

Best wishes in your detective work.

7

Hyperthyroidism

The thyroid is your metabolism gland and hypothyroidism slows down your metabolism. Hyperthyroidism, however, is the opposite of hypothyroidism in that your metabolism speeds up. Like hypothyroidism, hyperthyroidism can cause certain mental illnesses, especially anxiety, as well as depression, bipolar disorder, OCD, and hypomania (Bunevicius, & Prange, 2006). Not all studies, however, report mental problems with hyperthyroidism (Aslan, et al., 2005; Graber, et al., 2005).

In my counseling and psychiatric hospital experience, I had a few hyperthyroid patients who suffered from anxiety, depression, and OCD, and upon treatment, the mental symptoms abated. About 1% of the population suffers from hyperthyroidism; but it affects far more women than men—perhaps 5-10 times more (Bunevicius & Prange, 2006).

Causes: The most common cause is Graves' disease, an autoimmune disorder that affects the thyroid. There are other causes, but Graves' disease accounts for most hyperthyroidism (Leo, Lee, & Braverman, 2016; Bunevicius & Prange, 2006). Your endocrinologist can diagnose the cause.

Mental Symptoms: The mental symptoms often precede the physical symptoms, which leads to a delay in diagnosis (Dowben, et al., 2012). In fact, a person may go years before being diagnosed because health care professionals assume a mental cause for a mental problem. Thus, they miss the physical cause (Oz & Kilicarslan, 2003). Too often the treatment is an antidepressant or anti-anxiety medication which would not be the solution.

With a high metabolism, people often report having trouble concentrating and sleeping, and feeling warm when others don't. More severe mental problems are anxiety (the most common issue), depression, OCD, hypomania, bipolar disorder, and panic disorder (Bunevicius & Prange, 2006; Lee & Hutto, 2008).

Physical Symptoms: Sometimes physical symptoms are similar to the mental symptoms, such as sleep problems, shaking (tremors), and fatigue. Fatigue occurs because the body gets worn out from the excess metabolism. With a higher metabolism, people often lose weight without trying, despite eating far more than normal (Oz & Kilicarslan, 2003). Patients often present with an elevated heart rate (Bunevicius & Prange, 2006). As with hypothyroidism, there are often sexual difficulties with desire, arousal, and orgasm in women (Atis, et al., 2011). You don't have to have all of these symptoms, and many of them are common to other problems, such as hypoglycemia, anemia, etc.

Relation to Other Illnesses: With any thyroid problem, I always had my patients checked for B-12 deficiency and iron deficiency anemia—both of which may occur with hyperthyroidism (Hegazi & Ahmed, 2012). Hyperthyroidism can be confused with Polycystic Ovary Syndrome (PCOS) or pheochromocytoma, but testing will rule out those problems. There is evidence that low levels of vitamin D may play a part, although this is a new line of investigation (Wang, 2015, et al.; Vondra, Starka, & Hampl, 2015).

TESTING:

Physicians often use three tests for diagnosing thyroid problems, T-4 and T-3 (thyroid hormones) and TSH (thyroid stimulating hormone produced by the pituitary). There are, however, many more tests, including tests for Graves' disease. There is controversy regarding what levels of TSH are normal, but the American Association of Clinical Endocrinologists changed the "normal" levels from 0.5 – 5.0 to 0.3 – 3.0. They thought it would lead to better diagnosis, but pressure from doctors resulted in a change back to the 0.5 – 5.0 levels (Shomon, 2016).

Shomon suggests you find a doctor who agrees with the 0.3 - 3.0 levels, as the more sensitive the test, the better chance you have of getting the correct diagnosis. That way you won't have to wait until the problem gets worse and suffer from both mental and physical problems. Go online and put in "hyperthyroidism" and "symptoms" to learn more. Play special attention to the physical symptoms, since they can be more telling.

TREATMENT:

There are various treatments for hyperthyroidism: (1) removing the thyroid or part of it; (2) radiation to kill all or most of it; and (3) medication. See an endocrinologist for the latest treatments.

8

Cushing's

Cushing's disease is a real rascal for two reasons: it causes mild to severe mental problems and it is overlooked far too often. This is partially because many of the symptoms are common to other problems such as depression, weight gain, and fatigue, as well as the fact that many doctors aren't looking for it. Therapists are often not aware of this illness. I'll try to help you recognize Cushing's by listing the symptoms and what you can do if you might have it. If you read much about Cushing's, you'll find three terms used: Cushing's syndrome, Cushing's disease, and hypercortisolism. "Cushing's syndrome" includes all causes of the symptoms listed below, and the cause is sometimes from taking medicinal steroids. "Cushing's disease" has the same symptoms, but it's due to the body producing too much cortisol (a steroid) (Susmeeta & Nieman, 2011).

WHAT ARE THE MOST COMMON MENTAL ILLNESSES CAUSED BY CUSHING'S?

The major mental complications of Cushing's are depression, anxiety, bipolar disorder, and sometimes psychosis (loss of contact with reality), which would fit schizophrenia symptoms. I wonder how many Cushing's patients take antipsychotic medicine because of a missed diagnosis of Cushing's. One person labeled schizophrenic had excess cortisol (Zielaske, et al., 2002); I saw that problem at our hospital. Fortunately, our psychiatrists knew about Cushing's and sent such patients to an endocrinologist. How many missed diagnoses are there because no one is checking for a medical disease? We don't know. Check out Cushing's on YouTube for sad cases—sometimes patients went five years before a correct diagnosis.

Of course, doctors reduce or end steroid use if it causes Cushing's. Fortunately, physicians who prescribe steroids know the side effects and watch for it in their patients. My oncologist said their clinic doctors check for steroid-induced side effects.

If an individual is not taking steroids, but shows Cushing's symptoms, the astute doctor will look for the physical cause. The pituitary gone awry can produce Cushing's. There are several possible causes for a pituitary malfunction, including a blow to the head, fever, or a tumor. Tumors of the pituitary are usually benign (non-cancerous), but they can release the same hormone (ACTH) as the pituitary, itself. This hormone travels through the blood and stimulates the adrenal glands to make cortisol, which may cause Cushing's.

Cushing's can also be due to malfunctioning adrenal glands, which can produce excess cortisol without help from the pituitary. The culprit is often a tumor in this case, as well. About 60% of Cushing's is due to the pituitary, 25% due to the adrenal gland, and the rest due to miscellaneous other causes (e.g., Norman, 2014). Medical journals and websites give different percentages, but the numbers don't matter—getting help does. Researchers are unsure, but it looks like 15-25% of us might have pituitary gland tumors although few pituitary tumors result in Cushing's (Ezzat, et al., 2004). Don't fear; most are benign and harmless and easily treated.

Few doctors or therapists are looking for Cushing's, and a person may suffer from it for years before being diagnosed. If you want to see sad stories, go to YouTube and search "Cushing's disease patients" or "Cushing's advocates."

How common is Cushing's and who gets it?

Many estimates suggest 2-15 people per million suffer from Cushing's, but estimates vary depending on the source. Consider this, however: I live in the Tampa-St. Petersburg metro area, which has a population of around 2.7 million.

Does that mean we have 6-45 Cushing's sufferers in this area? I bet we have more! Furthermore, I'm not the only person who believes estimates are low (Guaraldi, & Salvatori, 2012). When I worked in a psychiatric hospital in a medium-sized city (100,000 people), I saw several Cushing's patients, so I believe it is more common than the medical literature estimates. Remember, however, that physicians seldom look for it, so the number of cases will be small.

Cushing's is sexist: women suffer 3 to 10 times more often than men (Singh, Kotwal, & Menon, 2011). Symptoms such as excess facial and chest hair are more noticeable in women than men. Children can also get Cushing's, but it is less common than in adults (Stratakis, 2012).

A major problem Cushing's patients face is that doctors and therapists aren't looking for it, because it's so rare. Especially with a mild form of Cushing's, doctors will try to solve the symptoms (depression, anxiety, or weight problems) with medication and therapy. If it's Cushing's, however, those approaches will fail in the long run and the Cushing's may get worse. As I've told my patients for the last 40 years, you need to become a detective for your health. No one cares as much about you as you do.

WHAT ARE THE SYMPTOMS OF CUSHING'S?

A major problem is that some Cushing's symptoms are common to other problems as you'll see below. Researchers suggest doctors should check the whole list of symptoms a patient has, so Cushing's doesn't get overlooked (e.g., Friedman, 2010). That's why, as Mr. or Ms. Detective, you need to arm yourself with a list of your symptoms and present it to your doctor. Look at the following symptom list and see if you or a loved one may experience any. You can also Google "Cushing's" and "symptoms" and find more. Make a list of those that apply to you.

I'm listing the mental illnesses first, but pay attention to all the symptoms, since the physical symptoms are more indicative of Cushing's than the psychological ones. Other biological problems cause the same mental problems. I put an asterisk* by the somewhat important ones and double asterisks** by those which I believe are especially important. List all symptoms which will help your doctor make a diagnosis.

Depression: This mental symptom is the most common psychological result of Cushing's. Of course, once depression rolls in, your self-esteem will drop or disappear and family and work relationships can suffer. Doctors and therapists may treat the depression rather than look for Cushing's.

Anxiety: When a person can't think well, worries about weight, and suffers from depression, it's easy to understand why anxiety would rear its ugly head. The cortisol alone can make one anxious, as well.

Manic Depressive Symptoms (Bipolar Disorder): The emotional ups and downs and anger outbursts from Cushing's can make an individual appear bipolar. Unless doctors look for Cushing's symptoms, they treat the unfortunate patient with bipolar meds with little success.

Psychosis*: The patient is out of contact with reality and may experience hallucinations and delusions (false beliefs). A Cushing's sufferer may be diagnosed with schizophrenia, which could result in medication for schizophrenia—not very helpful for the Cushing's sufferer.

Weight Gain:** A common symptom. You can gain weight with Cushing's without changing your diet, and people who want to lose Cushing's-induced weight will have a difficult time doing so. Of course, too many of us weigh more than we should, so a doctor may believe weight is the main presenting issue and try to solve that problem. Being overweight can cause mild depression, as well, so health care workers may overlook the real cause. The doctor should treat the weight problem if you have Cushing's, but not overlook the possibility of Cushing's as a contributor. Weight loss is one treatment that is suggested for Cushing's.

Facial Weight Gain**: This describes a rounded face called "moon face." Comparing old photos with how you look today is the easiest way to catch differences. Since it comes on slowly, neither the individual nor others may notice the change. Check YouTube for "moon face" and "Cushing's" to get a clearer idea of this symptom.

Buffalo Hump**: This is a fatty growth at the top of the back. The hump was noticeable in the patients I've seen. You can Google "buffalo hump" and "Cushing's" and get a good idea of how this looks.

Stretch Marks (Stria)*: These are found in many places: stomach, breasts, legs, back, etc. Unfortunately, patients often overlook this symptom because of weight gain, including pregnancy, both of which can produce stria for many people.

Ruddy Face: The face may appear redder than normal, due to the thinning of the skin and more elevated blood pressure.

Hypertension: Too much cortisol can raise blood pressure levels.

Excess Hair Growth (Hirsutism)*: Cushing's-induced hair growth can result in excessive hair on the face, chest, back, legs, and arms. As you might expect, hair growth is more noticeable in women, since men already have more hair in more places than women. One of my depressive patients didn't mention the hair problem until I asked her if there was anything physical she hadn't mentioned. She reported having to shave her face and arms almost every day. Don't be shy about this—tell you doctor. There are various causes of hirsutism other than Cushing's, but you should discuss any unusual hair growth, whether Cushing's is the culprit or not. Note: medically-induced Cushing's (from steroids) seldom exaggerates hirsutism as much as natural Cushing's (Peppa, Kraniz, & Raptis, 2011).

Hair Loss: Cushing's can cause scalp hair loss in women. It could also be a sign for men, but it's not as clear of a sign, since men lose hair for other reasons.

Legs and Arms are Often Thin*: The thinness contrasts with the weight gain in other areas (abdomen and face); a heavy-set Cushing's sufferer can have slender legs. This is a good symptom to share with the endocrinologist.

Easy Bruising*: A Cushing's sufferer can bruise more than most people due to thinning skin. There are other causes of easy bruising (e.g., alcoholism, excess aspirin consumption, excess Omega-3, and aging).

Muscle Weakness: Cushing's can result in muscle weakness.

Glucose Intolerance: Individuals may have abnormally elevated sugar levels. Cushing's patients often have diabetes, so watch the sugar metabolism. An Oral Glucose Tolerance Test my help suggest a problem.

Since depression, bipolar disorder, anxiety, and schizophrenia can result from Cushing's, you should know the physical symptoms I've listed. If Cushing's causes these mental problems, the mental labels won't apply once you correct the Cushing's. Be sure you list all the signs/symptoms to help the doctor diagnose you.

So, what's the treatment?

The treatment depends on the cause. Testing is necessary and some suggestions are in the medical literature (e.g., Loriaux, 2017)—a specialist will know the latest tests. Sometimes medicine can do the trick; other times, you'll need an operation. Treatment gets very involved, and you must see a specialist for such answers. It would take a short book to explain, so I'm passing the buck to the specialists: endocrinologists and neurologists.

How do I get help?

If you are near a large city, you can find an endocrinologist and a neurologist who specializes in problems of the pituitary and adrenals. Some endocrinologists only specialize in diabetes; others only work with thyroid problems. Be sure the doctor deals with the pituitary and adrenal glands. If you want to find a doctor who specializes in Cushing's, Google "patient advocate" and "Cushing's." There is much information out there with patients and doctors explaining symptoms, causes, and treatment.

As a final thought, not everyone who has an active tumor on the pituitary or the adrenal will have full-blown Cushing's. An individual could have a mild case resulting in depression and weight gain, but no other symptoms. The chance that a doctor will check for a tumor is remote. Many tests for those with mild Cushing's turn up negative, suggesting nothing's wrong (Friedman, et al., 2010). This is a problem, since Cushing's, even within an individual, can vary from time to time, making diagnosis difficult. When the problem is in remission, the person may have mild or no depression and blame the previous depression episode on stress. Mild cases go undetected and researchers warn about this (Giraldi, et al., 2007). Be the best detective for you or your loved ones.

9
Polycystic Ovary Syndrome (PCOS)

Polycystic Ovary Syndrome is a problem for females who have ovarian cysts. Some researchers suggest that one in 15 women suffer from this disorder (Norman, et al., 2007), while others suggest one in five (e.g., Teede, Deeks, & Moran, 2010), and yet others 6-7% (Bargiota & Diamanti-Kandarakis, 2012). Any of these numbers should keep women and doctors on their toes and looking for PCOS—it is the most frequent endocrine problem found in women.

There's no blood test or simple interview to identify a woman who has PCOS. You need to make a list of all of your symptoms and take it to a doctor familiar with this syndrome.

Mental Symptoms. These symptoms are similar to other illnesses and, therefore, don't tell us much.

1. Anxiety (the most common symptom)
2. Depression (common and mentioned by most researchers)
3. Bipolar disorder (Klipstein & Goldberg, 2006; Rassi, et al., 2010)
4. Anger (Balikci,, et al., 2014; Barry, Hardiman, Saxby, & Kuczmierczyk, 2011). Testosterone may be the culprit, but it's hard to know.
5. Low self-esteem (Livadas, S., Chaskout, S., Kandarakit, A.A., Skourletost, G., Economou,, et al., 2011). It's easy to assume that low self-esteem is due to weight gain, but studies show that is not the case; weight is independent of depression (e.g., Dokras, A., 2012).

Physical Symptoms. These are important in suspecting PCOS, since they differentiate from other illnesses more than the mental symptoms do. There is plenty of research on these. Of course, not everyone has all the symptoms, and they are similar to those of Cushing's disease. A doctor can test to discriminate the two. Hyperprolactinemia can also present with similar symptoms.

1. Excess hair growth (hirsutism) including on the face, chest, etc.

2. Hair loss from the scalp, like male pattern baldness.
3. Excess testosterone, which causes the hirsutism.
4. Menstrual problems.
5. Infertility (a reason many women first learn about PCOS).
6. Acne.
7. Weight gain. This might help explain why some women may be more prone to depression than women who don't have weight gain, but it's not the whole explanation. The messed up hormones also play a role. (Barry, et al., 2011; Himelein, & Thatcher, 2006).
8. Type II diabetes relationship due to insulin resistance. Sometimes doctors will prescribe metformin, which is a medication given to Type II diabetics who have insulin resistance. It may also help by lowering testosterone.

I've had several female patients with serious endocrine problems including PCOS. I referred them to a gynecologist; unfortunately, too many times this did not help, which discouraged them and me. Doctors told several of them that missing a period for 4-6 months is normal. After some disappointments, I then referred my patients to an endocrinologist with far better results. Be a detective and find a doctor who understands PCOS to get help. A recent study reported that cases may go undiagnosed for years! (Gibson-Helm, et al., 2016). How sad.

Testing and Treatment PCOS is difficult to treat and testing is complex. A doctor familiar with PCOS is the best way to go for education and help.

Weight loss is one of the most helpful things you can do, along with using metformin (a prescription medication). Metformin is cheap and may help PCOS folks lose weight. If one doctor isn't able to help, keep searching for one who can. Let no one tell you that it's all in your head.

Despite being a short chapter, PCOS is a major problem for women. Despite not being a medical doctor, I was the first to suggest this diagnosis in many patients, so don't let the brevity of this chapter make you think this problem isn't important. Be persistent! Check the following out for great information. Best wishes and don't give up!

http://www.ae-society.org/faq is a good place to check out. If you scroll thru the site, you might find a specialist in your area.

news@ovarian-cysts-pcos.com Give it a serious look and sign up for updates.

10

Iron Deficiency Anemia (IDA)

Iron deficiency anemia (IDA) is more common in women (9-20% and more depending on the study) but only 2% in men; unfortunately, healthcare workers often overlook it.

The most common symptom is fatigue, which occurs with many other medical problems covered in this book. IDA was the most likely cause of fatigue in my counselees, however, and was severe enough to disrupt their lives. I found depression in women with iron deficiency anemia, but this is not as frequent. Also, it was typically mild depression. That is, almost all could work, take care of family, etc. If you're the one, though, it is crucial to know that depression could result (Murray-Kolb, 2011; Stewart, & Hirani, 2012).

I will list IDA symptoms, but these are common to many illnesses, so don't read too much into them. Be aware, however, so you can share them with your healthcare professional.

Here are typical **mental symptoms**: fatigue, depression (*usually* mild), anxiety, confusion, concentration problems, irritability, and a few others.

Here are common **physical symptoms**: fatigue (I label this both as a mental and a physical sign), pale skin, sore tongue, desire to chew ice and crunchy foods (carrots/celery), low blood pressure, ringing in the ears (tinnitus), and brittle nails. Note: lots of people like to chew ice, but anemic sufferers often carry a cup of ice around with them. I've had counselees bring a cup of ice with them to a counseling session and many did not know it was a sign of iron deficiency anemia. I do not understand why ice-chewing relates to IDA, but it is. Get checked if you have a few symptoms—don't overlook IDA if you only have a couple.

Here are common causes of IDA, which might help you identify it before you get a blood test.

1. Too little iron in the diet. This is more common with vegetarians and vegans, because iron is most often found in animal products.

2. Poor absorption of the iron from your diet. Even meat eaters can have this problem as can those taking iron supplements.

3. Blood loss. This is most commonly from menstrual bleeding, but too much aspirin or other blood thinners and giving blood can cause it. If you have low iron levels, a blood bank may not take your blood. Many women first learn they are iron deficient when trying to donate blood.
4. Eating too much fiber. This doesn't affect everyone's iron level, and most people don't get enough fiber, anyway.
5. Crohn's disease or irritable bowel syndrome, since food goes through the system too fast to allow absorption. With these two bowel problems, deficiency in other nutrients is also common (e.g., vitamin B-12).
6. Drinking too much milk (not just two-three glasses a day) or taking too much calcium via supplements.
7. High caffeine intake.
8. Vegetarians may have a problem, because the iron from vegetables is not as absorbable as it is from animal sources (Sharma, & Mathur, 1995).

Remember: these are a few possible causes. There are many more (Goddard, McIntyre, & Scott, 2000)

As I stated earlier, iron deficiency anemia (IDA) is not as significant of a threat for depression as some of the other biological problems in this book. Don't overlook it, though. One study found that women who had low ferritin levels had more depression than women with normal ferritin levels (Shariatpanaahi, et al., 2007). One problem is that doctors may not know of low-grade deficiency causing such serious problems. In such cases, testing wouldn't seem to show IDA. A physician or therapist may say you're fine and explain it as getting older or being under too much stress. We're all getting older, and most of us have stress, so be careful of falling for such explanations.

Ferritin is something with which you should be familiar, since it should be on your blood tests. If it isn't, ask for it. One study found that iron supplementation (iron sulfate) helped women classified as "non-anemic" (Verdon, et al., 2003). Doctors wouldn't suggest supplementation to these patients, because they didn't appear to have IDA. Testing ferritin levels is the best test for checking iron deficiency, so insist on it (Short, & Domagalski, 2013). I asked my patients to bring blood tests with them; many had iron tests, but few had ferritin testing. There are other tests for IDA, as well. Find a **hematologist** who will help you.

Do not overlook the possibility that IDA may cause your fatigue and even depression. I've had patients whose doctors told them they were anemic, but suggested nothing, while a few suggested taking supplements. That lack of treatment is discouraging to me and unhelpful for patients. Fortunately, I could get most of them to doctors who understood the situation and corrected the deficiency.

10: Iron Deficiency Anemia (IDA)

Supplements help many, but I've had patients who failed to absorb them. Google "iron supplements" or talk to a healthcare practitioner about which type iron you should take. Vitamin C helps absorption, and absorption is often worse if you're vitamin-D deficient, so be sure to get your vitamin-D levels checked.

I've had patients who got iron shots. They told me they were painful, but the difference in their lives was incredible. They didn't realize how tired and listless they were until they got the shots, and those shots changed their lives. Some doctors recommend intravenous iron, as well (e.g., Khalafallah, et al., 2012).

Vitamin B12 is often low in diabetics and treatment can be necessary (Kibirige & Mwebaze, 2013). B12 deficiency can cause neuropathy just as diabetes can, so keep this in mind. When one part of the body is failing, there is often another part that's not doing too well, either.

See a specialist—a hematologist—and get the correct treatment. Go to Google and learn all you can about the symptoms, tests, and treatment to help your doctor get you back into the game of life.

11

Viruses, Bacteria, and a Parasite

INTRODUCTION

Researchers have known for many years that viruses cause mental illness (e.g., Menninger, 1926; Barry, 2005, Selton, et al., 2009; Crow, 1978). Most people, including doctors and therapists, have not heard, however, that viruses can cause mental illness like depression, schizophrenia, and anxiety. I used to ask my seminar attendees if they ever heard of viruses causing depression. Few and sometimes none had. True, a virus seldom causes depression, but when it does, that poses problems for the sufferer. Since inflammation has often been considered a problem in depression, it's good to seek the right help rather than just getting antidepressants or talk therapy.

There are many viruses, and the medical profession is discovering more and more viruses that affect our physical and mental status, but some authors say the research is inconclusive (Malhotra, Kaur, & Bhatia, 2012). I've seen virus-induced depression too often in my practice to dismiss it, though. Many researchers believe viral infections such as influenza, hepatitis C, and HIV are possible culprits of anxiety and depression (e.g., van den Pol, 2009) while others cite mood disorders (e.g., Benros, et al., 2013) and schizophrenia (Benros, 2011).

How do viruses cause mental illness? There are many hypotheses, including inflammation; if we get a virus, our brains and other organs get inflamed, leading to dysfunction in various ways (van den Pol, 2009; Schaefer, et al., 2008; Wandinger, et al., 2011). Sometimes, an autoimmune problem could affect our brains (Ramanthan, et al., 2014) just like our immune system can cause hypothyroidism or a B-12 deficiency.

The evidence is clear that viruses affect our mental status. I will relate a few of the more common ones. Some illnesses can cause depression, such as HIV, and will require medical and psychological help.

EPSTEIN-BARR:

Epstein-Barr is a virus that causes several illnesses, and the most common one you've heard about is infectious mononucleosis, the kissing disease—although you can get it without kissing (e.g., sharing a glass). I had mono when I was 52 years old, but I only suffered from fatigue, a common symptom (Petersen, 2006). I fell asleep five-10 times while driving the 50 miles from Tampa to Orlando—no wrecks, though. Other symptoms are fever, swollen glands, and a sore throat. Although not mentioned often, the virus can also cause depression (Wang, 2014; White and Lewis, 1987; Petersen, 2006). Depression is the most common mental problem, although schizophrenia may sometimes appear (Wang, 2011; Dubner, Durant, & Creech, 1989). I've only had a few patients whose depression appeared after mono. You can get tested for mono, like I did; however, about 95% of adults have the virus without symptoms (Saccomano, & Ferrara, 2013). Check the symptoms of mono and get to a doctor with a list of your symptoms.

INFLUENZA:

The flu can cause neurological problems, including depression, schizophrenia, and Parkinson's disease (Manjunatha, et al., 2011), although the evidence is not strong. The flu doesn't always carry mental consequences, so therapists and doctors aren't looking for it. The H1N1 (swine flu) is the most studied flu, and evidence for mental problems dates back years (e.g., Menninger, 1926). Recent studies also support the flu influence (Okusaga, et al., 2011; Borand, 2015).

Know that the flu can cause mental symptoms. If you get the flu and suffer from depression, contact a physician with a specialization in virology or microbiology. Look for a specialist in your area. Taking an anti-depressant may help, but try to get the best treatment for post-flu issues. I did not understand back in 1976 that a virus could cause depression until I heard from folks who had suffered from depression post-flu. Following that, I noticed many patients who had flu-induced depression.

LYME DISEASE:

Lyme disease is not a virus, but a bacterium. Researchers identified that Lyme disease resulted from a tick bite as far back as the early 1920s, but after almost 100 years and thousands of research articles, it is still confusing to diagnose and treat (Hurley & Taber, 2008; Dersch, et al., 2015). In fact, two researchers wrote an article on Lyme disease to help psychiatrists look for it as a possible cause of mental problems (Fallon & Nields, 1994). They point out that it's a tricky rascal and may remain dormant for months and years before affecting the sufferer. One of my students suffered from Lyme disease symptoms (depression) for three years before being diagnosed.

This tick is much more common in the eastern United States than in the western half, although there are cases from all over. Wild animals, such as mice and squirrels, carry the tick; if you go in the woods, you're in tick territory. If you notice a tick on you, take it off and take it to your doctor for identification.

Another problem is that Lyme disease shares many symptoms with other diseases. Typical symptoms are fever, arthritis, skin rash, fatigue, meningitis, nausea, and headaches. The flu has some of those symptoms. Make a list to present to your doctor; testing for it is not simple, but if you can convince a doctor that you were in the woods and had these symptoms, you have a better chance of getting tested.

Psychological symptoms include depression; 26-66% of patients had depression in one study, making it the most common mental symptom. Some people present with anxiety, manic episodes, and if severe, panic attacks and even psychotic episodes (Fallon & Nields, 1994; Garakani & Mitton, 2015; Barr, et al., 1999). Cases of Lyme disease have exploded (Hurley & Taber, 2008), but that could be because doctors are more aware of it.

Since the number of cases is small, the chance of you getting Lyme disease is slim. Again, if you spend time in the woods, live in the eastern United States, and especially if you have evidence of a tick bite—by finding a tick or sporting a red mark you can't explain—get to the doctor. Treatment will improve with time, I'm sure, but as of now, diagnosing is not a simple matter, nor is a treatment (Hurley & Taber, 2008; Dersch, et al., 2015).

Toxoplasmosis:

Toxoplasma gondii is a parasite that can affect humans and cause behaviors and thoughts that mimic schizophrenia, bipolar disorder, and depression (Duffy, et al., 2015; Yolken & Torrey, 2008). Many researchers study the connection between toxoplasmosis and schizophrenia, but bipolar disorder and depression can sometimes cause psychotic behavior (being out of touch with reality), and a psychiatrist or psychologist can discriminate those from schizophrenia. One researcher reported that one-fifth of schizophrenia may result from toxoplasmosis, although the literature is not clear on this (Torrey & Yolken, 2003).

Flu-like symptoms are typical, including fever and muscle soreness, but usually only last a few days (Whiteman, 2014). The parasite goes dormant, but remains in your system (McAuliffe, 2012). Dormant may not be the correct word, because, in some people, it affects the nerves, which may cause the psychiatric problems. Scientists are not sure what is happening, but there is a growing body of research that supports the toxoplasmosis theory of psychological involvement (McCauliffe, 2012). The problem is it causes problems years after the initial attack just as shingles results from the chicken pox virus that people had as a child (Yolken & Torrey, 2008). Thus, the flu-like symptoms help little in diagnosis, since most of us have had the flu. Discovering if you have the parasite requires testing. You must see a specialist for this, and researchers are working on better tests for correct diagnosis (Leweke, et al., 2004; Flegr, et al., 2013; Yolken & Torrey, 2008).

How do we get toxoplasmosis? The most common ways are by eating contaminated vegetables (always wash them), eating undercooked meat, working in the garden, or playing in sandboxes where contaminated soil or cat feces might be present (McCauliffe, 2012; Whiteman, 2014; Yolken & Torrey, 2008). Indoor cats are probably safe, if the cat has always been an inside cat. Those that go outdoors, however, are susceptible to problems. If the cat eats infected mice or other animals, they can bring the disease in with them. Changing the cat litter can be a danger to a human fetus, resulting in abortions and stillbirths, as the parasite can cross the placenta barrier (Torrey & Yolken, 2003).

If you or someone you know is having strange thoughts (e.g., hallucinations, paranoia, or delusions), getting tested might be a step in the right direction. Remember, however, that 30% of the worldwide population has the parasite (Flegr, 2013) and it doesn't always cause problems. You should see someone who specializes in parasitology. I listed the website for the Centers for Disease Control in the reference section.

There is a treatment for toxoplasmosis, but the research is confusing, since not everything works in every study. Researchers are continuing to look for new therapies in anti-microbial drugs (Leweke, et al., 2004; Torrey & Yolken, 2003).

Final Thoughts

Many other illnesses can cause mental problems, such as cytomegalovirus and HIV (Yolken & Torrey, 2008). The good news with those diseases is that patients and doctors look for and treat them based on the patient's history and symptoms. The doctors treat them often with good results, lessening their psychiatric issues. Cytomegalovirus often goes unnoticed, because it has few problems for most folks, even though about 60% of those in developed countries have the virus (Yolken & Torrey, 2008). I won't elaborate on these two illnesses, but the medical and psychological professions often overlook the ones I cover in this chapter.

If you think you might have one of these viruses (e.g., if you had a bad flu or mono), spent time in the woods or fields (Lyme disease), or have an indoor-outdoor cat, you should make the doctor aware of these possibilities. Don't just get an anti-depressant without investigating further—the biological factor is too important to overlook. I've had patients who took an anti-depressant and obtained some relief, but try to find the cause and correct treatment.

12

Pheochromocytoma

Pheochromocytoma is such a rare disease many cases go undetected (Zardawi, 2013). I've only identified one patient with this problem--I hope I didn't miss anyone. It's most often a problem of a tumor on the adrenal glands producing too much adrenalin. It also produces noradrenaline and dopamine. Medical researchers use the term epinephrine instead of adrenaline, but we all know what an adrenaline rush is. The tumor keeps the adrenaline rush constant, rather than just for a few moments like most of us experience when we get excited. For example, you can get excited for a football game, a movie, or when giving a speech. Pheochromocytoma bouts of anxiety may last for an hour, and there doesn't seem to be a psychological cause (Schildkrout, 2014). The symptoms may wax and wane, which would be less noticeable with mild cases.

Mental Symptoms

The most common mental symptoms from pheochromocytoma are anxiety, panic attacks, and depression. Unfortunately, if a person seeks help for anxiety or depression, the patient is more likely to get medication for the mental problems, rather than a test for pheochromocytoma. In one case, a woman suffered with depression and anxiety of 15 years, died, and was diagnosed for the first time during the autopsy. The author also states that physicians don't recognize half of the cases (Zardawl, 2013). Because the healthcare system thinks of psychological causes too often, rather than physical causes, it's no wonder that cases go unrecognized—all the more reason for folks to know their symptoms in order to help the doctor with the correct diagnosis.

Physical Symptoms

As with some of the other illnesses I cover in this book, physical symptoms may be more helpful with getting the right diagnosis than mental symptoms. Nearly everyone with this disease will have a few of the following symptoms: high blood pressure, mild to severe headaches, excess perspiration, shakiness, and elevated sugar levels (Schildkrout, 2014). If a doctor were to check an individual's adrenaline level, they might identify it. One problem with this illness is that there are various levels of seriousness. The person with a severe case is luckier in the sense that doctors will be more likely to identify pheochromocytoma.

Those who have a mild case may suffer from anxiety and mild depression their whole lives.

GETTING HELP

It's a gland problem, so you should see an endocrinologist and, if possible, one who specializes in pheochromocytoma. If you live near a research hospital such as you'll find at many large universities, they might be very helpful. Both blood and urine tests plus others types of tests are available. Correction of this problem often requires the removal of the tumor (Schildkrout, 2014).

I don't want you to get paranoid if you have unexplained anxiety or depression, as it could well have other causes. If you're the one, however, it's important for you to understand this disease. Hyperthyroidism can cause some of the same symptoms, but it is seldom as severe as pheochromocytoma. The tests for hyperthyroidism can distinguish between the two illnesses. See the chapter on PCOS (Polycystic Ovary Syndrome) which shares similar problems, as does Cushing's.

I suggest that you take time and make a list of your symptoms. Also, talk to significant others to see if they think you should be so anxious or depressed. You, as the sufferer, can think you have reasons, but others can often be more objective. Both suggestions can help you be a great detective. Any time anxiety and depression are present, the doctor should check for rare, but important diseases (Zardawi, 2013). Assist the doctor by doing your part with giving a list of your symptoms.

13

Hyperprolactinemia (also prolactinoma)

Hyperprolactinemia is an over-production of prolactin, which is most commonly produced by the pituitary gland. The hormone is best known for milk production. Pituitary tumors are the most common cause; fortunately, most tumors are benign. Research shows that hyperprolactinemia occurs in 9-17% of the female population, so it's not all that uncommon.

MENTAL SYMPTOMS

The most common psychological issues are:

- Anxiety
- Depression

- Fatigue, which occurs with depression and other medical problems
- Anger/hostility
- Psychosis, but this is rare. Medications prescribed for schizophrenia and manic episodes in bipolar disorder may cause an over-production of prolactin (e.g., Höfer, et al., 2010).
- There are research articles citing other mental symptoms of this problem (e.g., Reavley, et al., 1997; Fava, et al., 1981).

Although I was a counselor, I had many patients who had hyperprolactinemia. They came to me because they were experiencing signs of depression, anxiety, or OCD and sometimes more than one. In the initial interview with them, their symptoms pointed to excess prolactin.

Case A: She was experiencing mild depression, but it was bad enough that life wasn't enjoyable. I thought she might have been suffering from prolonged post-partum depression, since her depression began after giving birth. I was wrong in assuming she was breastfeeding. She said, "No, my child is four years old." So, I asked if she was still producing milk. My question shocked her, but she admitted she was and had to wear pads. I told her to go to her doctor and ask for a medication that reduces prolactin (some drugs prove useful). She did, and the depression lifted.

Case B: A woman who just had a baby (three months before) was suffering from severe depression. She was told it was post-partum depression and that it should improve soon, but after waiting for it to clear, she came to see me. I told her she might want to take an anti-depressant (Prozac was popular then). I told her she should quit breastfeeding, since we didn't know if the Prozac might affect the baby in negative ways. She quit breastfeeding, but she couldn't see a doctor for about a month, and in the meantime, the depression cleared. I presume it was due to reduced prolactin once she stopped breastfeeding. Please note that breastfeeding seldom causes depression, although levels rise during breastfeeding to produce milk.

Case C: A woman came to see me after attending my seminar regarding the biological causes of depression. She suffered extreme fatigue and, since fatigue occurs with hyperprolactinemia, I was suspicious that excess prolactin might be the problem (Weitzner, Kanfer, & Booth-Jones 2005). In my interview, I learned that she had been suffering from depression and not just fatigue—depression and fatigue are common bedfellows. She could hold a job, but would come home, make supper, and be in bed at 6:30.

In continued questioning, she said she was still producing milk. A doctor had put her on an anti-depressant, but the milk production had increased, so she stopped taking it. Again, I encouraged her to see a doctor, ask for a checkup, and get an anti-prolactin medication. The doctor said she was fine, except for her prolactin levels, and the drug worked within two weeks. Her depression lasted three years before she attended my seminar. Sad to think she suffered that long from not knowing about the prolactin problem; her doctor didn't check for it until I sent her back to him.

Men and babies can also have hyperprolactinemia, but it's not near as common as it is in women. I've only met one man suffering from this problem, and it was due to medication for treating a heart ailment.

Physical Symptoms

The most common physical symptoms with which you should be familiar are:

1. Galactorrhea. This is the milky discharge referred to above.

2. Lack of or irregular menses. This often points to hyperprolactinemia, but I've been wrong many times in my guessing because there are so many causes of irregularity. Irregular periods are not normal, so something needs to be checked. Excess prolactin is one possible cause.

3. Infertility, which relates to hormones causing lack of or irregular menses.

4. Sexual desire is sometimes lower in both sexes. (LaMarre, A.K., Paterson, L.Q., & Gorzalka, B. B.; 2003).

5. Eye problems, if the tumor gets large, since it messes with the nerves going from the eye to the back of the brain. This is rare, but specialists can treat it with good success.

Treatment is excellent and often simple. Of course, if you don't know the symptoms, you won't be able to help your doctor find the problem. A doctor, after hearing some of the psychological symptoms, could diagnose you with depression or anxiety, but incorrectly assume you need an anti-depressant or an anti-anxiety medication. Don't fall for that. Take note of the symptoms and get to an endocrinologist who specializes in pituitary problems.

An endocrinologist can check you for this issue and will understand the medications for lowering prolactin levels. If you have tumors (remember that most are benign), however, they may want to use a different medication or operate on the pituitary. Review the symptoms above (both psychological and physical) and do a Google search--you don't have to read medical journals to learn what you need to know.

14

Porphyria: High Carbs May Be Good for You!

Porphyria is a blood problem due to a missing gene or genes that allow porphyrins to accumulate. It can cause both mental and physical symptoms. There are genetic tests for this inherited disorder, although most people have the recessive gene and problems never develop. Others suffer from the dominant gene and have the symptoms below. There are sub-types of porphyria, but this list of symptoms includes the most common types, especially acute intermittent porphyria (AIP). Women experience porphyria more than men—perhaps 83% are female and most develop symptoms between 20 and 40 years of age (Cardenas, et al. 2009; Bonkovsky, 2014). It's another sexist illness, although some men have it (Cardenas, 2009).

Porphyria is a rare disease and may only affect 1 in 100,000 people (Cardenas, 2009). Others, however, believe it may be more common (Bonkovsky, 2014). Unfortunately, as with many of the diseases discussed in this book, health workers often overlook it and delay diagnosis, which means the patient may suffer from serious problems (Ellencweig, 2006).

The three most prominent symptoms of porphyria are abdominal pain, neuropathy (pain or numbness in the hands and feet), and mental symptoms (Cardenas, 2009; Ghosh, et al. 2006). Since so many of the symptoms are common to other problems, it's understandable why doctors miss or delay diagnosing porphyria (Nia, 2014). Furthermore, the attacks come and go, which also makes diagnosing difficult. Attacks might last for days or weeks and then retract; the person could be symptom-free for months. It's best to get a diagnosis when you have an attack, since doctors will be more apt to check, then, especially if you provide a list of your symptoms to help in the diagnosis.

Not everyone will have all the symptoms, but keep them in mind. I discovered only one depressive patient with porphyria in all of my years of counseling and never remember any inpatient being diagnosed with it in my 13 years serving in a psychiatric hospital. I hope we didn't miss anyone.

SYMPTOMS OF PORPHYRIA

Mental Symptoms Mental symptoms present in 24-80% of the cases (Ghosh, et al. 2006). These symptoms are not in any order.

1. Depression is rather common (Mercan, et al. 2003; Klobucic,)

2. Anxiety (Bonkovsky, 2005; Cardenas, et al., 2009, Mercan, 2003)

3. Irritability (Cardenas, 2009; Auchincloss, 2001)

4. Psychosis, including paranoia, hallucinations, delusions, and mania (Mercan, 2003) Bonkovsky, 2005; Mehjta, 2010; Ellencweig, 2006; Crimlisk (1997); Cardenas, 2009)

5. Phobias (Nia, 2014)

PHYSICAL SYMPTOMS

1. Pain in the gut is the most common physical symptom with perhaps a 90% incidence (Cardenas, 2009; Mehta, 2010). This symptom is a biggy, but many folks have tummy issues, so a physician might overlook it. Abdominal problems from porphyria can include nausea, vomiting, and a lack of appetite (Klobucic, et al., 2011; Auchincloss, 2001). Frequent vomiting can cause dehydration and result in mineral imbalance due to low sodium, which can be serious. Many patients receive a diagnosis of appendicitis or gall bladder problems because

symptoms are similar (Bonkovsky, 2014). Constipation is another symptom that occurs from abdominal issues (Cardenas, 2009).

2. Hypertension (rapid heartbeat) is common during an attack (Bonkovsky, 2005; Cardenas, 2009). This symptom, like most, is not specific to porphyria (e.g., hyperthyroidism and diabetes).

3. Peripheral neuropathy, which could be numbness or pain in the hands and feet (Cardenas, 2009). Again, this symptom is not unique to porphyria (e.g., B-12 deficiency, nerve conduction issues, or diabetes).

4. Seizures from porphyria are rare, but do occur (Bronkovsky, 2005; Mehta, 2010).

5. Muscle weakness or pain (Mehjta, 2010).

6. Dark urine (purplish) is another physical sign (Cardenas, 2009). You must, however, allow the urine to sit in the sun for the color to show. If it turns dark, you should tell your doctor.

What triggers or makes porphyria more active? These factors are part of the treatment plan for porphyria. Keep track and note if you had a possible flare-up from any. You can avoid some of these.

1. Alcohol, including red wine and whiskey (Crimlisk, 1997; Cardenas, 2009; Mercan, 2003)

2. Barbiturates and anti-convulsants (Marcan, 2003). If you take anti-convulsants, talk to your doctor about one that may not affect porphyria.

3. Prescribed hormones, including estrogen and progesterone (Cardenas, 2009; American Porphyria Foundation)

4. Starvation diets can trigger attacks (Crimlisk, 1997; Bonkovsky 2014). As you see in the treatment recommendations, a high carbohydrate diet is helpful. Diets that limit carbs can be dangerous to the porphyria sufferer.

5. Sun exposure can be a problem for some (Bonkovsky, 2014; Cardenas, 2014; Klobucic, 2011).

6. Menstrual cycles can trigger an attack (Mercan, 2003). Birth control pills can exacerbate symptoms, so it is not a good idea to take them for menstrual problems or as birth control if you have the dominate gene for porphyria.

DIAGNOSING PORPHYRIA

Because of its rarity and symptoms common to other maladies, discovering that someone has porphyria is not a simple matter. One journal article's main thrust was to show how difficult it is to diagnose (Cardenas, 2009). One patient received psychiatric medications for seven years before these doctors discovered porphyria, and she returned to work and lived a normal life. In another study, researchers found patients averaged 15 years before being diagnosed (Bonkovsky, 2014). Many of those patients had had appendectomies or their gall bladders removed. One individual went to the emergency room and then to an internal medicine doctor, suffered a seizure, was referred to neurology and then to the Department of Internal Medicine. Through all of this, she had a seizure and persistent pain. Finally, they made the correct diagnosis (Klobucic, 2011). She had many signs of porphyria—hypertension, nausea, vomiting, extreme muscle pain after sun exposure, and seizure—but many of the typical lab tests proved negative. See how difficult it is to get diagnosed, despite showing symptoms? Make a symptom list for your doctor.

Fortunately, there are many medical tests to help diagnose porphyria. The doctor can check for porphyrins in your urine (Mehjta, 2010), but sometimes those don't appear at the time of the attack (Auchincloss, 2001). Don't give up—there are more diagnostic tools. Check with the American Porphyria Foundation for more.

Treatment for Porphyria There is much you can do. Be sure to understand possible triggers of your attacks and avoid them, if possible. Here are some tips.

1. As mentioned before, a high-carbohydrate diet is helpful (Cardenas, 2009). My patient was pleased that she could eat carbohydrates! Ask your doctor which carbohydrates are good and which aren't, if you have porphyria.

2. Glucose infusions provide help for acute attacks (Crimlisk, 1997). Of course, that fits with the need for high carbohydrates.
3. Hematin infusions are effective (60%) for acute attacks and for avoiding attacks (Bonkovsky, 2014).
4. Go the American Porphyria Foundation website for more on treatments.

It's up to you!

Remember: most medical personnel are not looking for porphyria because it's rare and symptoms are similar to other problems. Be understanding with the medical professionals—you'll just have to help them, and I'm holding you responsible.

The American Porphyria Foundation also provides a list of tests for diagnosing, medications to avoid, and a diet to live by. Don't skip this website (see references)—it's fabulous.

15

And There's More!

If I cited every connection made between physical and mental illnesses, this book could be over a thousand pages. I've covered what I believe are the most significant physical illnesses that escape diagnosis. However, as you might suspect, there are more. Here are a few short summaries of other triggers of mental illnesses. Are these triggers important? They are if you're the one.

Anger. Anger is a major problem that hurts all kinds of relationships, but it's only classified as a mental illness if severe. The American Psychiatric Association' classifies anger as either "oppositional defiant disorder" (children) or "intermittent explosive disorder" when an adult's anger is out of proportion to the circumstances (American Psychiatric Association, 2013). Most of us learned to be angry, e.g., how to react to slow drivers, long lines, a spouse or a child doing something we don't like, etc. We've probably learned to be angry from watching others (parents, friends, and TV/movies). The problem of anger in our society merits its inclusion as a mental illness; if the problem worsens, perhaps it will earn another diagnostic classification. Since we learn most of our anger, therapy/counseling can help us unlearn it. But therapy is not the whole answer if our biological state contributes to that anger.

Certain biological causes make people's tempers worse, but few seem to know about them. This information would require a chapter too long to include in this book. Hence, I wrote a short book on the biology of anger: *Temper, Temper: An Effective Strategy to Conquer Your Anger and Hostility.* It explains biological problems that increase or contribute to anger and violence. As you read in this present book, flu caused my depressive episode, but a different biological problem made me angry. That experience got me researching biologically-induced anger and enabled me to help others who had anger problems. I can't say I enjoyed either my depression or anger, but those experiences allowed me to help others, which turned out for good. As a third problem, I get "migraine with aura" headaches. Contact my website for how I conquered those—I haven't had a migraine since 1992 and have been able to help many with that problem, too. If you or a loved one seems to have too much anger, check out my anger book which is available on Amazon.

Knowing the biological contributors can be a real relationship saver.

Seizures. The problem with seizures is they can be silent—that is, neither the individual affected nor those close by may know the seizure even happened. The person with absent seizures (petit mal) may go years without a diagnosis. So he deals with depression and anger problems while having no idea what caused them. Grand mal seizures cause muscle jerking, and the person may lose consciousness. These seizures are visible, so the individual gets treatment. I've seen only about ten to fifteen patients who presented with depression and anger from seizures, but they experienced incredible relief once diagnosed and treated. Aside from one of them, they all had petit mal seizures unrecognized by family, friends, or doctors.

No one wants to have seizures, so it's understandable that someone would experience anxiety and depression if they have them. The person might wonder: When will the next occur? Should I marry? Should I have children? But, few know that depression, anger, or both can result from a seizure—a biological cause with a mental effect. On the other hand, a person with depression may find that the depression lifts after having a seizure. So, a seizure may make one person depressed and bring another out of depression. Go figure. But people with absent seizures would be denied this insight since they wouldn't know they had a seizure

I write in depth about seizures in my book on anger, since seizures can trigger extreme anger. And if the seizures are causing depression, the correct treatment will help a great deal. An interesting, informative read is *A Remarkable Medicine Has Been Overlooked*, by Jack Dreyfus. The medicine he recommends is Dilantin (phenytoin)—anti-seizure medication. Dreyfus's depression badgered him for years before his doctor prescribed Dilantin. Dreyfus spent thousands on research and offered his book free to physicians. The book covers many other psychological problems that phenytoin helped.

OTHER MEDICAL ILLNESSES ASSOCIATED WITH MENTAL ILLNESSES

In previous chapters, I noted that when a person seeks help for depression, she is usually treated for depression and not tested for a possible medical cause. She may be hypothyroid but receive an anti-depressant rather than get treated for the underlying physical disease. Conversely, patients visit doctors to receive treatment for a medical illness instead of a mental illness and physicians treating these patients often know of the psychological problems that can accompany the physical disease. Thus, they look for and treat the psychological symptoms as well which is great unlike when the patients came to me with depression, and I discovered the physical illness.

Sometimes, depression or other mental problems are the first sign of these diseases (Cosci, Fava, & Sonino, 2015; Hall, et al., 1978);

however, please don't get paranoid. I don't want you to think because you're depressed or anxious that you may have one of these problems. Make sure you consider other symptoms. Sometimes, the depression results from negative thoughts about having one of these diseases. Occasionally, it's due to the chemical changes occurring and is a harbinger of these diseases. I did not discover any of these diseases in patients I saw. Nonetheless, the following information is necessary to know, in case you're the one.

Diabetes. Depression is twice as common in people with diabetes as it is in the general population (Conti, et al., 2017). Whether the chemical changes in the body or the problems associated with diabetes result in depression is a matter of debate. Both could play a part (Mezuk, et al., 2008).

I worked with diabetics suffering from depression, and it's hard to know what caused what. With proper diet and exercise—and often medication—they lost weight and could then limit medication. The depression I saw in patients with both types of diabetes (I and II) was mild and often cleared (in about 75% of the patients) when they lost weight and exercised. Many people with diabetes reported that their fatigue, which is strongly related to depression, also lifted after they lost weight, as did their mood. Again, it's hard to say if their biology (i.e., off-kilter sugar and insulin levels) caused the depression, or if their worries did. I presume getting better control of their sugar levels and the counseling both helped.

I recommend that those with diabetes join a diabetic support group and see a nutritionist and an endocrinologist. Some practitioners don't address depression in diabetes, but therapy and, sometimes, anti-depressants can help (Holt, Groot, & Golden, 2014). The high rate of comorbidity between diabetes and depression should tell practitioners to care for the depression, too.

Hypogonadotropic Hypogonadism (males). I never had a patient in whom I discovered low testosterone causing depression; however, I did have two students share their stories with me. Their doctors found low testosterone and corrected the problem. One student applied testosterone gel to his skin, and the other took shots. Both said they were tired, depressed, and lacked sexual desire before treatment; one also had temper problems. Anxiety often accompanies low testosterone (Aydogan, et al., 2012). Low testosterone is rare for young people but worth checking in case you're the one. Older men suffer from low testosterone more often, and testosterone supplementation has proven helpful in such situations (Jung & Shin, 2016). Although males have more problems with this, females with low testosterone can also present with depression, anxiety, and tiredness; testosterone treatment often helps (Miller, et al., 2009).

Multiple Sclerosis (MS). A high percentage of people with MS experience delayed diagnosis—75% in one study. One reason? The health-care professionals treat them for depression since it was the presenting symptom (Byatt, et al., 2011). Depression is one mental illness that precedes MS, but doctors have reported psychotic episodes, too—again, the problem of misdiagnosis (Carrieri, Montella, & Petracca, 2011).

Depression and anxiety are two early signs of MS, but both have many causes. Thus, it's useful to Google other symptoms. You'll find fatigue is common. Since MS affects the nervous system, numbness, vision issues, and sometimes cognitive problems may be issues as well. These are also signs of many other medical conditions though (e.g., B12 or folate deficiency), so they don't determine an MS diagnosis; only medical tests will do that. Just know the symptoms and get tested. In the beginning stages of MS, the symptoms can wax and wane, and depression, anxiety, and other mental symptoms often occur between the physical ones (Castro & Billick, 2013).

At present, there is no cure for MS, but researchers are developing new medicines; Ocrevus (ocrelizumab and other meds) shows promise in arresting the progression. Anti-depressants, anti-anxiety meds, and psychotherapy can be useful for easing the depression or anxiety that often accompanies the MS. I've known MS patients who smiled through the whole ordeal; others not so much. I advise getting into a support group, therapy, or both. See Ann Romney's book, *In This Together: My story* for great information (2015).

Heart issues. Depression often accompanies heart problems. Sometimes it's psychological, a result of negative thinking. For example: "I know I'm mortal. Life is over. What can I do? What about my spouse? My children?" Such worries can depress one. However, evidence suggests that chemical changes in the body's system can also bring on depression (Trebatická, et al., 2017). Fortunately, doctors now know it's important to treat the depression that accompanies heart issues. Just to be safe, Google symptoms of silent heart attacks and see if you have some of them. It bears repeating: many problems have similar symptoms, so don't get paranoid.

Strokes. Depression after a stroke is common. It's likely that the mental part ("I'm mortal") is the primary cause of depression. But as is the case with heart attacks, the person's physiology often changes due to the stroke, and the brain doesn't work as it should. Both psychotherapy and anti-depressants can be valuable.

Systemic Lupus Erythematosus (SLE). Lupus is an autoimmune problem, and depression and anxiety are common in 50% of people who suffer from it. Of course, some of this depression and anxiety results from worrying about the complications as well, but chemical changes from the body's response to lupus may also cause mental issues. Hence, there are both psychological and biological aspects (Marian, et al., 2010). Some symptoms of lupus are similar to other medical illnesses. Fatigue is common, but skin rashes separate it from the diseases I've covered. Muscle pain and (sometimes) paralysis are present. Google "SLE symptoms" for more common symptoms. Again, I believe most of the mental issues are due to psychological worries rather than the chemical changes.

Normal Pressure Hydrocephalus (NPH). NPH, a medical illness, imitates senility and too often, dementia is the diagnosis. Unfortunately, once a person gets the senility label, the search for a cause often ceases. Vitamin B12 deficiency can also cause dementia, but the most common causes are Alzheimer's and minor strokes. Too often, mental health practitioners overlook NPH. Symptoms of NPH include problems with walking (a critical one), issues with memory and other cognitive functions, and urinary incontinence. It is insidious (progression is slow), so family, friends, doctors, and therapists may attribute the behaviors to old age. Thus, doctors don't diagnose and therefore, don't treat (Factora & Luciano, 2008; Chaudhry, et al., 2007).

NPH is much more widespread than the reported .3% to 3% of the population over 65, due to that senility label. The Hydrocephalus Association believes 700,000 Americans have NPH but fewer than 20% get diagnosed (Hydrocephalus Association, 2017). Too many practitioners aren't looking for it (Nassar & Lippa, 2016). The good news is that most times, the proper treatment can reverse the so-called senility. This is not the case with Alzheimer's. Google the symptoms and go over your list with a neurologist.

Medications. Drugs often have side effects; this is evident from advertisements. Psychological problems are common side effects (MacHale, 2015). The list of side effects is long, and I don't know what you take; check your meds on Google. Don't obsess on side effects—just be aware of them. Two meds I'm taking can lead to cancer. Without them, I'd have been dead and crippled by this time—not in that order.

The number of medical issues that cause or contribute to psychiatric problems could fill many books—and they do. Others I've not discussed include Wilson's disease, Addison's disease, hyperparathyroidism, hypoparathyroidism, Creutzfeldt-Jakob disease, vitamin D deficiency, folate (folic acid) deficiency, gluten sensitivity, tumors (benign or cancerous), and more (e.g., Hall, et al., 1978; Castro & Billick, 2013)!

Remember: the medical community and those working in counseling often overlook the medical causes of and contributors to mental problems. Do your homework; you don't want to miss the correct diagnosis. Best wishes in your hunt for answers.

16

The Mental Health Dilemma

Psychologize:
to speculate in psychological terms or on psychological motivations to explain or interpret in psychological terms

Retrieved from http://www.merriam-webster.com/dictionary/psychologize

Go to Google and put in "psychologize" and see various comments.

THE PSYCHOLOGIZING OF AMERICAN MENTAL HEALTH

I like the word "speculate" in that definition, because much of psychology is speculation. If you Google, "Is psychology a science?" you'll find articles bashing and extolling psychology. I think part of psychology is scientific, but much of it is speculation. Despite my having a Ph.D. in psychology, I'm not sold on much of it, and you can see that others aren't, either.

The movie, *The Snake Pit*, was about a mental hospital patient with therapy based on Freudian theory. It's laughable now, but I bet most folks who watched it the in the 1940s and 1950s believed that the Freudian analysis was correct. Some therapists still follow Freud, but there are many changes in the psychoanalytic approach. Freud presented his ideas and, through persistence, got many people to believe what he said. He also, however, thought a boy at the third stage of development (phallic stage) wanted to kill his father and marry his mother (Oedipus complex).

More important was his view that the unconscious—the unaware part of our personality—rules much of our lives. The problem with scientific psychology is that research has a tough time proving or disproving what Freud said. The reason I went into psychology was that I wanted to help people—or did I sublimate my sexual energy into going to school? I don't know, but I got a Ph.D., which makes me wonder how sexual I might be! Scary. Fortunately, it's unconscious, so I don't know what a bad person I could have been!

That sounds silly, of course, but Freud didn't think so. Here's another example I read in a journal back in the 1970s. A mother was anxious about buying a four-door car. She wanted a four-door, because it makes a family outing much easier. She worried, however, that as they drove, her two-year-old might open a door by mistake,

16: The Mental Health Dilemma

fall out, and get hurt. That was a serious question before child locks became popular.

The therapist said she wanted her son to die. Of course, the mother argued against that (denial, in Freud's view), but the therapist convinced her with this question: "Were you happy when you found out you were pregnant?" She said they'd been hoping to wait another year, and he said her answer proved her desire for her son's death but it was an unconscious desire. Wouldn't that be fun to hear from a therapist? Again, she couldn't disprove his hypothesis. To a simple person like me, however, concern about a child opening the door makes sense, since it happened back in the day and children were hurt and sometimes killed.

Here's another Freudian example. I was a great bed-wetter (please tell no one) and didn't stop until I was about twelve. When I was eleven, my mother asked me if I thought they were good parents. Puzzled by such a question, I said, "Yes, you're great parents." She then said, "I read a magazine article saying the reason children might wet the bed is to express anger toward their parents." At eleven, I thought, "Whoever thought that is a looney." I didn't want to wet the bed—the only kids I could enjoy a sleepover with were other bed-wetters!

On a more somber note, one of my fellow high school students killed her parents when I was 16. There were six psychiatrists involved in the trial. Three who were for the defense stayed at my parents' motel and the other three stayed at our competitor's. On the trial's off-day, my dad asked me to take a psychiatrist fishing. While fishing, he told me that the girl was insane. Furthermore, he said the psychiatrists for the prosecution had it all wrong. How could such learned doctors champion two different viewpoints? Because, that's what psychiatrists thought back then, probably due to Freud's theory. I thought the whole thing was puzzling, but when I got to grad school and learned about Freud, I understood why they could take either side. (For a bit more positive view of psychoanalysis, see Barth, 2010.)

Psychologists make up reasons for why people act as they do. Years ago, many believed that depression resulted from pent-up anger. Anger often occurs with depression, so it made sense; unfortunately, they could never prove that anger caused the depression. Others said depression was due to low self-esteem. It's much more likely; however, that feeling depressed was what ruined their self-esteem, as it did for me when I went through depression.

I've counseled many women whose therapists told them they picked loser men to date because they didn't have good relationships with their fathers. Can that be true? Yes, but there are many reasons for choosing a spouse. I had a young lady crying because her dorm mates said she was only kind to people to win friends. She was a nice person, but they interpreted her behavior from a negative slant.

Years ago, therapists told new mothers that their post-partum depression proved that they didn't want their child. Sweet and comforting, right? Of course, some women don't want a child, but they don't always get depressed. My mother told me that she and my father weren't ready for another child when I came along. My parents had just gone through bankruptcy, Germany was raping Europe, and the Japanese had just bombed Pearl Harbor. Had depression engulfed my mother, it would have made sense. She said she was happy when I appeared. Phew! Fortunately, we now know that factors other than wishing you hadn't had a baby can cause depression.

Another scientific-sounding explanation is stress. It can be a noun (I am under stress), verb (I am stressed), and adjective (my son's illness was a stressful event). Psychologists and magazine articles, however, too often explain mental and physical problems as being due to stress. I once read that stress causes 90% of medical illnesses. No one has ever proven that. More recently, I heard a preacher who was more modest by saying that 50-60% of medical illnesses are due to stress. There's no evidence for such claims, either.

Can you see how easy it is to use stress to explain all kinds of problems? Most of us are under stress. The hypothesis is that it weakens our immune systems and leaves us vulnerable to many problems. I agree that stress can cause problems and exacerbate others, but the explanation is too facile (See Salleh, 2008). Think of how easy it is to say stress causes depression. What about schizophrenia or bipolar disorder? Many of these sufferers have stress immediately before seeking help. Is their deterioration due to stress? Possibly, but consider this: when a person is shifting into a schizophrenic or bipolar episode, the illness can cause difficulties at work, home, and with friends. Thus, the symptoms make for stress, rather than stress causing the episode.

The stress explanation is an important hypothesis for counselors and doctors. It sounds logical, but is way overdone. For example, had I gone to counseling for my depression, the counselor may have helped me reduce stress with various techniques. Of course, after my six-day depressive experience, I was back to happy Dave. I would have assumed the therapist getting me to be less stressed was what had helped. Obviously that was wrong, since I never did go to the therapist, but I might have believed it if I had done so.

Many counselees have shared how learning how to handle stress helped them. I know relieving stress can help all kinds of problems, such as anxiety disorders and some depression. Certainly it's helpful for marriage and parenting issues. I've used de-stressing techniques many times to help counselees, so I'm not against the stress explanation, but we should use it in moderation. What I oppose is the stress explanation when there is something physical causing the issue. If the cause is physical, a person may spend unnecessary money or take medication that doesn't help.

Psychology is full of such explanations, which I can't go into—it'd be another book. (See Dawes, 1994, for an excellent expose of psychology.) The problem is that such explanations may not help

16: The Mental Health Dilemma

at all. You are in the present and need to solve the problem now. Learning when a problem started helps few folks solve a problem.

Psychologists often label behavior, as if that explains it. It is, however, just a label. I'm not against all labels, because they can be shortcuts for treatment, but they must be accurate. If a person suffers from schizophrenia, that gives doctors a clue as to which medication might be best for them. It could also help a therapist determine what talk therapy might help (e.g., cognitive-behavioral therapy, family therapy). The problem is when a person is labeled with schizophrenia when a physical problem is what is causing their thoughts and behaviors. When we discover the medical reasons, we work on those to help reduce or eliminate the schizophrenic problems, at which point we wouldn't say the person was schizophrenic, but that they suffered from a medical illness.

Psychology can be scientific when we can see cause-effect. Psychologists have done well in explaining individual personality traits that might fit one job or another. If you love working with numbers, like to work alone, and are fastidious, you'll enjoy accounting more than someone like me, who is not a detail person and not in love with numbers. Personality testing is not a perfect approach, but it can be helpful. On the other hand, I've had people with personality test results which said they were sociopaths or schizoaffective or had a borderline personality. In those cases, none of those conclusions fit the individuals, and they came to me fearful of what their future might hold with such a label.

Scientific psychology is helpful with IQ testing, but it's not perfect. Similarly, entrance tests are also valuable for college and grad school entrance, but not perfect by any means. Personality tests such as the Minnesota Multiphasic Personality Inventory help diagnose mental problems. They are not perfect, but they are helpful. There are many other tests that are a boon to diagnosing and assisting medical and psychological personnel to aid treatment.

Unfortunately, much research has little relevance to helping others, but is sometimes only to promote a favorite theory or hypothesis. Psychologists also have pressure to cheat on their research. Some get caught, but many do not. Put fabricated psychology research into Google and see what problems they had with cheating. Psychologists are not the only researchers who cheat—other scientists do, too. See http://retractionwatch.com/ for lists of the retractions of faked research.

THE MEDICALIZATION OF MENTAL HEALTH

Years ago, psychiatrists offered to counsel their patients. With better medications, however, which were cheaper than talking to a doctor, the field changed. Most psychiatrists are medication managers and often work with a therapist who does the therapy part. I believe psychiatric medication has been a boon to mental health. In fact, many general practice doctors prescribe these drugs to good effect.

So, what's my problem? Patients receive prescriptions too often for mental problems without considering if there's something biological causing the problem (Diamond, 2002). Thus, if Susan suffers from depression, her doctor is much more likely to prescribe an anti-depressant than look for something medical that is causing the problem. If she has high anxiety, she'll receive anti-anxiety medication. I agree that medications are necessary for many sufferers, but doctors and therapists should also look for the biological contributors I mention in this book. See the chapter on chemical imbalance for more insight.

THE DE-VALUE-ING OF MENTAL HEALTH

Psychology has a history of avoiding the important values of life. I believe there are two main reasons for this:

1. Psychology often tries to be scientific, and science has difficulty fitting values into the science mode. Early psychologists sought to figure out what affects how you perceive visual phenomena, pain, or touch, and a myriad of other body relationships. Values didn't fit the scientific model for years.

2. Psychology grew out of philosophy and religion. Modern psychologists seldom have

religious leanings, and religious teachings became out-of-bounds for the counseling office. After all, we are scientists, not philosophers or theologians. Therapists, however, often push values in counseling, even without a scientific basis. For example, should I put me first? Although therapists often teach that, a scientific approach wouldn't be able to tell that you should live by that maxim. That is a value statement, but is it a good value? It might be in some circumstances, but not in others. In marriage counseling, many counselors encourage each person to praise and do nice things for the other. There is research to back up such statements and I'm all for them, but they are value statements and not scientific ones (see Gottman & Silver, 1999).

Most religions have excellent values that therapists could use in counseling, but therapists often avoid them. I used biblical concepts in counseling, although I didn't quote chapter and verse, unless the person showed that they wanted spiritual counseling. I used the principles and even my atheist counselees appreciated them. Who wouldn't think forgiveness and gratitude wouldn't be helpful for a normal marriage? I've been to psychology conferences, however, and found few practitioners who were interested in values. There has been a recent resurgence in using values to help others, and I find it heartening. One of these major movements is positive psychology. Again, the problem of defining something like happiness is difficult, but the research is promising.

Is Psychology Useful for Mental Health Issues?

I'm not against counseling, which can be very helpful, but I don't believe it will help much with biologically-caused depression or anxiety such as a thyroid or B-12 problem. Likewise, if a person has a broken bone, counseling (except educational) would not help. Of course, if a person suffered from depression—even if due to hypothyroidism—counseling could help to a degree.

A good therapist can help many psychological problems, such as marriage and family, parenting, bereavement, and others (Gottman & Silver, 1999). Biological problems can exacerbate these issues, but psychological therapy can help. Much depression is a mental problem, rather than biological, and determining whether depression is biological or learned is a tough call. Sometimes, it's a little of both. After all, if a person has depression from some illness, one's thinking changes to depressive thinking and makes matters worse.

I have preferences for recommending therapists. The orientation I like best is the cognitive-behavioral therapy (CBT) approach, but, any approach might work well. CBT works on your thinking and your behaviors, which are both critical in making changes. Some therapists use hypnosis with CBT, which can be a quick-change therapy for many. Sometimes we just need a good listening ear.

I'm all for counseling for problems in living. Marriage counseling can be helpful as can working with parenting issues. Much of depression results from irrational thinking and therapy is a boon for such. My main point in this book is to look for biological-induced mental problems which need medical help rather than counseling.

I wish you the best in your search for answers. Feel free to contact me via my website. I answer questions as much as time allows.

References and Further Reading by Chapter

1: WHAT IF YOU'RE THE ONE?

Auchincloss, S. & Pridmore, S. (2001). Vomiting, burns, and irrational behavior. *The Lancet, 358*, December 1. 1870.

Barry, J. M. (2004). *The Great Influenza.* New York: Penguin Books. The numbers of deaths I mentioned in my text vary from one source to another. I've read three books about the pandemic of 1918-19, and this is one of the best. A fabulous read regarding an event of which too many are unaware. The recent "bird flu" scare of the early 21st century opened the eyes of many since it made big news.

Baron, R.J., & Braddock, III. (2016). Knowing what we don't know—improving maintenance of certification. *New England Journal of Medicine, 375,* 2516-2517. DOI: 10.1056/NEJMp1612106.

Bar-Shai, M., Gott, D., & Marmor, S. (2011). Acute psychotic depression as a sole manifestation of vitamin B-12 deficiency. *Psychosomatics: Journal of Consultation and Liaison Psychiatry, 52* (4), 384-386.

Cahalan, Susannah. (2012). *Brain on Fire: My Month of Madness.* New York: Free Press. This book is an incredible look at being diagnosed with "mental illness" when the cause was a rare, physical disease. If you want to see how easy it is to label a person with any variety of mental problems when the cause is physical, this is one great book to read. She will inspire you to look for the physical cause of your problem or that of a loved one.

Castro, J., & Billick, S. (2013). Psychiatric presentations/manifestations of medical illnesses. *Psychiatric Quarterly, 84,* 351-362. DOI: 10.1007/s11126-012-9251-1. The authors cite various cases of labeling a patient with a psychiatric problem. Many weren't diagnosed with the medical illness until months or years later. Think how many patients never get the right diagnosis

Gold, M.S. (1988). *The Good News about Depression.* New York: Bantam. Dr. Gold's book as a great inspiration to me back in the 1980s when I was researching biological causes of mental illness.

Patterson, P.H. (2011). *Infectious Behavior: Brain-Immune Connections in Autism, Schizophrenia, and Depression.* Cambridge, MA: The MIT Press. This book covers immune problems including the 1918 flu outbreak and other infections plus immunization issues. An excellent read.

Taylor, R.L. (2007). *Psychological Masquerade: Distinguishing Psychological from Organic Disorders (3rd ed.).* New York: Springer. Warns the reader that there is no way to know from psychological symptoms if a problem is psychologically caused or physically caused. Covers many of the issues in my book and more.

Schildkrout, B. (2014). *Masquerading Symptoms: Uncovering physical illnesses that present as psychological problems.* Hoboken, NJ: John Wiley & Sons. As I mentioned in the text, the book is meant for professionals; however, it's a great read and the cases she gives point out the problems with looking for a physical cause when a mental label is applied first. I recommend it to medical personnel, therapists, and anyone working in the mental health field.

2: How to Tell If You Have a Biology Problem

Aneshensel, C. S., Frerichs, R. R., & Huba, G. J. (1984). Depression and physical illness: A multiwave, nonrecursive causal model. *Journal of Health and Social Behavior*, 25 (4), 350-371.

Brousseau, Kristin, Arciniegas, David, & Harris, Susie. (2005). *Neuropsychiatric Disease and Treatment, 205*, 1(2). 145-149.

Cosci, Fava, and Sonino (2014). Mood and anxiety disorders as early manisfestations of medical illness: a systematic review. *Psychotherapy and Pschosomatics, 84*, 22-29.

Hall, R.C.W., Popkin, M.K., Devaul, R.A., Faillace, L.A., & Stickney, S.K. (1978) Physical illness presntng as psychiatric disease. *Archives of General Psychiatry, 35*(11) 1315-1320.

Perez-Stable, E. J., Miranda, J., Munoz, R.F., & Ying, Yu-Wen, (1990). Depression in medical outpatients underrecognition and misdiagnosis. *Archives of Internal Medicine. 150* (5), 1083-1088.

Schulberg, H. C., McClelland, M., & J. Burns, B. (1987.). Depression and physical illness: The prevalence, causation, and diagnosis of comorbidity. *Clinical Psychology Review,* 7(2) 145-167.

3: WHAT DOES CHEMICAL IMBALANCE MEAN?

Coupland, C., Hill, T., Morriss, et al. (2016). Antidepressant use and risk of cardiovascular outcomes in people aged 20-64: cohort study using primary care database. *BMJ,352:* I1350. Http://dx.doi.org/101136/bmj.i1350

Dronavalli M., Bhagwat MM., Hamilton, S., Gilles M, Garton-Smith, J., Thompson, SC. (2016). Findings from a clinical audit in regional general practice of management of patients following acute coronary syndrome. *Australian Journal of Primary Health* (Abstract). 2016 Sep 20, 9 pages. DOI: 10.1071/PY15191.

Ioannidis, J.P.A. (2008). Effectiveness of antidepressants: an evidence myth constructed from a thousand randomized trials? *Philosophy, Ethics, and Humanities n Medicine, 3,* 3-14. DOI: 10.1186/1747-5341-3-14.

Liu, H., Luiten, P.G., Eisel, UL., Djongste, MJ., Schoemaker, RG. (2013) Depression after myocardial infarction: TNF-a-induced alterations of the blood-brain barrier and its putative therapeutic implications. (Abstract) *Neuroscience & Biobehavioral*

Reviews, 37, 561-72. DOI: 10.1016/j.neurbiorev.2013.02.004

Pigott, H. E., Leventhal, A.M., Alter, G.S., & Boren, J.J. (2010) Efficacy and effectiveness of antidepressants: Current status of research. *Psychotherapy and Psychosomatics, 79,* 267-279.

4: HYPOTHYROIDISM

hypothyroidmom.com is a wonderful blog. Sign up and read. Great stuff—patients sharing with patients, too.

Bathla, M., Singh, M., & Relan, P. (2016). Prevalence of anxiety and depressive symptoms among patients with hypothyroidism. *Indian Journal of Endocrinology and Metabolism, 20* (4). 468-474. DOI: 10.4103/2230-8210.193476/

Chaker, L., et al., (2016). Thyroid function and risk of type 2 diabetes: a population-based prospective cohort study. *BMC Medicine, 14,* 150ff. DOI 10:1186/s12916-016-0693-4.

Gupta, et al. (2017). Rapid response to loading dose levothyroxine in myxedema psychosis. *Primary Care Companion CNS Disorder, 19* (1), January 12, 2017. https://doi.org/10.4088/PCC.16l01974

Kharrazian, D. (2010). *Why do I Still have Thyroid Symptoms? When my lab tests are normal.* New York: Morgan James. An interesting read—very nutritionally-oriented.

Rubin, Allen L. (2006). *Thyroid for dummies. (2nd Ed.).* Hoboken, NJ: Wiley. Rubin is a well-respected endocrinologist. You'll like his book.

Shomon, Mary J. (2005) *Living well with hypothyroidism (2nd Ed.).* New York: HarperCollins/HarperResource. Mary Shomon's book has probably helped more hypothyroid patients get help than any other book. Great! Excellent website, too. http://www.thyroid-info.com/

Trentini, D., & Shomon, M. (2016). *Your healthy pregnancy with thyroid disease.* Boston: Perseus Books/Ca Capo Press. Your body changes during pregnancy (I presume that's not news), and the thyroid sometimes has issues, too. This book will help you.

Welsh, K.J., & Soldin, S.J. (2016). How reliable are free thyroid and total T_3 hormone assays? *European Society of Endocrinology, 175,* R255-R263. DOI: 10.1530/EJE-16-0193.

Wu, P., (2000) Thyroid disease and diabetes. *Clinical Diabetes, 18,* (1), Winter. Retrieved from http://journal.diabetes.org/clinical-diabetes/v18n12000/pg38.htm

5: Vitamin B-12 Deficiency

Allen, L.H. (2009). How common is vitamin B-12 deficiency? *American Journal of clinical Nutrition, 89 (suppl)*, 693S-396S.

Bar-Shai, M., Gott, G., & Marmor, S. (2011). Acute psychotic depression as a sole manifestation of vitamin B-12 deficiency. *Psychosomatics: Journal of consultation and Liaison Psychiatry, 52*, 384-386.

Berry, N. Sagar, R., & Tripathi. (2003). *Acta Psychiatrica Scandinavica, 108*, 156-159.

Brown, H.E., & Roffman, J.L. (2014). Vitamin supplementation in the treatment of schizophrenia. *CNS Drugs, 28*, 611-22. DOI: 10.1007/s40263-014-172-4.

Campbell, M. (2006). Metformin and risk for vitamin B12 deficiency. Diabetes Self-Management (blog)Retrieved on 1/8/17 from www.diabetesselfmanagement.com/blog/metformin-and-risk-for-vitamin-b12-deficiency/

Castelli, M.C., Friendman, K., Sherry, J., et al. (2012). Comparing the efficacy and tolerability of a new daily oral vitamin B-12 formulation and intermittent intramuscular vitamin B-12 normalizing low cobalamin levels: A randomized open-label, parallel-group study. *Clinical Therapeutics, 33,* 358-371.

Dngelborghs, S., Vloeberghs, E., Maertens, et al. (2004). Correlations between cognitive, behavioral and psychological findings and levels of vitamin B-12 and folate in patients with dementia. *International Journal of Geriatric Psychiatry, 19,* 365-370.

Gariballa, S. & Forster, S. (2007). Effects of dietary supplements on depressive symptoms in older patients: A randomized double-blind placebo-controlled trial. *Clinical Nutrition, 26,* 545-551.

Kale, A., Naphade, N., Sapkale, S., et al (2010). Reduced folic acid, vitamin B-12 and docosahexaenoic acid and increased homocysteine and cortisol in never-medicated schizophrenia patients: Implications for altered one-carbon metabolism. *Psychiatry Research, 175,* 47-53.

Kibirige, D. & Mwebaze, R. (2013). Vitamin B12 deficiency among patients with diabetes mellitus: is routine screening and supplementation justified? *Journal of diabetes & Metabolic Disorders, 12,* 17 (6 pages)

Available on line at http://www.jdmdonline.com/content/12/1/17.

Kocer, B., Engur, S., Ak, F., & Yilmaz, M. (2009). Serum vitamin B12, folate, and homocysteine levels and their association with clinical and electrophysiological parameters in multiple sclerosis. *Journal of clinical Neuroscience, 16,* 399-403.

Lanska, D.J. (2009). Chapter 30: Historical aspects of the major neurological vitamin deficiency disorders: the water-soluble B vitamins. In *Handbook of clinical Neurology, Vol. 95 (3rd series) History of Neurology.* Finger, S., Boller, F., and Tyler, K.L. (Eds), 445-475.

Mansueto, P., Di Stefano, L., D'Alcamo, A., & Carroccio, A. (2012) Multiple sclerosis-like neurological manifestations in a coeliac patient: nothing is as it seems. *BMJ Case Reports,* July 4. DOI: 10.1136/bcr-2012-006392.

Morris, M.S., Selhub, J., & Jacques, P.F. (2012). Vitamin B-12 and folate status in relation to decline in scores on the mini-mental state examination in the Framingham heart study. *Journal of the American Geriatrics Society, 60,* 1357-1357.

Ortuno, J.M. & Cerveera-Enguix. (2003). The patient that changed my practice: A rare case of organic psychosis. *International Journal of Psychiatry in Clinical Practice, 7,* 147-150.

Pacholok, Sally M., & Stuart, Jeffrey J. (2011). Could it be B-12?: An epidemic of misdiagnoses. (2nd Ed.). Fresno: Quill Driver Books. An excellent book that will explain much about B-12 which I couldn't cover in this short chapter. Read the reviews on Amazon. It's an eye-opener and not just for mental problems—it covers about everything a book could regarding vitamin B-12. At $14.95, it's a steal. I was thinking of writing a book about B-12 until I read theirs.

Pawlak, R., Parrott, S.J., Raj, S., Cullum-dugan, D., & Lucus, D. How prevalent is vitamin B(12) deficiency among vegetarians? *Nutrition Review, 71,* (2), 110-117.

Prodan, C.I., Cowan, L.D., Stoner, J.A., & Ross, E.D. (2009). Cumulative incidence of vitamin B12 deficiency in patients with Alzheimer disease. *Journal of the Neurological Sciences, 2814,* 133-148.

Reynolds, E. (2006). Vitamin B12, folic acid, and the nervous system. *Lancet Neurology, 5,*

949-60. Available at http://neurology.thelancet.com.

Robinson, D.J., O'Luanaigh, C., Tehee, E., et al., (2011). Associations between holotranscobalamin, vitamin B12, homocysteine and depressive symptoms in community-dwelling elders. *International Journal of Geriatric Psychiatry, 26,* 307-313.

Sahoo, M.K., Avasthi, A., & Singh, P. (2011). Negative symptoms presenting as neuropsychiatric manifestation of vitamin B12 deficiency. *Indian Journal of Psychiatry, 53,* (4), 370-371.

Schildkrout, B. (2014). *Masquerading Symptoms: Uncovering physical illnesses that present as psychological problems.* Hoboken, NJ: John Wiley & Sons.

Solomon, L.R., (2007). Disorders of cobalamin (vitamin B12) metabolism: Emerging concepts in pathophysiology, diagnosis and treatment. *Blood Reviews, 21,* 113-130.

Spiegel, D.R., & West, S. (2008). Successful treatment of megaloblastic mania with cobalamin in a patient with pernicious anemia. *Clinical Schizophrenia & Related Psychoses, 2,* 155-157. DOI: 10.3371/CSRP.2.2.5.

Torrey, E. Fuller. (2013). *Surviving Schizophrenia: A Family Manual (6th ed.).* New York: HarperCollins. Torrey's sister suffers from schizophrenia; hence, I presume his interest in the subject. I suggest this book for families to help them understand this dread disease. Torrey uses the term 'schizophrenias' since there are so many causes—it's not just a simple disease. Heredity is major contributor, but there are other causes (e.g., influenza, mumps). Torrey, understandably, has some harsh critics in the mental health arena because too many psychologists and psychiatrist want to explain schizophrenia as a learned behavior from harsh parenting or other trauma. There are a few such cases, but the biological factor plays heavy in causation. We're still in the infancy of understanding causes and treatments despite the steps made in the past fifty years.

6: HYPOGLYCEMIA

Hofeldt, F.D. (1989). Reactive hypoglycemia. *Endocrinology Metabolism Clinics of North America, 18* (1), 185-201.

Hunt, L.M. (1985). Relativism in the diagnosis of hypoglycemia. *Social Science and Medicine, 20,* (1), 1289-1294. DOI: 10.1016/0277-9536(85)90383-1

Johnson, D.D., Door, K.E., Swenson, W.M., & Service, J. (1980). Reactive hypoglycemia. *JAMA, 243,* 1151-1155.

Leichter, S.B. (1979). Alimentary hypoglycemia: a new appraisal. *American Journal of Clinical Nutrition, 32,* 2104-2114.

Messer, S.C., Morris, T.L., & Gross, A.M. (1990). Hypoglycemia and psychopathology: A methodological review. *Clinical Psychology Review, 10,* 631-648.

Peroutka, S.J. (2002). Serum glucose regulation and headache. *Headache, 42,* 303-308.

Pourmotabbed, G., & Kitabchi, A.D. (2001). Hypoglycemia. *Obstetrics & Gynecology Clinics of North America, 28,* 383-400.

Ritholz, M.D., & Jacobson, A.M. (1998). Living with hypoglycemia. *Journal of General Internal Medicine, 13,* 799-804.

Salzer, H. M. (1966). Relative hypoglycemia as a cause of neuropsychiatric illness, *Journal of the National Medical Association, 58,* (1), 12-17.

Skaer, D.H. (2017). Temper, Temper: An Effective Strategy to Conquer your Anger and Hostility. Amazon.

Yager, J., & Young, R.T. (1974). Non-hypoglycemia is an epidemic condition. *New England Journal of Medicine, 291,* 907-908.

Wilson, V. (2011). Non-diabetic hypoglycaemia: causes and pathophysiology. *Nursing Standard, 25,* (46), 35-39. https://doi.org/10.7748/ns2011.07.25.46.35.c8637

7: HYPERTHYROIDISM

Aslan, S., Ersoy, R., Kuroglu, A.C., et al. (2005). Psychiatric symptoms and diagnoses in thyroid disorders: a cross-sectional study. *International Journal of Psychiatry in Clinical Practice. 9,* (3), 187-192. DOI:1080/13651500510029129.

Atis, G., Dalkilinc, A., Altunatas, Y., et al. (2011). Hyperthyroidism: A risk factor for female sexual dysfunction. *Journal of Sexual Medicine.8,* 2327-2333. DOI: 10,1111.H,1743-6109.2011.02354.

Bunevicius, R., & Prange, A.J. Jr. (2006). Psychiatric manifestations of Graves' hyperthyroidism. *CNS Drugs, 10* (11), 897-909.

Dowben, J.S., Steele, D., Froelich, K.D., et al. (2012). Biological perspectives: Remember the thyroid. *Perspectives in Psychiatric Care. 48,* 65-69.

Grabe, H.J., Volzke, H., Ludemann, J., et al. (2005). Mental and physical complaints in thyroid disorders in the general population. *Acta Psychiatrica Scandinavica, 112*, 286-293.

Hegazi, M.O., & Ahmed, S. (2012). Atypical clinical manifestations of Graves' Disease: An analysis in depth. *Journal of Thyroid Research, 2012,* Article ID 768019. DOI:10.1155/2012/768019.

Hu, L-H., Shen, C-C., Hu, YW., et al. (2013). Hyperthyrodism and risk for bipolar disorders: A nationwide population-based study. *PLOS ONE, 8,* (8), e73057.

Iglesias, P., devora, O., Garcia, J., et al. (2010). *Clinical Endocrinology, 72,* 551-557. DOI: 10.1111/J.1365-2265.2009.03682.x

Lee, C.S-N, & Hutto, B. (2008). Recognizing thyrotoxicosis in a patient with bipolar mania: a case report. *Annals of General Psychiatry, 7,* 3ff.

Hyperthyroidism (n.d.). American Thyroid Association. retrieved from http://www.thyroid.org/wp-content/uploads/patients/brochures/ata-hyperthyroidism-brochure.pdf

Leo, S.D., Lee, S.Y., & Braverman, L.E. Hyperthyroidism. *Lancet, August 27, 388*, (10047) 906-918. DOI: 10.1016/SO140-6736 (16) 00278-6.

Nath, J., & Sugar, R. (2001). Late-onset bipolar disorder due to hyperthyroidism. *Acta Psychiatrica Scandinavica, 104*, 72-75.

Oz, S.G., & Kilcarslan, A. (2003). Subclinical hyperthyroidism. *Journal of Ankara Medical School, 25,* (4), 191-198.

Shomon, M. (2016). "When Endocrinologists Briefly Narrowed the TSH Reference Range" retrieved from https://www.verywell.com/tsh-thyroid-stimulating-hormone-reference-range-wars-3232912 Go check Shomon's article explain the whys and wherefores of the argument. She suggests finding a doctor who is more open-minded about change. Excellent article as is her website.

Vondra, K., Starka, L., & Hampl, R. (2015). Vitamin D and thyroid diseases. *Physiological Research, 64,* (Suppl. 2). S95-S100.

Wang, J., Lv, S., Chen, G., et al. (2015). Meta-analysis of the association between Vitamin D and autoimmune thyroid disease. *Nutrients, 7,* 2485-2498. DOI: 10.3390/nu7042485.

8: Cushing's Syndrome

Ammini A.C. Tandon, N., Gupta, N., Bhalla, A.S., Davensapathy, K. et al. (2014). Etiology and clinical profile of patients with Cushing's syndrome: A single center experience. *Indian Journal of Endocrinology and Metabolism, 18,* (1), 99-105.

Blevins, L.S., Jr. (2014). *Pituitary patient resource guide (6th Ed.).* Thousand Oaks, CA: Pituitary Network. This has a wealth of information about everything pituitary. Some of it is a bit technical—actually, a lot is. Reasonably priced.

Ezzat, S., Asa, S., Couldwell, W.T., Barr, C.E., Dodge, W.D., Vance. M.L., & McCutcheon, I.E. (2004). The prevalence of pituitary adenomas: A systematic review. *Cancer 101,* (3), 613-619.

Feelders, R.A., Pulgar, S.J., Kempel, A., & Pereira, A.M. (2012). The burden of Cushing's disease: clinical and health-related quality of life aspects. *European Journal of Endocrinology, 167,* 311-326.

Friedman, T.C., Ghods, D.E., Shahinian, H.K., Zachery, L., Shayesteh, N. Seasholta, S., Zuckerbraun, E., Lee, M.L., & McCutcheon, I.E. High prevalence of normal tests assessing hypercortisolism in subjects with mild and episodic Cushing's syndrome suggests that the paradigm for diagnosis and exclusion of Cushing's syndrome requires multiple testing., *Hormone and Metabolic Research Journal, 42*, 874-881.

Gadelha, M.R., &U Neto, L. V. (2014). Efficacy of medical treatment in Cushing's disease: a systematic review. *Clinical Endocrinology, 80,* 1-12.

Giraldi, F.P., Pivonello, R., Ambrogio, A. G., De Martino, M.C., De Martin, M., et al. (2007). The dexamethasone-suppressed corticotropin-releasing hormone stimulation test and the desmopressin test to distinguish Cushing's syndrome from pseudo-Cushing's states. *Clinical Endocrinology, 66,* 251-257.

Guaraldi, F., & Salvatori, R. (2012). Cushings syndrome: Maybe not so uncommon of an endocrine disease. *Journal American Board of Family Medicine, 25,* 199-208.

Millian, M., Teufel, P., Honegger, J., Gallwitz, B. Schnaudert, G., & Psaras, T. (2012). The development of the Tuebingen Cushing's disease quality of life inventory (Tuebingen CD-25). Part II: normative data from 1784 healthy people. *Clinical Endocrinology, 76,* 861-867. Doi: 10.1111/j.1365-2265.2011.04280.x

Nieman, L.K., Biller, B.M.K., Findling, J. W., Newell-Price, J., Savage, M.O., Stewart, P.M., & Montori, V.M. (2008). The Diagnosis of Cushing 's syndrome: An Endocrine Society Clinical Practice Guideline. *Journal of Clinical Endocrinology & Metabolism,* 93, 5, 1526 –1540. (As of this writing, the article is available on Google.)

Norman, J. (2014). Diseases of the Adrenal Cortex: Cushing's Syndrome. Retrieved from http://www.endocrineweb.com/conditions/cushings-syndrome/diseases-adrenal-cortex-cushings-syndrome on July 19, 2015.

Peppa, M., Kraniz, M., & Raptis, S.A. (2011). Hypertension and other morbidities with Cushing's syndrome associated with corticosteroids: a review. *Integrated Blood Pressure Control, 4.* 7-16.

Sharma, S.T. Nieman, L.K., Feelders, R.A. (2015). Comorbidities in Cushing's disease. *Pituitary, 18,* 188-194. DOI 10.1007/s11102-015-0645-6.

Singh, Y., Kotwal, N., & Menon, A.S. (2011). Endocrine hypertension—Cushing's syndrome. *Indian Journal of Endocrinology Metabolism, 15* (Supple4), S313-S316.

Sonino, N., & Fava, G. (19198). Psychological aspects of endocrine disease. *Clinical Endocrinology, 49,* 1-7.

Stratakis, C. A. (2012). Cushing syndrome in pediatrics. *Endocrinology Metabolism Clinics of North America, 41* (4), 793-803.

Susmeeta T. S., & Nieman, L. K. (2011) Cushing's syndrome: All variants, detection, and treatment. *Endocrinology Metabolism Clinics of North America, 40* (2): 379–391. doi:10.1016/j.ecl.2011.01.006.

Tang, A., O'Sullivan, A.J., Diamond, T., Gerard, A., & Campbell. (2013). Psychiatric symptoms as a clinical presentation of Cushing's syndrome. *Annals of General Psychiatry. 12,* 23. Retrieved from http://www.annals-general-psychiatry.com/content/12/1/23.

Wolkowitz, O.M., Burke, H., Espel, E.S., & Reus, V.I. (2009). Glucocorticoids and mood. *Annals of New York Academy of Science, 1179,* 19-40. Doi: 10.1111/j.1749-6632.2009.04980.x

Zielaske, J., Bender, G., Schlesinger, S., Friedl, P., Kenn, W., Allolio, B., & Lauer, M. (2002). A woman who gained weight and became schizophrenic. *The LANCET, 360,* November 2, 2002.

9: Polycystic Ovary Syndrome

Balikci, A., Erdem, M., Keskin, U., Bozkurt Zincir, S., G ulsun, M. et al. (2014). Depression, anxiety, and anger in patients with polycystic ovary syndrome. *Archives of Neuropsychiatry, 51,* 328-333.

Bargiota, A., & Diamanti-Kandarakis, E. (2012). The effects of old, new and emerging medicines on metabolic aberrations in PCOS. *Therapeutic Advances in Endocrinology and Metabolism, 3* (1), 27-47. DOI: 10.1177/2042018812437355.

Barry, J.A., Hardiman, P.J., Saxby, B. K., & Kuczmierczyk, A. (2010). Testosterone and mood dysfunction in women with polycystic ovarian syndrome compared to subfertile controls. *Journal of Psychosomatic Obstetrics & Gynecology, 32* (2), 104-111.

Dokras, A. (2012). Mood and anxiety disorders in women with PCOS, *Steroids, 77,* 338-341.

Gibson-Helm M, Teede, H., Dunaif, A., Anuja Dokraset, A. (2017). Delayed diagnosis and a lack of information associated with dissatisfaction in women with polycystic ovary syndrome. *Journal of Clinical Endocrinology and Metabolism, 102 (2),* 604-612.

Himelein, M.J., & Thatcher, S.S. (2006). Depression and body image among women with polycystic ovary syndrome. *Journal of Health Psychology, 11,* 613-625.

Kerchner, A. (2009). Risk of depression and other mental health disorders in women with polycystic ovary syndrome: a longitudinal study. *Fertility and Sterility, 91* (1). 207-212.

Klipstein, K.G., & Goldberg, J.F. (2006). Screening for bipolar disorder in women with polycystic ovary syndrome: A pilot study. *Journal of Affective Disorders, 91,* 205-209.

Livadas, S., Chaskout, S., Kandarakit, A.A., Skourletost, G., Economou, F., et. Al., (2011). Anxiety is associated with hormonal and metabolic profile in women with polycystic ovarian syndrome. *Clinical Endocrinololgy, 75,* 698-703.

Mansson, M., Holte, J.,Lndin-Wilhelmsen, K, Dahgren, E., Johansson, A., & Landen, M. (2008). Women with polycystic ovary syndrome are often depressed or anxious—A case control study. *Psychoneuroendocrinology, 33,* 1132-1138.

Norman, R. J., Dewailly, D., Legro, R.S., & Hickey, T. E. (2007). Polycystic ovary syndrome. *The Lancet, 370,* August 25. 685-697.

Rasgon, N.L., Rao, R.C., Hwang, S., Altshuler, L.L., Elman, S., et al. (2003). Depression in women with polycystic ovary syndrome: clinical and biochemical correlates. *Journal of Affective Disorders, 74*, 299-304.

Rassi, A., Veras, A.B., dos Reis, M., Pastore, D.L., Bruno, L. M., et al, Prevalence of psychiatric disorders in patients with polycystic ovary syndrome. *Comprehensive Psychiatry, 51*, 599-602.

Teede, H., Deekds, A., & Moran, L. (2010). Polycystic ovary syndrome: a complex condition with psychological, reproductive and metabolic manifestations that impacts on health across the lifespan. *BMC Medicine, 8*, 41-50.

10: Iron Deficiency Anemia

Goddard, A.F., McIntyre, A.S., & Scott, B.B. (2000). Guidelines for the management of iron deficiency anaemia, *Gut, 46 (Supple IV)*, iv1-iv5.

Khalafallah, A.A., Dennis, A.E., Ogden, Kath, et al, (2012). Three-year follow-up of a randomized clinical trial of intravenous versus oral iron for anaemia in pregnancy. *BMJ Open* 2:e000998. Doi:10.1136/bmjopen-2012-000998.

Kilbirige, D., & Mwebaze, R., (2013). Vitamin B12 deficiency among patients with diabetes mellitus: is routine screening and supplementation justified? *Journal of Diabetes & Metabolic Disorders, 12*, 17-22.

Murray-Kolb, L.E. (2011). Iron status and neuropsychological consequences in women of reproductive age: What do we know and where are we headed? *The Journal of Nutrition, 141* (4), 747S-755S. doi:10.3945/jn.110.130658.

Shariatpanaahi, M. V., Shariatpanaahi, Z. V. Moshtaaghi, M., Shahbaazi, S.H., & Abadi, A. (2007). "The relationship between depression and serum ferritin level," *European Journal of Clinical Nutrition, 61*, 532-535.

Sharma, D.C., & Mathur, R. (1995). *Indian Journal Physiological Pharmacology, 39*(4), 403-406.

Short, M.W., & Domagalski, J. E. (2013). Iron deficiency anemia: Evaluation and management. *American Family Physician, 82* (2), 98-104. Iron supplementation for unexplained fatigue in non-anaemic women: double blind randomized placebo controlled trial. *British Medical Journal, 326*, May 24, 1-4)

Stewart, R. & Hirani, V., (2012). Relationship between depressive symptoms, anemia, and iron status in older residents from a national survey population. *Psychosomatic Medicine, 74* (2), 208-13. Doi: 10.1097/PSY.Ob013e3182414f7d. Epub2

Verdon, F., Burnand, B., Fallabu Stubi, C-L, Bonard, C., Graff, M., Michaud, A., Bischoff, T., de Vevey, M., Studer, J-P., Herzig, L., Chapuis, C., Tissot, J. Pecoud, A., & Favrat, B. (2003). Iron supplementation for unexplained fatigue in non-anaemic women: double blind randomized placebo controlled trial. *British Medical Journal, 326,* May 24, 1-4.

11: Viruses, Bacteria, & a Parasite

Here are a few websites with information about some of what's covered in this chapter. You can check the Internet for websites and blogs that have a ton of information on any subject covered herein.

http://www.aldf.com/ This is the American Lyme Disease Foundation. Check out the website for helpful information.

http://www.cdc.gov/parasites/toxoplasmosis/gen_info/faqs.html

https://microbewiki.kenyon.edu/index.php/Borna_Disease_Virus_(Human)

Barr, W.B., Rastogi, R., Ravdin, L., & Hilton, E. (1999). Relations among indexes of memory disturbance and depression in patients with Lyme Borreliosis. *Applied Neuropsychology, 6*(1), 12-18.

Barry, J.M. (2004). *Influenza: The epic story of the deadliest plague in history.* Penguin Group: New York. If you don't know about this plague that killed 60-100 million people worldwide back in 1918-19, you should read this book.

Benros, M.E., Nielsen, P.R., Nordentoft, M, et al. (2011). Autoimmune diseases and severe infections as risk factors for schizophrenia: A 30-year population-based register study. *American Journal of Psychiatry, 168,* 1303-1310.

Benros, M.E., Waltoft, B. L., Nordentoft, M., et al. (2013). Autoimmune diseases and severe infections as risk factors for mood disorders: A nationwide Study. *JAMA Psychiatry, 70,* (8), 812-820. DOI: 10.1001/jamapsychiatry.2013.1111.

Bornand, D., Toovey, S., Jick, S.S., & Meier, C.R. The risk of new onset depression in association with influenza—A population-based observational study. *Brain, Behavior, and Immunity, 53,* 131-137. DOI: 10.1016/j.bbi.2015.12.005.

Coughlin, S.S. (2012). Anxiety and depression: Linkages with viral diseases. *Public Health Review, 34,* 2, 13 pages. Retrieved from https://www.ncbi.nlm.nih.gov/pmc/articles/PMC4175921/pdf/nihms407997.pdf

Crow, T.J. (1978). Viral causes of psychiatric disease. *Postgraduate Medical Journal, 54,* 763-767.

Dorsch, R., Freitag, M.H., Schmidt, S., et al. (2015). Efficacy and safety of pharmacological treatments for acute Lyme neuroborreliosis—a systematic review. *European Journal of Neurology, 22,* 1249-1259.

Dubner, N.P., Durant, D.L., & Creech, F.R. (1989). Epstein-Barr antibodies in three psychiatric syndromes. *Psychiatric Hospital, 20* (4), 167-170.

Duffy, A.R., Beckie, T.M., Brenner, L.A., et al. (2015). Relationship between toxoplasma gondii and mood disturbance in women veterans. *Military Medicine, 180,* (6). 621-625. DOI: 10.7205/MILMED-D-14-00488.

Fallon, B.A., & Nields, J.A. Lyme disease: a neuropsychiatric illness. *American Journal of Psychiatry, 151,* 1571-1583.

Flegr, J. (2013). How and why Toxoplasma makes us crazy. *Trends in Parasitology, 29,* (4), 156-163. DOI: 10:1-16/j.pt.2013.01.007

Garakani, A., & Mitton, A.G. (2015). New-onset panic, depression with suicidal thoughts, and somatic symptoms in a patient with a history of Lyme disease. *Case Reports in Psychiatry,* 2015, Article ID 457947, 4 pages. Retrieved from http://dx.doi.org/10.1155/2015/45794.

Holub, E., Flegr, J., Dragomirecka, E., te al. (2013). Differences in onset of disease and severity of psychopathology between toxoplasmosis-related and toxoplasmosis-unrelated schizophrenia. *Acta Psychiatrica Scandinavica, 127,* 227-238. DOI: 10.1111/acps.12031.

Hurley, R.A., & Taber, K.H. (2008) Acute and chronic Lyme disease: controversies for neuropsychiatry. *The Journal of Neuropsychiatry and Clinical Neurosciences. 20,* (1), iv-6. Retrieved from http://dx.doi.org/10.org/10.1176/jnp2008.20.1.iv

Leweke, E.M., Gerth, C. W., Koethe, D., et al. (2004).Antibodies to iknfectious agents in individuals with recent onset schizophrenia. *European Archives of Psychiatry and Clinical Neurosciences, 254,* 4-8. DOI: 10.1007/s00406-004-0481-6.

McAuliffe, K. (2012). How your cat is making you crazy. *The Atlantic,* March 2013, 36-44.

Malhotra, S., Kaur, N., Kumar, P., et al. (2012). Viral infections and depression. Delhi Psychiatry Journal, 15 (1), 188-194.

Manjunatha, N., Bath, S. B., Kulkarni, G. B, & Chaturvedi, S.K. (2011). The neuropsychiatric aspects of influenza/swine flu: A selective review. *Indian Psychiatry Journal, 20,* 83-90. DOI: 10.4103/0972-6748.102479.

Menninger, K.A. (2006, reprint). An analysis of post-influenzal "Dementia Precox," as of 1918, and five years later. *American Journal of Psychiatry.* Retrieved from http://dx.doi.org/10.1176/ajp.82.4.469. This article was first published in the journal in volume 82, Issue 4, April 1926, 469-529. This was post influenza of 1918 and Dementia Precox was the term for schizophrenia back then.

Okusaga, O., Yolken, R.H., Langenberg, P., et al. (2011). Association of seropositivity for influenza and coronaviruses with history of mood disorders and suicide attempts.

Journal of Affective Disorders, 130, 220-225. DOI: 10.1016/j.jad.2010.09.029.

Petersen, I., Thomas, J.M., Hamilton, W.T., & White, P.D. (2006). Risk and predictors of fatigue after infectious mononucleosis in a large primary-car cohort. *Quarterly Journal of Medicine, 99,* 49-55.

Ramanathan, S., Mohammad, S.S., Brilot, F., & Dale, R.C. (2014). Autoimmune encephalitis: Recent updates and emerging challenges. *Journal of Clinical Neuroscience, 21,* 722-730.

Saccomano, S.J., & Ferrara, L. R. (2013, June). Infectious mononucleosis. *Clinician Reviews, 23,* 42-49.

Schaefer, S., Boegershausen, N., Meyer, S., et al. (2008). Hypothalamic-pituitary insufficiency following infectious diseases of the central nervous system. *European Journal of Endocrinology, 158,* 3-9.

Selton, J-P, Frissen, Lensvelt-Mulders, G., & Morgan, V.A. (2009). Schizophrenia and the 1957 pandemic of influenza: Meta-analysis. *Schizophrenia Bulletin, 36* (2), 219-228. DOI: 10.1093/schbul/sbp147 Downloaded from http://schizophreniabulletin.oxford-journals.org/content/36/2/219

Torrey, E. F., & Yolken, R. H. (2003). Toxoplasma gondii and Schizophrenia. *Emerging Infectious Diseases, 9* (11), 1375-1380. Retrieved from https://dx.doi.org/10.3201/eid0911.030143.

Wang, H., Yolken, R.H., Hoekstra, P.J., et al. (2011). Antibodies to infectious agents and the positive symptom dimension of subclinical psychosis: The TRAILS study. *Schizophrenia Research, 129,* 47-51.

Wandinger, K-P, Saschenbrecker, S., Stoecker, W., & Dalmau, J. (2011). Anti-NMDA-receptor encephalitis: A severe, multistage, treatable disorder presenting with psychosis. *Journal of Neuroimmunlogy, 231,* 86-91.

Van den Pol, A.N. (2009). Viral infection leading to brain dysfunction: more prevalent than appreciated? *Neuron, 64,* (1), 17-20. DOI: 10.1016/j.neuron.09.023.

Wang, X., Zahang, L., Lei, Y, et al. (2014). Meta-analysis of infectious agents and depression. *Scientific Reports, 4,* #4530. DOI: 10.1038/srep04530. Retrieved from: http://www.nature.com/srep/2014/140331/srep04530/full/srep04530.html

White, P.D., & Lewis, S.W. (1987). Delusional depression after infectious mononucleosis. *British Medical Journal, 295,* 97-98.

Whiteman, H. (2014, November 2). "A fifth of schizophrenia cases 'may be attributable to T. gondii infection'." *Medical News Today*. Retrieved from http://www.medicalnewstoday.com/articles/284681.php.

Wong, D., & Fries, B. (2014). Anti-NMDAR encephalitis, a mimicker of acute infectious encephalitis and a review of the literature. *IDCases 1*, 66-67. Retrieved from http://dx.doi.org/10.1016/j.idcr.2014.08.003

Yamato, M., & Kataoka, Y. (2015). Fatigue sensation following peripheral viral infection is triggered by neuroinflammation: who will answer these questions? *Neural Regeneration Research, 10* (2), 203-204. Retrieved from: http:///.nrronlikne.org IP: 207.30.62.198.

Yolken, R.H., & Torrey, E.F. (2008). Are some cases of psychosis caused by microbial agents? A review of the evidence. *Molecular Psychiatry, 13*, 470-479.

12: PHEOCHROMOCYTOMA

Schildkrout, B. (2014). *Masquerading Symptoms: Uncovering physical illnesses that present as psychological problems.* Hoboken, NJ: John Wiley & Sons. I've mentioned this book several times—it will help you realize how many physical diseases present as a mental disease. A great read.

Zardawi, I.M. (2013). Phaeochromocytoma masquerading as anxiety and depression. *American Journal of Case Reports, 14,* 161-163.

13: HYPERLACTATEMIA

Fava, G.A., Fava, M., Kellner, R., Serafini, E., Mastrogiacomo, I. (1981). Depression hostility and anxiety in hyperprolactinemic amenorrhea. *Psychotherapy and Psychosomatics, 36* (2), 122-128. (Abstract)

Höfer, P., Friedrich, F., Vyssoki, B., et al. (2010). Hyperprolactinaemia and acute psychosis: Prolactinoma or medication-induced phenomenon?" The *World Journal of Biological Psychiatry, 11,* 759-761.

Hyperprolactinaemia and prolactinoma. (no author but a bunch of UK docs). Retrieved on 7/21/15 from http://patinet.iknfo/doctor/hyperprolactinaemia-and-prolactinoma.

LaMarre, A.K., Paterson, L.Q., & Gorzalka, B.B. (2003) Breastfeeding and postpartum maternal sexual functioning: A review. *The Canadian Journal of Human Sexuality, 12* (3-4), 151-168.

Liao, W.T., & Bai, Y.M. (2014). Major depressive disorder induced by prolactinoma—a case report. *General Hospital Psychiatry, 36* (2) e1-e4.

Reavley, A., Fisher, A.D., Owen, D., Creed, F.H., & Davis, J.R. (1997) Psychological distress in patients with hyperprolactinaemia. *Clinical Endocrinology (Oxford), 47* (3), 343-348.

Schaefer, S., Boegershausen, N., Meyer, S., Iva, D., Schepelmann, K., & Kann, P.H. (2008). Hypothalamic-pituitary insufficiency following infectious diseases of the central nervous system. *European Journal of Endocrinology, 158,* 3-9. DOI: 10.1530/EJE-07-0484.

Weitzner, M.A., Kanfer, S., & Booth-Jones, M. (2005). Apathy and pituitary disease: It has nothing to do with depression. *Journal of Neuropsychiatry and Clinical Neuroscience, 17* (2), 159-166. Although this title sounds like there's no link between pituitary problem and depression, they are saying don't call this illness depression, when it is a pituitary problem. Therefore, treatment with anti-depressants is NOT the treatment of choice.

14: Porphyria

American Porphyria Foundation

http://www.porphyriafoundation.com/about-porphyria/types-of-porphyria/AIP

This website gives you everything you need to know and more. You can see testimonials, testing suggestions, treatment and more. You can even call them and get a referral to a doctor who specializes in porphyria. Please check it out.

Auchincloss, S., & Pridmore, S. (2001). Vomiting, burns, and irrational behavior. *The Lancet, 358*, December 1, 2001, 1870.

Bonkovsky, H. L. (2005). Neurovisceral porphyrias: What a hematologist needs to know. American Society of Hematology, (1), 24-30. DOI: 10.1182/asheducation-2005.1.23ASH Education Book.

Bonkovsky, H.L., Maddukuri, V.C, Yazici, C., Anderson, K.E., Bissell, D.M., et al. (2014). Acute porphyrias in the USA: Features of 108 subjects from porphyria consortium. *American Journal of Medicine, 127* (12), 1233-1241. DOI: 1-.1016/j.amjmed.2014.06.036.

Cardenas, G.E., Almaguer, M.D.H., Guerra, R.R., & Alcaraz, M.G.A. (2009). Psychiatric complications of a late diagnosis of acute porphyria in an affected male. *Salud Mental, 32,* 365-369.

Crimlisk, H.L. (1997). The little imitator— porphyria: a neuropsychiatric disorder. Journal of *Neurology, Neurosurgery, and Psychiatry, 62,* 319-328.

Ellencweig, N. Schoenfeld, N., & Zemishlany, A. 2006). Acute intermittent porphyria: Psychosis as the only clinical manifestation. *Israel Journal Psychiatry Related Sciences, 43* (1), 52-56.

Ghosh, S., Chaudhury, P.K.R., & Goswmi, H. (2006). An analysis of six cases of acute intermittent porphyria (AIP). *Indian Journal of Psychiatry, 48,* (3), 189-192. DOI: 10.4103/0019-5545.31584. PMCID: PMC2932991.

Griswold, K.S., Del Regno, P.A., & Berger, R.C. (2015). Recognition and differential diagnosis of psychosis in primary care. *American Family Physician, June 15; 91 (12),* 856-863. http://www.aafp.org/afp/2015/0615/p856.html

Klobucic, M., Sklebar, D., Ivanac, R., Matkovic, D.V., Jug-Klobucic, A., & Sklebar, I. (2011).

Differential diagnosis of acute abdominal pain—acute intermittent porphyria. *Medicinski Glasnik, 8*, (2), 298-300.

Mehjta, M., Rath, G.P., Padhy, U.P., Marda, M., Mahajan, C., & Dash, H.H. (2010). Intensive care management of patients with acute intermittent porphyria: Clinical report of four cases and review of literature. *Indian Journal of Critical Care and Medicine, 14* (2), 88-91. DOI: 10.4103/0972-5229.68222.

Mercan, S., Karamustafalioglu, O., Tanriverdi, N. & Oba, S. (2003). Safety of fluoxetine treatment in a case of acute intermittent porphyria. *International Journal of Psychiatry in Clinical Practice, 9*, 281-283.

Nia, S. (2014). Psychiatric signs and symptoms in treatable inborn errors of metabolism. *Journal of Neurology, 261* (Suppl 2): S559-S568. DOI: 10.1007/s00415-014-7396-6

15: And There are More!

American Psychiatric Association. (2013). *Diagnostic and statistical manual of mental disorders* (5th ed.). Washington, DC: Author.

Aydogan, U., et al. (2012). Increased frequency of anxiety, depression, quality of life and sexual life in young hypogonadotropic hypogonadal males and impacts of testosterone replacement therapy on these conditions. *Endocrine Journal, 59,* 1099-1105.

Byatt, N., Rothschild, A.J., Riskind, P., Ionete, C., & hunt, A.T. (2011) *Journal of Clinical Neuropsychiatry and Clinical Neurosciences, 23,* (2) 198-200.

Carrieri, P. B., Montella, S., & Petraccca, M. (2011). Psychiatric onset of multiple sclerosis: Description of two cases. *Journal of Clinical Neuropsychiatry and Clinical Neurosciences, 23,* 23 (2). E6.

Castro, J., & Billick, S. (2013). Psychiatric presentations/manifestations of medical illnesses. *Psychiatric Quarterly, 84,* 351-362. DOI 10:1007/s11126-012-9251-1 I encourage every doctor and therapist read this journal article to see the wide array of medical illnesses that cause psychiatric problems. Wonderful article and kudos to the authors.

Chaudhry, P., et al., 2007). Characteristics and reversibility of dementia in normal pressure hydrocephalus. *Behavioural Neurology, 18,* 149-158.

Conti, et al., (2017). Clinical characteristics of diabetes mellitus and suicide risk. *Frontiers in Psychiatry, 8* (40). DOI: 10.3389/fpsyt.2017.00040.

Cosci, F., fava, G., & Sonino, N. (2015). Mood and anxiety disorders as early manifestations of medical illness: A systematic review. *Psychotherapy and Psychosomatics, 84*, 22-29. DOI: 10.1159/000367913.

Dreyfus, J. (2001). *A Remarkable Medicine Has Been Overlooked.* New York: Lantern Books. Great book.

Facora, R., & Luciano, M. (2008). When to consider normal pressure hydrocephalus in the patient with gait disturbance. *Geriatrics, 2008, 63*, 32-37.

Hall, R.C.W., et al., (1978). Physical illness presenting as psychiatric disease. *Archives of General Psychiatry, 35*, 1315-1320.

Holt, R.I.G., de Groot, M., & Golden, S.H. (2014). Diabetes and depression. *Current Diabetes Reports, 14* (6). DOI: 10.1007/s11892-014-0491-3.

Hydrocephalus Association (2017). http://www.hydroassoc.org/symptoms-and-diagnosis-nph/ This is an organizations for NPH that provides great information.

Jung, H.J., & Shin, H.S. (2016). Effect of Testosterone Replacement Therapy on Cognitive Performance and Depression in Men with Testosterone Deficiency

Syndrome. *World Journal of Men's Health, 34*(3), 194-199. doi: 10.5534/wjmh.2016.34.3.194.

Kirsch I, Deacon BJ, HuedoMedina TB, Scoboria A, Moore TJ, et al. (2008) Initial severity and antidepressant benefits: A metaanalysis of data submitted to the Food and Drug Administration. *PLoS Med 5* (2): e45. doi:10.1371/journal.pmed.0050045

MacHale, S. (2002). Managing depression in physical illness. *Advances in Psychiatric Treatment, 8,* 297-305. DOI: 10.1192/apt.8.4.297

Marian, G., et al., (2010). Depression as an initial feature of Systemic Erythematosus? A case report. *Journal of Medicine and Life, 3,* (2). 183-185.

Mezuk, et al., (2008). Depression and type 2 diabetes over the lifespan: A meta-analysis. *Diabetes Care, 31,* 2383-2390. DOI: 10.2337/dc08-0985.

Miller K.K. et al. (2009). Low-dose transdermal testosterone augmentation therapy improves depression severity in women. *CNS Spectrums, 14,* 688-94. PMID: 20394176

Nassar, B.R., & Lippa, C.F. (2016). Idiopathic normal pressure hydrocephalus: A review for general practitioners. *Gerontology & Geriatric Medicine, 1,* 1-6. DOI: 10.1177/2333721416643702.

Romney, Ann. (2015). *In this together: My story.* New York: Thomas Dunne Books. Ms. Romney also supports a program working with neurological diseases including others than MS.

Skaer, D.H. (2017). *Temper, Temper: An Effective Strategy to Conquer your Anger and Hostility.* Amazon.

Trebatická, J., Dukát, A., Ďuračková, Z., & Muchová, J. (2017, Feb 28). Cardiovascular diseases, depression disorders and potential effects of omega-3 fatty acids. *Physiological Research.* Abstract. PMID: 28248536.

16: THE MENTAL HEALTH DILEMMA

Barth, F. D. (2010). Does talk therapy really work? Retrieved on 7-30-16 from https://www.psychologytoday.com/blog/the-couch/201011/does-talk-therapy-really-work. Barth extols the greatness of psychoanalysis. But the reasons she reported that make psychoanalysis so useful are cognitive-behavioral techniques. I'm not big on psychoanalysis, but that doesn't mean it doesn't work for some. The research on therapeutic effectiveness is difficult to do well.

Dawes, R.M. (1994). *House of Cards: Psychology and Psychotherapy Built on Myth.* New York: The Free Press. This book will open your eyes to the severe limitations of psychology. He says there are good research applications of the scientific psychological approaches but points out many theories and hypotheses that are not scientific at all.

Diamond, R.J. (2002 revision). Psychiatric presentations of medical illness: An introduction for non-medical mental health professionals. Retrieved from http://www.alternativementalhealth.com/psychiatric-presentations-of-medical-illness-2/ This is an incredible source to help practitioners consider the biological causes of mental problems.

Gottman, J.M. & Silver, N. (1999). *The Seven Principles for Making Marriage Work.* New York: Three Rivers Press. Gottman approached the study of marriage, divorce, and relationships with a scientific approach. I believe Dawes (above) would agree. He has other books, too. Go to ww.gottman.com for excellent blogs, e.g., 'Debunking 12 myths about relationships.' Great stuff on all kinds of relationships.

http://retractionwatch.com/ This website gives a list of retractions of journal articles because of cheating.

Salleh, M. R. (2008). Life Event, Stress and Illness. *The Malaysian Journal of Medical Sciences : MJMS, 15* (4), 9–18. This article covers about every hypothesis regarding stress causing mental and medical illnesses. He is honest about citing limitations of inferring causation; however, I still think it goes too far.

Meet the author

Dr. Skaer has a Ph.D. in psychology from the University of Miami (FL). He's been a therapist for over 20 years including work at a psychiatric hospital and as an adjunct college professor. He's presented over a thousand seminars on parenting, marriage, mental illness, humor, and stress management among others. In 1976, the flu bug hit him which brought on severe depression and helped him understand that physical illnesses could cause mental illness. He then researched other biological causes/contributors to depression and other mental illnesses. This book is the result. He is a member of the International Positive Psychology Association.

Dr. Skaer learned that experience, although not always pleasant, is a great teacher and motivator. Another of his books, *Temper, Temper* (2017) results from learning, years ago, that low blood sugar made him prone to anger. Further research and his counseling experience proved he wasn't the only one who encountered anger from biological issues—of which there are many.

He also suffered from "migraine with aura" headaches since a young child—more experience. When he was 50 years old, he discovered how to avoid those and hasn't had one since 1992. He will soon share this good news with others—not the headache, the technique to stop them.

Please contact him on his Webpage for more information. His goal is to provide solutions for problems at a reasonable price (or free), so anyone can afford the help they need. Check it out: www.DavidSkaer.com

Printed in Great Britain
by Amazon